PUPPY CARE

PUPPY CARE

A Complete Guide to Raising a Happy Puppy in a Positive Environment

Joan Capuzzi, VMD

Technical Review by Elizabeth Bunting, VMD

Photographs by Stephen Gorman and Eli Burakian

LYONS PRESS

Essex, Connecticut

An imprint of Globe Pequot, the trade division of
The Rowman & Littlefield Publishing Group, Inc.
4501 Forbes Blvd., Ste. 200
Lanham, MD 20706
www.rowman.com

Distributed by NATIONAL BOOK NETWORK

Interior Design: Paul Beatrice
Layout: Melissa Evarts
Interior Photos by Stephen Gorman and Eli Burakian with the exception of those listed on page 236. Thank you to all the dogs who appear in this book, with special thanks to A.J., Arlo, Bella and Cosmos, Franklin, Orion (Boston terrier), Richard and Rianna, and Tallulah.

British Library Cataloguing in Publication Information available

The Library of Congress previously cataloged this book under LCCN 2010011821

Printed in India

For my two little puppies, Michael and Natalie.

Acknowledgments

A number of people helped me with this book, lending me their knowledge, technical guidance, let-me-run-this-by-you opinions, and/or love and encouragement. My thanks go to Rich DePiano Jr., Katie Benoit, Beth Bunting, VMD, Michele Campellone, VMD, Stacey Conarello, VMD, Kristin Dance, VMD, Mike Giresi, Gregory Joo, DVM, Joan Kanes, Kathy Liez, VMD, Kathryn Michel, DVM, Ilana Reisner, DVM, Helma Weeks, and my parents, Ruth and David Capuzzi.

Photographer Acknowledgments

The photographers would like to thank Tamara Sullivan, Kate Harbaugh, Elizabeth Greene, Upper Valley Humane Society—Enfield, NH, Lorelei Westbrook, and Lebanon Pet and Aquarium Center—West Lebanon, NH.

CONTENTS

INTRODUCTION

This is not a book about puppies so much as it is a book about decisions. You'll find, as you read, so many options, choices, and decisions. Who would have thought that getting a puppy would present such dilemma?

There's the choice between wet versus dry food, choke collar or buckle collar, shedding blade or undercoat rake, crate or gate.

And leash options: Leather? Nylon? Chain? Braided? Six-foot? Ten-foot? Retractable?

Should you register for puppy class or hire a personal trainer? When you teach manners to puppy, is it "down" or "off"? When you go out of town, kennel or dog sitter?

What about car trips? Bark collars? Sterilizing? Paper training? Flea products? Raw food diets? Health insurance? Electric fences? Dog shows?

Whoa! Let's backtrack for a minute. You still haven't decided between a lap dog and a jogging buddy, a male and a female, a mutt and a purebreed, a rescue pup and a breeder pup, a Rottweiler and a pug and a Bedlington and a Lab and a Chinese crested and a boxer and a shih tzu and a pit bull and a Jack Russell and a Gordon setter and . . . the list goes on, up to about 400 different breeds!

This book will guide you through all these choices and more. But the most important decision you have to make is addressed in the first few pages: Should you get a puppy in the first place?

A puppy will be your dog for life

The companionship of a cute puppy can certainly amplify your life. But timing is everything.

Bringing a puppy into your home is a huge, life-altering commitment. Having a dog changes the way you go through life—the way you live each day—for upwards of fifteen years. This puppy that you are contemplating today

will give way to an adult dog and then a senior. His life will—over the long term—represent a discrete chapter in your own life.

It always fascinates me, as a veterinarian, to hear elderly clients recount the dogs of their lives: the dog that taught their child self what a dog was, the dog that became their parents' when they went off to college or the military, the dog they handpicked once they had a chance to start building a life of their own, the dog they raised alongside their children, the hand-me-down dog they received from a child departing for college, and the empty-nester dog that came to fill a void.

And it's a beautiful thing to see an owner bring in a creaky old dog with white face and cloudy eyes that she raised from a puppy. She might be looking for meds to quell her dog's arthritis pain or curtail urinary leakage. Or she may be asking how she'll know "when it's time . . ."

I have to respect this owner who was patient enough to turn a boisterous puppy into a well-behaved dog that meshed with her life, and who stuck by the dog even when it wasn't so convenient. This person made sacrifices for her dog over the years: bringing the dog along after being transferred out of state for a job, forsaking the perfect apartment because it didn't allow dogs, keeping the dog, even when she was busy with babies or elderly parents or work deadlines or home remodeling, and shelling out money

for emergency surgery when the credit cards were already maxed.

But I also give credit to the person who looks into the future and acknowledges early on that these choices are not for them, and makes responsible decisions.

I think of the young woman who recently came into my office with an adorable mutt that looked just like Benji. As I administered her puppy's first vaccines, she said, in an exasperated voice, "My boyfriend bought me this puppy as a surprise, and I don't think I want him." Caressing the puppy's face, she went on to describe her grueling work schedule, and to explain that she is more of a cat person, besides. She inquired about how to find a good home for the puppy. This woman recognized the importance of commitment, and had enough respect for the puppy's life and for her own needs to make a responsible—albeit difficult—decision.

The benefits of man's best friend

For anyone with the necessary raw materials—time, patience, desire, and some discretionary funds—a puppy can enrich life beyond measure. A puppy can help to nurture a child's developing personality, and serve as a companion whom he or she can play with and help to train and care for.

Puppies add life to any home, and may even prolong our own lives. Research shows that the presence of a pet can significantly reduce an owner's heart rate and blood

A puppy is not a necessity, nor is it a rite of passage. A puppy will not teach your children about responsibility—that is really your job. And certainly, a puppy will not take care of himself. I commonly see dogs who are shortchanged on attention because their often well-meaning owners simply don't have the time for them. Too frequently, I witness dog owners making inferior medical decisions because they are trying to save money. And I see the dismal statistics on shelter euthanasia because we—as a population—breed and acquire dogs that, for one reason or another, we are unable or unwilling to care for.

But for all the reasons *not* to get a puppy—expense, time commitment, and so forth—there are far more reasons *to* get a puppy.

pressure. And dogs bring psychological benefits as well. The poet Lord Byron described the dog as "the firmest friend, the first to welcome, foremost to defend."

So, as you can see, dogs are good for people. We have kept them by our sides for over 10,000 years, capturing our food, culling the vermin, guarding our encampments, and warming our laps. Dogs are part of human history in every culture, from one end of the Earth to the other, and they come in so many different shapes and sizes that it's surprising they even share a common species link.

The modern dog breeds we see today would not likely have developed in the wild, and there are several that would not survive for very long without us. The different varieties of *Canis lupus familiaris*—the domestic dog—were adapted by us, and for us: They are, in effect, our followers. In the early days of dog clubs like the American Kennel Club, around the late 1800s, the general public had only a hazy understanding of the breed distinctions. Today, we talk of the stamina of our Weimaraners, the intelligence of our border collies, the beauty of our Samoyeds, and the affable nature and hypoallergenic coat of the mixed packages we fondly call "labradoodles."

Getting a puppy once meant preparing a comfortable spot out back and setting out chow and water each day. Today, indoctrinating a dog is akin to expanding the family.

There is so much available to the puppy owner, in terms of products, services, theories, and experts available to help

you put these canine theories into place. This book is loaded with information on do-it-yourself training, grooming, and general care, plus tips on finding the right professionals to help you with things like clipping, training, pet sitting, and doctoring your puppy.

In this book, you will also discover how to have fun with your puppy, whether you want to walk him along the Appalachian Trail or parade him around a show ring.

UNDERSTAND THE COMMITMENT
Are you ready for over a decade of caring for a dog?

Bringing a puppy into your home is a marriage of sorts—a commitment for the lifetime of the dog. Behind those rolls of puppy fat, the oversized paws, and the delightfully clumsy totter is over ten years of your time, money, and patience.

With good care, your dog will live many years, and he will expect to live them with you. For many owners, keeping a dog for his total life span is a tall order. In fact, the median amount of time a dog is kept by his owner is less than five years. Unfortunately, one in twenty owned dogs enters a shelter each year.

The owner must provide care for his dog *every single day* of the dog's life. The work of owning a dog is typically front-end loaded. Puppies need to be fed three or four times a day and taken outside to eliminate every few hours—even in the middle of the night! They have potty training mishaps that require cleaning *ad nauseum*. And supervision is needed

Canine needs:

- Housing
- Food and water
- Veterinary care
- Safety
- Regular walks/outdoor access
- Exercise
- Training
- Socialization

Puppy to Adult

- The average life span of a dog is ten to thirteen years (six or seven for some giant breeds and approximately fifteen or so for several toy breeds).

- Before selecting a pup, find out what its adult version looks like.

- The work of owning a dog is usually concentrated at the beginning and end of his life.

- Most dogs relinquished to shelters are five months to three years old. Slog through the puppy stage, and you'll probably have a companion for life.

to ensure the safety of pup, your human friends, and your belongings.

But remember that it's puppy today, dog tomorrow. So if you're going to take the "puppy plunge," you'll need to embrace the entire canine life cycle: from today's unruly youngster to tomorrow's infirm "twilight" dog. With realistic expectations and careful early planning, you can lay the foundation for a beautiful partnership that both you and your dog will come to cherish.

· · · · · · · · · · GREEN ● LIGHT · · · · · · · · · · · ·
Before getting a puppy, test-drive dog ownership by pet sitting for a friend, fostering a dog, raising a service dog (i.e., Seeing Eye), or joining a dog-rental service that allows you to lease —and potentially adopt—a rescue animal.

Living with Pup

- Here are the worst-case scenarios, to give you some perspective: See what it feels like to have a puppy by puddling water onto your carpet and walking on it barefoot.

- Shred your undergarments, and then try wearing them.

- Dump the contents of your trash can all over the floor. Step back. Behold the sheer mess.

- Set your alarm clock for 2:00 a.m. Wake up. Walk around outside in a "fog" for five minutes. Repeat every two hours.

Think Long-term

- Your dog may live for fifteen years. Think about where household members will be in their lives throughout this period.

- Do you expect to remain healthy enough to care for your dog throughout his lifetime? If not, have a contingency plan for his care.

- Might you relocate during your dog's life? Are you willing to bring him along?

- If you're planning any other additions to your family over the next decade or so, will your pup still have a place in your household?

COST OF OWNERSHIP

Dogs cost money: Here's what you'll need to spend and where you can cut costs

If you're thinking about bringing a dog into your life, seriously consider your budget. Should your dog attain the age of fourteen, plan to spend $10,000 to $15,000 on his needs throughout his life. Stretched out over time, that's about $70 a month. And figure on high start-up fees—$500 to $1,000, excluding acquisition costs, in the first six weeks of ownership: Puppies are surely Mother Nature's way of showing us that cute comes at a premium.

There are the infrastructure costs that you can plan for, things like pens, bowls, grooming tools, and such. There are the added medical costs inherent to puppyhood. And then there are the surprises: the many pairs of chewed shoes you

Dog Beds

- Dog beds run the gamut, from curved to chaise, organic fleece to vinyl, heated to chewproof.

- Costs range from $20 to $300.

- There is no need to spend a lot of money. A folded quilt, a blanket, or the corner of your bed may do just fine.

- If you do buy a dog bed, look for one that is easily washable and/or waterproof.

Stocking Up for Pup

- A variety of paraphernalia is available for puppies.

- Every puppy supply cabinet should include a grooming brush, shampoo, nail clipper, toothbrush, extra leash and collar, carpet stain cleaner, and chew toys.

- Save money by passing on things like gem-studded collars, doggie garments, and vitamin supplements not recommended by your veterinarian.

- Pet supply superstores generally offer a better price and selection on pet products than do pet shops and veterinary offices.

had to replace; and the $1,500 surgery to remove that one piece of mauled shoe leather that got stuck in your puppy's intestines.

Want to curb costs? Supervise pup closely in order to minimize the chances that he will hurt himself and damage your belongings. And understand the difference between essential and bells-and-whistles in pet supply stores.

Finally, plan for the unexpected. Puppies, like all animals, are basically unpredictable. They'll surprise you at every turn. And those surprises can be costly.

MAKE IT EASY

Save money through adoption versus purchase; small dog versus large dog (you'll trim costs on food, medication, grooming, and boarding); durable dog supplies that will last longer; instructional books and DVDs, for do-it-yourself grooming and training; homemade dog treats; and pet insurance, which may save you up to 80 percent on veterinary care costs.

Veterinary Expenses

- Puppies require extra veterinary services, including an initial vaccine series, fecal exams, deworming medication, and spay/neuter surgery.

- Schedule an early veterinary exam to check for pricey birth defects like cleft palate and cataracts.

- Providing the right quality food may save you money down the road in treatment costs for maladies like allergies, skin problems, diabetes, and arthritis.

- Veterinary care in the first year generally runs $400 to $700.

Average dog-related costs:

Acquisition fees:

Purchase (breeder/pet store)	$500 to $750
Adoption	$50 to $200

One-time expenses:

Spay/neuter	$100 to $200
Collar/leash/tags/bowls	$30 to $50
Bed	$50 to $200
Crate	$100 to $200
Fencing	$100 to $2000
Microchipping (implantation + registration)	$20 to $35

Ongoing expenses (annual):

Food	$150 to $350
Treats/toys	$25 to $150
Medical bills (after year 1)	$150 to $300
Boarding/pet sitting	$100 to $300
Grooming	$150 to $300
Training	$100 to $300
Pet health insurance	$240 to $480
License	$20

EVALUATE YOUR LIFESTYLE

Dog ownership will enrich your life, but you need to make room for a dog

A puppy brings a new aura to your household, one of vivacity and utter silliness. But like any addition to the family, a puppy produces a major life change. Before you take on a puppy, evaluate your lifestyle and decide whether a dog can mesh with the scaffolding of your life.

The idea of a puppy is palatable to most, but the reality of a puppy is certainly not for everyone. Depending on your personal infrastructure, your stage of life, and the way you like—and need—to spend your time, a dog could elevate you . . . or weigh you down. If you have a dog, bid adieu to spontaneous overnights at the seashore. Vacation getaways become luxuries that require careful choreography—finding

Proper Accommodations

- Dogs are generally safer and happier when housed indoors with their family.

- Have a convenient spot to take your dog outside to eliminate. In a pinch, using an apartment balcony is better than leaving a puddle in the elevator.

- A fenced yard can simplify your life immeasurably, and enhance your dog's: Just open the door and let him run.

- Designate a few exercise areas, such as a fenced yard, public park, beach, or hiking trails. Follow dog restrictions and leash laws.

Doggie Time

- Decide how much time you have to spend each day with your dog.

- Restructure your schedule to incorporate dog-related responsibilities, such as feeding, walking, and cleaning.

- Develop a daily routine for quality doggie-and-me time, such as training, playing, exercising, and cuddling.

- Designate a backup person to help you on those days that work or personal commitments cut into your doggie time.

a reputable kennel, gathering the necessary health records for boarding, and so on.

How would you feel about dog hairs on your pillow? Or a cascade of barks whenever someone comes to the door? Or late-night runs to the vet when the dog ingests one of your garments?

The main reasons owners surrender their dogs to shelters concern lifestyle incompatibility. Evaluate your life first, so that when you do welcome a puppy into your home, it will be a truly welcome addition to your life.

Labor of Love

- The time you spend caring for your dog can be extremely rewarding for you both.

- Some breeds require more work, such as extra grooming or exercise.

- Just as you have a preferred lifestyle, so too does each different breed of dog.

- If you do your homework, you can probably find a breed that suits your lifestyle—and who your lifestyle would suit.

· · · · · · · · · · RED ● LIGHT · · · · · · · · · · ·

Don't get a dog if your landlord prohibits dogs or if you have no place to exercise him; not enough time to care for him properly; an unpredictable schedule; physical limitations that would impair your ability to meet his needs; or a household member with an illness (i.e., dog dander allergy; immune disorder) that could make exposure to dogs dangerous.

Top 10 reasons dogs are relinquished to animal shelters:*

#1 Owner is moving

#2 Landlord forbids pets

#3 Cost prohibitive

#4 No time to care for dog

#5 Inadequate facilities

#6 Too many other pets in household

#7 Dog is ill

#8 Personal problems

#9 Dog bites

#10 No homes for littermates

*National Council on Pet Population Study & Policy

GOALS FOR YOUR PUPPY

Dog for the kids? Sporting companion? Determine your goals and pick the right puppy

So you've decided that you want a puppy, as well as the adult dog it will turn out to be. Now you have a whole host of other decisions to make, such as breed, gender, and timing. You also have to prepare the home and family for puppy, and develop a realistic set of expectations for life with him. Your reasons for wanting a dog—the role that he will fill in your life—will dictate how you go about acquiring and prepping for him.

Certain breeds, like shelties, are highly trainable and can often be taught to do tricks. Others, like cavalier King Charles spaniels, are not only docile and good with kids, but they are also great lap dogs—for cuddling in front of the TV. Want a

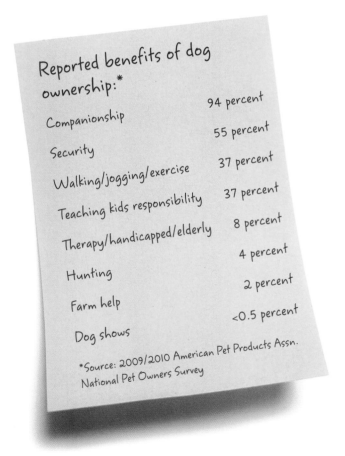

Reported benefits of dog ownership:*

Companionship	94 percent
Security	55 percent
Walking/jogging/exercise	37 percent
Teaching kids responsibility	37 percent
Therapy/handicapped/elderly	8 percent
Hunting	4 percent
Farm help	2 percent
Dog shows	<0.5 percent

*Source: 2009/2010 American Pet Products Assn. National Pet Owners Survey

Bonding

- Forging a bond between puppy and household members is the key first step.

- Bonding with puppy gives him a sense of security, paves the way for obedience training, shapes his temperament, and brings joy to you both.

- Bond with pup through calm, friendly talk, tender touch, gentle play, and taking him on errands.

- Each household member can bond with puppy uniquely by assuming their own puppy-related responsibility, like feeding him, or walking him.

loyal companion that will make you feel safe? Perhaps a German shepherd? A puppy that could have some future use as a therapy dog, maybe working with disabled children? Consult with social workers who might be able to give you some advice.

Remember that all your best-laid plans could go to the dogs. The puppy buzzword is unpredictability. That pup that you acquire as a future jogging buddy could end up a canine couch potato.

ZOOM

The "working group," as defined by most kennel clubs around the world, consists of larger breeds traditionally bred for physical labor, such as guarding, police work, rescue, and herding. The American Kennel Club (AKC) includes breeds like Akita, boxer, Doberman pinscher, Newfoundland, and Rottweiler in this group.

Role Playing

- A "dog" is almost anything you want it to be. What would a dog mean in your life?

- Whatever her function, she must be a companion above all else.

- Her primary role as buddy will enhance her desire to perform for you, whether in the field, the stream, the show ring or the backyard.

- As you train your dog to perform specific tasks, you cement the bond that will endure once she becomes too old or infirm to perform those tasks.

Showing Off

- In most dog shows, purebred competitors are judged for conformation: The judge assesses how closely each dog conforms to the breed standard, which consists of externally observable canine qualities like appearance, movement, and temperament.

- In all-breed shows, competitors are divided into seven groups: sporting, non-sporting, working, herding, hounds, terriers, and toys.

- Every family member can participate, as handlers, trainers, drivers, groomers, or eager spectators.

THE FAMILY DOG

Whatever your family situation, everyone needs to be behind the idea of a dog

Dogs take up space, whether they are spinning circles in your living room or balled up tightly on your pillow. They make noise, from their yappiest bark to their softest breath. They choreograph your life, from *when* you need to feed them to *when* you need to take them out. And they color your world with their individual idiosyncrasies. With their commanding presence, a dog can set the tone for your household.

This is why the decision to adopt a puppy is one of the most important choices a family can make. According to the American Veterinary Medical Association (AVMA), 54.3 percent of dog-owning households consist of five or more human members—that's a lot of people needed to give the

Family style

- A "family" can consist of any grouping of people and animals, even just you and your dog.

- Dog-owning households are more likely to include children under eighteen and be larger in size than their non-dog-owning counterparts.

- There is no rule for what constitutes the best family dog. Match the characteristics of your household with breed features and individual puppy temperament.

- Do you have children? Remember that cuteness and "ideal" size are bested by right breed and good disposition.

Group Decision

- Involve every household member in the major decisions associated with getting and raising a puppy.

- The puppy is more likely to become a permanent fixture if everyone in the household is involved in the decision to acquire him.

- Each individual should have a say in the type of puppy and its source.

- Give everyone in the home dibs on a puppy-related task, and don't force the participation of anyone who does not wish to be closely involved with the puppy.

thumbs-up to getting a puppy.

Puppies require 'round-the-clock care, and dogs need daily care and consistent attention. There may be some house-mates who are not *invested* in the idea of a puppy (at least not yet!). That's okay—not everyone loves dogs. But all family members need to be willing to tolerate a puppy, and to do so pleasantly. Those who do not wish to participate in the puppy's care need to make this clear beforehand, so that everyone knows his or her role from the outset.

· · · · · · · · · · · · · RED ● LIGHT · · · · · · · · · · · · ·

Surprises are wonderful, when they come in the form of a party or a job promotion. Surprising a loved one with a puppy—a really sweet idea—can backfire! The all-too-frequent fallout: family strife and a displaced dog. Seek consensus *before* getting a dog.

Family Time

- All household members should be on hand in the initial weeks after puppy's arrival.

- Adopt the puppy at a time when it is convenient for everyone's schedule.

- Summer months are an opportune time for many people to adopt, since school is not in session.

- Do not bring in the puppy at a time when you have out-of-town vacation or business travel on the horizon.

Family puppy discussions should include:

- Puppy's breed, age, and gender
- Cost of puppy
- Where to get puppy
- Divvying up jobs
- Training styles
- Where in house/yard puppy will stay
- Dog names
- Who will keep/take puppy if a household member moves out

BABY OR TEENAGER?

You don't have to get a "baby" puppy; there are advantages to older puppies, too

Baby puppies are learning how to become dogs, and their lack of life experience shows. A ten-week-old pup is like a toddler—clumsy, undisciplined, and hard to communicate with. A nine-month-old puppy is somewhat akin to a teenager. He comes equipped with the basics of social conduct, learned from mom. For this reason, puppies benefit from more time spent with their mothers and littermates, and separating them before eight weeks deprives them of critical lessons in good doggie behavior.

A puppy over six months is more sure of its environment than is a youngster. A larger, sturdier puppy will be better able to withstand a child's rough play.

What defines a "puppy"?

- Puppies become "dogs" between nine months and two years.

- Bone growth ceases between eight and twelve months (later in large breeds).

- Puppies erupt baby teeth between thirty and forty-five days, and permanent teeth from two to seven months.

- Males reach full sexual maturity at around one year.

- Bitches have their first heat cycle at six to eighteen months old.

- Small breeds reach sexual maturity earlier than large breeds.

Teenaged Pup

- By nine months of age, the worst of the puppy stage is over.

- Feeding intervals have increased.

- Older puppies can fully concentrate their urine, so they produce less, and have better bladder muscle control.

- Older pups eat and excrete less often, and can stay alone for longer periods of time.

10

In case you're wondering, there is no evidence that the human-dog bond is lesser if the dog was brought into the home as an older puppy or even an adult. But if you decide to get an older puppy, make sure there's been adequate human socialization between eight weeks of age and his homecoming. An older puppy could be imprinted with some emotional baggage that a newbie probably will not have.

Puppy's Head

- Puppies learn the nuts-and-bolts of behavior from their mothers and littermates.

- These behavior lessons include the rules of hierarchy and appropriate play.

- An eight- to twelve-week-old puppy can begin to learn rudimentary commands like "no" and "come."

- By twelve weeks, a puppy's mental capacity is well developed and primed for experiential learning.

Advantages of an older puppy:

- May be easier to gauge adult size

- Teething possibly finished; adult teeth not needle-sharp like puppy teeth

- Possibly housetrained and socialized

- Temperament and behavior may be better defined

- Vaccination, deworming, and spay/neuter possibly completed

- Health problems possibly apparent

- Less fragile

THE BREED GROUPS
From the "scentsible" hounds to the cuddly toys, dogs come in many varieties

There are over 400 recognized dog breeds worldwide. Breeds are a reflection of different human societies and cultures, and each was created to fill distinct human needs. Popular breeds mirror the times and the trends. From 1905 until 1935, the Boston terrier held the #1 or #2 position, and from 1925 until 1936, the German shepherd was most popular. From there, the cocker spaniel held rank, giving way to the beagle as the dog of the '50s. Poodles took center stage after that, and the Labrador retriever has topped the list since 1991.

The last decade has seen an increase in AKC registrations for dogs under twenty-five pounds, like the cavalier King Charles spaniel, the French bulldog, and the Brussels griffon. There has

Dogs over Generations

Unique Breed Characteristics

- Dogs have been domesticated for over 10,000 years.

- Early uses for dogs included hunting, guarding, and companionship.

- Creation of breeds—subspecies of *Canis lupus familiaris*—grew out of the desire to have dogs that specialize in different tasks.

- Breeds are classified as such once they have been reproduced with consistent characteristics for many generations. Over 150 breeds are recognized by the American Kennel Club (AKC) today.

- Chondrodystrophied breeds, such as the basset hound and dachshund, feature shortened legs.

- Brachycephalic breeds, including the pug, bulldog, and shih tzu, have pushed-in faces.

- Breed coat types include silky (Afghan hound), curly (Irish water spaniel), tightly kinked (Komondor), double (husky), and smooth (Doberman pinscher).

- Breed abilities include sprinting, search-and-rescue , hunting, water work, and scenting.

also been a general decline in larger breeds, possibly reflecting the appeal of dogs that are more transportable and less time intensive. And there has been an amplified demand for "hypoallergenic" breeds like the Portuguese water dog, the soft-coated wheaten terrier, and the Chinese crested.

Like each civilization that produced its own breeds, your home is its own civilization, and has specific canine needs. It is incumbent upon you to match the breed of dog to your household. In your quest for a puppy, *your breed choice is probably the most important decision you'll make.*

Researching Breeds

- Read about the characteristics of the different breeds in the AKC publication, *The Complete Dog Book* (See page 235 Resources).

- Search breeds online.

- Talk to friends about their breeds of dog.

- Talk to breed rescuers and breeders about the pros and cons of their breed; keep in mind that these people will likely be biased toward their breed.

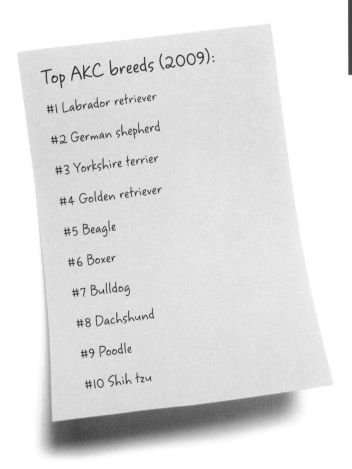

Top AKC breeds (2009):

#1 Labrador retriever

#2 German shepherd

#3 Yorkshire terrier

#4 Golden retriever

#5 Beagle

#6 Boxer

#7 Bulldog

#8 Dachshund

#9 Poodle

#10 Shih tzu

HIGH-MAINTENANCE BREEDS
Some breeds require more work and commitment than others

PUPPY CARE

Your selected breed will impact your life beyond imagination. So get the right breed for you. Both the Weimaraner and the greyhound are large, short-haired, athletic dogs bred for hunting. But the spunky Weimaraner needs lots of room to run. The greyhound, though capable of sprinting 45 mph, is a great apartment dog because he's a couch potato.

Breeds sometimes don't look their part. Lap dogs are small.

But just try putting the typical Jack Russell terrier on your lap: This little guy will use it as a launching pad. And if your lifestyle is sedentary, then watch out. Bred for fox hunting, the Jack is wiry, stubborn, and on the go.

Finally, don't choose a breed based on what others are getting. Labrador retrievers are the most popular breed in America. They generally have lovely temperaments. But most

High-energy Breeds

- Some breeds require room to run and a lot of physical interaction/playing time. Without this, they can develop nervous habits and become destructive.

- These breeds include Labrador retrievers, Weimaraners, vizslas, boxers, German shorthaired pointers, Dalmatians, shelties, and border collies.

- Plan on at least three fifteen-minute walks (or free time in the yard) plus some heavy exercise daily. Do not get a high-energy breed if you do not have the adequate time, interest, stamina, and exercise space.

Breed Disposition

- To best predict how a dog will behave, look at what jobs it was bred for.

- A herding dog, for instance, is calm and consistent, but tenacious. Remember this when considering a border collie, who will shadow you and possibly nip your heels.

- Some breeds are strong-willed and dominant, with the tendency toward aggression. These include the Rottweiler and the chow chow.

- Interdog aggression is commonly seen in breeds like the spitz and the fox terrier.

behave like energetic puppies until they're *at least* two. Their long, heavy tails can topple vases as well as small children. And they can be indiscriminate eaters, devouring everything from undergarments to toys.

Before settling on a specific breed, find out about its temperament, habits, and requirements. Are they diggers? Constant barkers? Major shedders? If you want a positive dog-owning experience, be sure to research the breed first!

ZOOM

Breeds vary in their ease of upkeep by temperament, energy level, athleticism, size, strength, hair coat, physiology, health problems, odor, even saliva (slobber).

A Worthy Choice?

- Just because a breed is high maintenance does not mean you shouldn't choose it if that's the breed you have your heart set on.

- Every breed (that's *every*) has its downsides.

- Establish reasonable expectations based on what you have learned about your chosen breed.

- Make proper household, scheduling, and budgetary accommodations for your breed's characteristic flaws.

High-maintenance breed features:

- High energy
- Demands a lot of attention
- Disruptive breed-related behavioral quirks (i.e., aggression and separation anxiety)
- Requires ongoing training
- Health problems in breed
- Heavy grooming requirements
- Sheds
- Size issues
- Temperature sensitivity

LOW-MAINTENANCE BREEDS

Find out which breeds are content to go with the flow and just hang out

A low-maintenance dog is hard to find. But some breeds are a little easier to manage than others. If you spend a lot of time at work and/or have a busy household, low maintenance is especially important when bringing in a puppy: He needs to blend in as unobtrusively as possible.

What could be an easier dog than the beagle? Bred to hunt in a pack, he must work pleasantly with other dogs, and meet commands with obedience. At twenty to thirty-five pounds, he comes in a sturdy but compact package. And his hair coat is short and maintenance free. However, beagles can be stubborn and very independent. They have a tendency to dig, escape, and howl.

Mellow Breeds

- A mellow dog is one that is friendly to family as well as visitors.

- He is calm, unobtrusive, malleable, and obedient.

- Placid breeds generally include greyhounds, beagles, basset hounds, dachshunds, Boston and wheaten terriers, Malteses, corgis, pugs, and spaniels.

- Individual variations exist within every breed. High-octane breeds can have easygoing individuals (and vice versa!); you may be able to locate serene exceptions within a litter via temperament testing.

Advantages

- An easily maintained breed does not deplete your time.

- An easily maintained breed is a welcome sight to visitors at your home and is not an inconvenience to your neighbors.

- An easily maintained breed does not drain your wallet with medical expenses, training fees, grooming costs, and home repair bills.

- An easily maintained breed is a joy to be around, rather than a nuisance.

So the beagle is a living example of the adage: No dog is perfect. While most people would consider the beagle easy to maintain, some would not. It depends on your personal preferences, sticking points, and home infrastructure.

This aside, every dog—regardless of breed— needs attention and positive interaction with his owner. If you don't have the time or motivation to do this, then a good "breed" to get is *Carassius auratus:* the goldfish.

Identifying Easy Breeds

- Use word-of-mouth from friends whose lifestyle demands are similar to yours and whose judgment you trust.

- Talk to social workers at nursing homes and rehab facilities where therapy dogs visit. If there's anywhere that mandates breeds that are well behaved and unencumbered, it's here.

- Breed hype does not mean breed ease: Think Dalmatian, Jack Russell terrier, and Chihuahua! They're great breeds, but media images don't always reveal downsides.

Low-maintenance breed features:

- Calm

- Somewhat independent

- Not generally dominant

- Good with other animals

- Easy to train

- Right size for your household

- Low/no grooming requirements

- Generally healthy

17

BREED HEALTH

Each breed has ailments; know what health problems and idiosyncrasies run in your chosen breed

The basset hound was created by hunters in medieval France. They needed a dog of short stature whose gait was slow enough to keep up with on foot. But the basset's disproportioned physique—elongated back seated atop squatty legs—predisposes it to spinal disc herniation and resulting paralysis.

Likewise, the cute, pushed-in faces of some breeds, like bulldogs, essentially result in squashed airways. These dogs tend to snort their way through life, and can be prone to life threatening breathing obstructions and heat stroke.

The Chinese shar-pei has impressive rolls of skin that give the dog its desired look, but skin problems flourish in the

Hereditary Health Problems

- Breeds are prized for their unique physical characteristics. But with good comes bad. Most purebred dogs have at least one health problem to which they are prone.

- Some breeds are particularly plagued by medical problems.

- Breed-related ailments include bloat (deep-chested breeds), congenital deafness (i.e., Dalmatian, Australian shepherd), kidney disease (i.e., cairn terrier, Samoyed), and respiratory problems (brachycephalic breeds like Boston terrier and shih tzu).

In the Genes

- All breed-related health disorders are essentially "genetic." But they are manifested as primary (i.e., metabolic, neoplastic [cancer]) and secondary (related to physical construction [i.e., bloat, osteoarthritis]).

- There are individual exceptions; just because a disorder is common in a breed does not mean that every individual within that breed will be affected.

- If possible, find out if any heritable health problems are present in your puppy's line.

breed largely as a result of the skin folds. By creating such extreme traits—ones that would not likely develop in a wild, freely breeding population—we have inadvertently produced health problems.

Some breed-related—or heritable—health problems are lifelong and/or potentially serious. Others are merely a bother.

But even the nuisance problems, like prolapsed third eyelid—or "cherry eye"—of the cocker spaniel can be quite disturbing for dog owners.

Healthy-breed Features

- While not all medical conditions are preventable, there are breeds with fewer innate health risks.

- You'll simplify your life with a breed not predisposed to orthopedic problems, heart and respiratory disorders, skin and ear problems, and dental disease.

- If you choose to get one of these breeds anyway, prepare to spend extra time and money at the vet, administer meds, and perhaps make at-home accommodations.

ZOOM

There are about 1,000 known heritable (breed-related) health conditions in dogs. It is critical that you inform yourself of any potential health problems in the breed of puppy you select before bringing her home. These problems need not be deal breakers, but you can avoid surprises by making an informed decision.

Tips for addressing breed-prone ailments:

- Research your breed so you're aware of potential health problems.

- If a health screen is available for your breed's problems, have puppy tested as early as possible.

- Follow your veterinarian's recommendations for monitoring.

- Ask your vet about surgeries, medications or lifestyle modifications to address or stall the problem.

MIXED-BREED PUPPIES
The all-American puppy can do just about anything a purebreed can

Every nation in the world has mutts. They're called "pot cake dogs" in the Bahamas, "poi dogs" in Hawaii, "vira lata" in the Dominican Republic, and "crackies" in Newfoundland. Closer to home, it's the "Heinz 57," the "mongrel," or the more tasteful "mixed-breed dog."

Mixes are of multiple-breed or unknown ancestry. They come in an endless variety of sizes, shapes, and colors.

If you're reading this section, you probably are including mixes in your puppy search. And that's good. One of the greatest assets of a mix is *hybrid vigor:* genetic superiority resulting from combining features of several breeds and muting deleterious recessive traits.

Much research has borne out the hybrid vigor of mixes. Swedish studies have shown that mixes are generally less

PUPPY CARE

Pluses

- The physical and behavioral extremes of purebreeds are muted.

- Mixed breeds have a lower incidence of genetic diseases characteristic of their purebred predecessors.

- Mixed breeds are prevalent in shelters, and easy to obtain.

- Mixed breeds can usually be acquired at lower cost than purebreeds.

Minuses

- Mixed-breed puppies can be a mystery. There's no saying what a mixed-breed puppy's appearance or temperament will be as an adult, and unless you know his parents, you probably won't be able to find out if health problems exist in his line.

- You cannot handpick different traits, as you can with a purebreed.

- Your mix probably won't come with a genealogical history.

- Your mix is not eligible to compete in conformation shows.

prone than purebred dogs to many diseases. A German study found that mongrels required less veterinary treatment than purebreeds. And a longevity study, published in 2007, showed that mixed-breed dogs live at least one year longer than their purebred counterparts.

Health aside, the mixed-breed dog can make a wonderful companion. Though he might not be able to track a scent like a bloodhound, he will have desirable traits from every breed that comprises him. Whether of mixed or pure descent, no dog is a cookie cutter—each one is a little different!

Fun with Your Mix

- Mixes come in a wide variety of body types and colors.

- Each mixed-breed puppy, even within a single litter, is distinctive.

- Mixed-breed dogs, as a group, can excel in sports, agility, and obedience just as much as purebred dogs can.

- Mixed-breed dogs can compete in obedience and agility trials.

Obtaining a Mix

- Shelters are full of mixes. There are also adoption organizations that deal only with mixes.

- If the pups are not weaned, ask to see the dam (mother).

- Teeny puppies can grow into thirty- or seventy-pounders. If you adopt your mix when he's over six months old, you can better gauge his adult size.

- Minus a breed history, it will be difficult for your veterinarian to assess potential problems. An *early* veterinary exam will flag obvious congenital defects.

DESIGNER DOGS

Designer dogs are a hot item; do your research and make an educated decision

A new type of mix has become trendy. Known as "designer dogs," crossbreeds are deliberate combinations of two different purebreeds. These dogs are named in the "portmanteau" style, which blends two different words into one. Their clever monikers reflect their breed combinations (i.e., "shih-poo" [shih tzu–poodle], Afador [Afghan hound–Labrador retriever], dorgi [dachshund–Welsh corgi], and—a personal favorite—"taco terrier" [Chihuahua–toy fox terrier]).

Designer-dog breeders aim to fuse the positive traits of component purebred parents into a single dog. These dogs further benefit from hybrid vigor, the combo effect resulting in progeny that are healthier than their parents.

Some Popular Varieties

- Goldendoodles and labradoodles: The golden retriever– and Labrador retriever–poodle hybrids are low- or non-shedding dogs with good temperaments.

- Puggles: These pug-beagle crosses have sweet dispositions and are very cute.

- Morkies: These Maltese-yorkie blends do not shed, and are gentle yet playful.

- Yorkiepoos: Yorkies combined with poodles, these small dogs are also non-shedders, playful, and generally good lap dogs.

Hypoallergenic Dogs

- Hypoallergenicity is one of the most sought-after traits in a dog.

- Hypoallergenic dogs are non- or low-shedders, with low dander.

- Poodles, Malteses, bichons, Yorkshire terriers, and shih tzus are common components in hypoallergenic crossbreeds.

- A hypoallergenic breed combination does not guarantee that the individual puppy has inherited a non-shedding coat. You may not know this until the puppy is between six and eight months old.

So in theory, the labradoodle would be a medium-size dog, docile, and playful like the Labrador retriever, and non-shedding like the poodle.

But the labradoodle, like all designer breeds, is a bit of a gamble. Here's why: Crossbreeds do not necessarily breed "true." The first labradoodle breeding in the late '80s was a success—pleasant dogs that were hypoallergenic (non-shedding, low dander). But among the second litter, seven of the ten pups were shedders.

Unlike purebreeds, which have bred true over many generations, designer dogs of the same mix do not always share the same features. In fact, even crossbreeds of the same litter can differ greatly from one another.

There are over 300 recognized designer breeds. Popular ingredients include the beagle, shih tzu, golden retriever, poodle, and bichon frise. These reflect a variety of widely held preferences, such as hypoallergenicity, pleasant temperament, and manageable size. During your search for a puppy, consider designer breeds, as they offer the opportunity to mix and match different traits.

Finding Puppy

- Decide what breeds you like or what canine traits you desire.

- See if that breed combination has been produced, or if those traits are available in a hybrid.

- Designer breed registries keep a record of puppy/litter pedigrees.

- Understand that the puppy you select might not have the combined breed traits you are seeking.

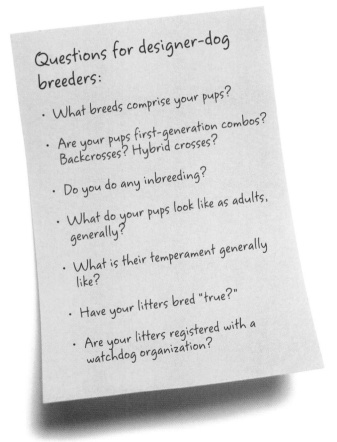

Questions for designer-dog breeders:

- What breeds comprise your pups?

- Are your pups first-generation combos? Backcrosses? Hybrid crosses?

- Do you do any inbreeding?

- What do your pups look like as adults, generally?

- What is their temperament generally like?

- Have your litters bred "true?"

- Are your litters registered with a watchdog organization?

GENDER GAP
The male-female choice can really make a difference in your dog-rearing experience

Puppy gender is a personal choice. Hidden in your psyche could be perceptions and personal expectations for a male "dog" versus a female "bitch." A dog might perpetuate your male sense of self or make you feel protected; a bitch could make you feel nurtured. Whether or not these sentiments are well founded, you must maximize your dog-owning experience for the sake of both you and your dog. If that means choosing a male instead of a female, or vice versa, then figure it out and go with it.

Psychobabble aside, there are discrete differences between living with a male and living with a female. Bitches are generally easier to train—including housebreaking—but spayed

Advantages of a Male

- If you're going through a breeder, male puppies are often cheaper and more obtainable. It is less expensive to neuter a male than to spay a female.

- Males do not go into heat/bleed, and do not gain weight from sterilization, like females often do.

- Males experience less urinary incontinence than females.

- They tend to win more ribbons at dog shows.

Advantages of a Female

- Females are generally smaller than their male counterparts. They earn higher scores for being docile, affectionate, and obedient, and for ease of housetraining.

- They are easier to walk: While a male might sniff every leaf and spurt urine in twenty different spots, a female generally squats once and empties her bladder.

- They are less likely to roam.

- They are less prone to expressing x-linked hereditary diseases.

24

females can become incontinent and dribble their urine involuntarily, especially as they age. Unspayed females have heat cycles throughout their lives, and yes, they have periods! Intact bitches are also at risk for reproductive cancers and can manifest the behavioral quirks associated with false pregnancy.

Males are more prone to aggression than are females. Testosterone is a behavior modulator that makes dogs react more quickly and more intensely. So an intact male might bark or growl with less provocation, and for a longer period of time, than would its female counterpart.

Castration often decreases certain types of aggression, as well as other male behaviors like roaming, mounting, and urine marking. Both intact and neutered males will, at times, extrude (expose) their penis from the skin that covers it.

In general, male dogs *tend to be* more active and playful, while females *tend to be* more affection seeking. But there are male dogs that brim with affection, and there are females that could chase a ball around the equator. These are just general guidelines—with animals, there are no absolutes.

Aggression

- Male dogs show higher rates of overall aggression.

- The majority of human dog bites are caused by male dogs.

- Interdog aggression is more common between same-sex dogs. If you already have a female dog, it might be better to get a male than a female puppy (and vice versa).

- Studies have shown neutering *can* decrease aggression in male dogs, and spaying *can* increase aggression in females *showing aggressive tendencies before the age of six months*.

Physical differences:

- Males of a breed are usually larger than females.

- Males tend to be more muscular.

- Facial features can differ slightly between the genders.

- In some breeds, like Rottweilers, differences in appearance are exaggerated.

- Most females squat to urinate; most males lift a hind leg to urinate.

PUPPIES, PUPPIES EVERYWHERE

Classifieds, shelters, rescues, and pet stores—your puppy may be a mouse click away

Each year, Americans acquire 7.3 million dogs. We get them from breeders, shelters, breed rescues, pet stores, Internet sites, and newspaper ads. We get our puppies from the family across town that whelped a litter in their dining room. And we fly them in from the mystery breeder across the country who advertised online.

Where you get that puppy may or may not ultimately affect your overall experience of owning a dog. But a seller who does not safeguard the welfare of the dogs they are breeding and the puppies they are selling might be someone you don't want to reward with your business.

This said, you can love a dog from a pet store as much as a

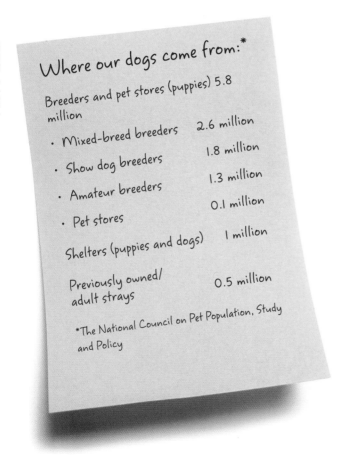

Where our dogs come from:*

Breeders and pet stores (puppies) 5.8 million

- Mixed-breed breeders 2.6 million
- Show dog breeders 1.8 million
- Amateur breeders 1.3 million
- Pet stores 0.1 million

Shelters (puppies and dogs) 1 million

Previously owned/ adult strays 0.5 million

*The National Council on Pet Population, Study and Policy

Shelter Adoption

- The quality of a shelter puppy can be every bit as high as one from a breeder.

- Most shelters spay/neuter, vaccinate, and deworm their dogs before sending them home.

- A pup's "shelter personality" is often very different from its actual disposition.

- Adopting from a shelter can save a life—over two million dogs are euthanized at U.S. shelters yearly.

- Web sites like www .petfinder.com list shelter dogs available around the country.

PUPPY CARE

26

dog from a chichi breeder as much as a dog from the streets. Whatever the source, a puppy can have an inbred genetic disorder or, if it has not been properly vaccinated, a potentially lethal infectious disease like parvovirus.

One outlet to scrutinize is pet stores. These are usually supplied by "puppy mills," which churn out puppies by over-breeding dogs kept in inhumane conditions. The pups that don't sell are usually destroyed. Pet store pups show higher incidence of congenital and infectious disease than the general population.

If you are determined to buy that "puppy in the window," ask if the kennel where she was bred is USDA licensed to wholesale dogs. While no guarantee that she wasn't whelped at a puppy mill, a USDA license indicates that her kennel is regulated.

So when looking for a pup, research the sources. And don't pin your hopes on where you got your puppy. The bond you form with your dog will probably not be affected by whether she came from a breeder or from a shelter.

Seller Litmus Test

- Will the seller let you see the puppy's parents?

- Inquire about genetic screenings and certification status for the parents, and recent veterinary health certificates for the pups.

- Will the seller let you visit the breeding facility?

- Test the knowledge of whomever bred the puppies. Is he or she well-versed on the breed, and its temperament, health issues, and habits?

How to identify a puppy mill:

- Large-scale commercial dog breeding facility

- Substandard: crammed dog quarters, poor hygiene, low-quality breeding stock, no genetic testing, inbreeding, and unsocialized pups

- Sell puppies through pet stores and/or brokers

- Produce multiple breeds

- Their newspaper classified ads feature different breed headings, all with same phone number.

- Do not allow consumers to tour facilities or visit sire or dam

FINDING A BREEDER
Winnowing out the responsible breeders for your purebred puppy

You want a breeder who is in the business because he values the features of his breed and wishes to share his line of dogs with others, and not just to make money.

The Internet has become a giant puppy supermarket. It sounds exotic to fly your dog in from a breeder on the opposite coast, but there's value in being able to visit the breeder, tour the premises, and meet your puppy's parents and the other adult dogs. For this reason, try to go local.

And remember that your total dog-owning experience is impacted by many factors. Your pup's breeder and heritage are only pieces of the overall picture. Look for hybrid vigor in the breeder's pedigrees: Do the last few generations contain many common ancestors? Does the breeder health-screen his dogs? If he has large breeds prone to hip dysplasia, for

Criteria for a good breeder:

- Lets you tour home/kennel
- Adult dogs look healthy, happy, and well cared for.
- Bitches have no more than one litter a year.
- Clean environment
- Knowledgeable about breed
- Asks about your lifestyle and home situation
- Will provide references and contract
- Concerned for pup's well-being; will take pup back for any reason
- Is experienced at breeding

AKC

- The American Kennel Club (AKC) is the only *non-profit*, all-breed dog registry in the U.S.

- The AKC registers and keeps pedigrees on over 400,000 litters and over 700,000 puppies yearly.

- AKC inspects breeders producing over four litters annually.

- AKC certification means that a puppy is purebred and has AKC registered parents; it does not guarantee a puppy's health or quality.

instance, does he hip-certify his breeding stock by PennHip or the Orthopedic Foundation of America (OFA)?

Finally, a responsible breeder does not breed a bitch until she has reached her second birthday (can be earlier in small breeds); minimizes contribution to dog overpopulation through reasonable breeding volume; is active in breed clubs and breed rescues; gives pups human socialization; and doesn't send pups home until they are a *minimum* of eight weeks old.

Finding a Breeder

- Go to www.AKC.org for breed clubs, breeder referral, breed rescues, and general breed information. Also, contact breed clubs and dog fancier organizations for referrals.

- Attend a dog show and talk to exhibitors—most of them are breeders.

- Ask your veterinarian if he or she knows of a reputable breeder.

- Looking for a specific breed? Almost every breed has a breed rescue you can locate online through the breed club.

Peddling Paper

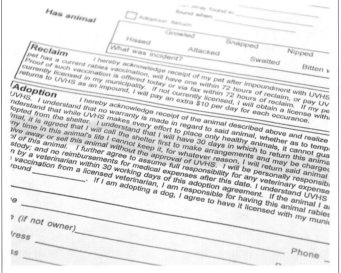

- A good breeder will probably load you up with papers, and not the kind used to line the crate.

- The most important thing is the sales contract.

- The breeder should include a pedigree going back at least three genera- tions, through the great-grandparents.

- Also included should be complete medical records (including recent health certificate), feeding information, properly completed AKC registration application (if applicable), and breed information.

PUPPY PACT

Understand the obligations, guarantees, and rights set forth by your purchase or adoption contract

The breeder's contract exists to protect you as well as the breeder. This contract typically provides a health guarantee, outlining a refund/return policy for a pup diagnosed with an illness during a specified period of time following purchase.

Think twice before returning your puppy: It's destiny unknown for a sick pup who is returned to a seller. Also, remember that a puppy is not a television, but a living thing. Do you really want to return him because he's "broken"? Check your state's puppy lemon law—it may stipulate refund *without* having to return the puppy.

The breeder's contract may also set forth buyer's obligations. Often the buyer must agree to notify the breeder if the

Seven things to look for in breeder's contract:

1. Seller's and buyer's names

2. Names of puppy, sire, and dam

3. Pup's breed, gender, color, and birth date

4. Purebreed registration number or statement that puppy is registerable

5. Health guarantee

6. Refund/return policy

7. Buyer's responsibilities (i.e., sterilizing, showing)

Price

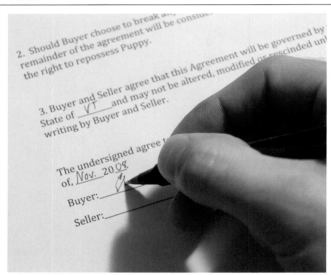

- Price is a key ingredient in the breeder's contract.

- Puppy prices run the gamut, anywhere from a few hundred dollars to $1,500+.

- Expect to pay more for a pup from a quality breeder than from a backyard breeder or a pet shop.

- A pup sold with a spay/neuter mandate will probably cost under $800.

- Puppies with health certifications or show/working/ sporting/obedience titles in their pedigree could run $1,500 or more.

dog becomes sick. (The breeder wants to make sure he is not breeding abnormalities into his line.) To avoid breeding of "inferior" individuals the seller could require you to sterilize your puppy. Breeder contracts can require anything. Remember, you can always walk away from the table.

Shelter or breed rescue adoption contracts typically list an adoption fee, and state that the dog will be a family pet and provided adequate housing, veterinary care, spaying/neutering, and collar with ID/license/rabies tag. They may state the shelter's right to inspect the premises, and release of liability.

Health Guarantee

•••••••••••• GREEN ● LIGHT ••••••••••••

One in three states has a puppy lemon law setting forth rules for refunds, replacement, and reimbursement of veterinary expenses should your puppy be diagnosed with an infectious or hereditary disease within a specified time frame. Check to see if your state has a puppy lemon law.

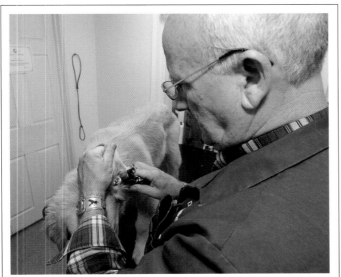

- Every breeder contract should contain a health guarantee.

- This stipulates terms for refund, puppy replacement, and reimbursement of veterinary expenses should the puppy become sick.

- For compensation, a puppy would need to be diagnosed with an infectious illness within about a week, and a congenital/hereditary disease by about a year.

- Make sure your contract gives you at least forty-eight hours to have your puppy examined by a vet.

AKC registration

- Reputable breeders generally offer AKC registration papers.

- Typically, the breeder will provide you with your puppy's AKC registration application at the time of sale, and you the buyer complete and send it in with a fee.

- Sometimes the breeder requires the buyer to meet certain conditions, like spaying/neutering, in order to receive AKC papers.

- Do not buy a puppy from a breeder who is asking a higher price "with papers" than without.

31

CONSIDER YOUR OTHER PETS

With the right introduction, your puppy can grow in harmony with other pets

When adopting a new puppy, you must factor in the other household members. The average dog-owning household has 1.7 dogs, so in most cases, when a new puppy comes into the house, there is a dog already there to "greet" him. And often, there's a cat or two, plus other smaller pets.

The prospect of mixing pets makes many owners anxious.

They wonder, will the older pet tolerate a puppy? Without even trying it, many rule out bringing in a new puppy.

There might be some initial apprehension, jealousy, protectiveness, maybe even a little territorial aggression. Sometimes older dogs become annoyed with overexuberant puppies. And individual chemistry plays a huge role: Not

Puppy and Your Adult Dog(s)

- Though your new puppy may be vexing to your older dog, they might become the best of friends.

- Allow your resident dog to have a role in training puppy in acceptable dog behavior.

- Sometimes an older dog will growl or bite a puppy who exhibits annoying behaviors like nipping.

- Although this interdog reprimand is normal and usually effective, monitor these interactions so no one gets hurt.

Puppy and Your Cat

- Adopting from a shelter? Ask the staff to perform a cat-tolerance test on puppy before adopting him.

- Young puppies tend to be more playful than aggressive with cats. Regardless, most cats shun rough puppy play.

- Just because your cat does not enjoy high-voltage puppy energy, there's no reason that kitty won't grow fond of your puppy as he matures.

- Reserve a puppy-free zone in your house, where your cat can go if he wants to be away from puppy.

every pair will become fast friends, and some will never be friends. But animals usually work out their differences over time. They make the appropriate accommodations in the interest of harmony and self-preservation. Rest assured that these adjustments will not harm your pets—change is part of life, even for animals.

As your pets adjust, do not punish their behavior. Your older dog may scold puppy for inappropriate conduct— allow him to do so, but monitor the situation so everyone stays safe. And be patient—these adjustments may take time.

Puppy and Your Pocket Pets

- Keep puppies and rodents separated.

- Never leave a small animal near your puppy unsupervised. Even if they have "met," the puppy can hurt your lizard or bird, intentionally or not.

- Habituate puppy to your small pets by letting him see and sniff the aquarium or cage. Before long, he'll probably ignore them.

- A mouthy puppy could contract infectious diseases, like *Salmonella* and *Campylobacter,* from infected reptiles and rodents.

· · · · · · · · · · · · RED ● LIGHT · · · · · · · · · · · ·

Remember that certain breed groups, like terriers, retrievers, and sighthounds, were created specifically to hunt. If you don't supervise things closely, your smaller pets, like cats and rodents, might become your puppy's quarry.

Safety first:

- Never leave your new puppy unattended with your resident pets.

- Separate them using baby gates, crates, doors, and tethers.

- Prevent disease transmission: Before coming home, take your pets—new and old—to the veterinarian for an exam, and ensure they are current on their vaccinations and free of parasites.

- Be sure any frightened animals have means for retreat.

- An energetic, clumsy puppy can unwittingly injure a frail older dog.

- Don't put yourself in the middle of an animal fight.

PUPPY VIGOR

Healthy choices are key, especially when picking a puppy out of a litter

Choosing a puppy out of a litter is kind of like choosing a flower out of a garden. Every one is appealing. It's hard to appreciate that each puppy is unique in temperament and fitness.

Since even experts can't always identify which puppy is truly the healthiest, you need only ensure that the puppy you pick doesn't have any glaring abnormalities. Look for a pup that is bright and alert, and explores her surroundings. Social interaction is key as well—the pup that cowers in the corner might have a passive personality, or a fearful one. The pup that burrows its muzzle into your ankles like a power drill might be very gregarious and need lots of interaction.

Pick of the litter:

- The breeder's "pick of the litter" is the pup that most closely conforms to the AKC standard for the breed.

- The breeder rates each pup "show quality" or "pet quality."

- Breeders usually pair show-quality pups with owners who show and breed.

- The choice pup for you is the one that best matches the tempo of your household.

- Ask the breeder if temperament testing was done on the pups.

Puppy Litter

- Canine pregnancy lasts sixty-one to sixty-three days.

- Litter size usually runs from five to ten pups, but can be as few as one or two in small breeds.

- Pups can usually be counted via palpation by five or six weeks' gestation.

- Many breeders obtain a puppy count by having the pregnant dam x-rayed. If the dam was x-rayed while pregnant, think twice about this litter: Radiation can damage DNA, particularly in developing fetuses.

The puppy that tramples the others to latch onto a teat might be strong willed and dominant. A yappy puppy could turn out to be a boundless barker. A puppy that nips constantly might become an orally fixated adult that licks or—worse—bites.

Visit the litter several times and take notes on each puppy. Consider your needs and try to eliminate puppies that exhibit extremes of any behavior, be it biting or barking, licking or chewing, jumping or cowering, running or resting.

After doing your own assessment, elicit the breeder's input.

Choosing

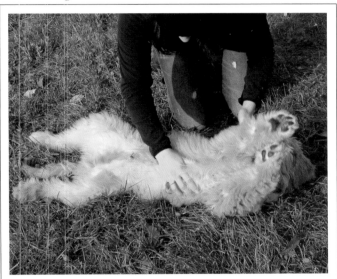

- Once you select a breed and a breeder, get your name on a list for a puppy.

- Decide on gender.

- Write the breeder a letter describing your household, your lifestyle, and how you intend to use the dog.

- If you trust the breeder, let him match you up with the best puppy for you, based on his getting to know the pups for the last eight weeks and based on the information you have provided about yourself.

Healthy Selection

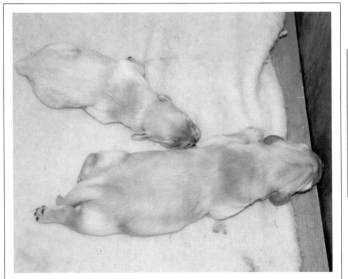

- Steer away from a pup that has abnormal stature, lameness, diarrhea, breathing problems, runny eyes, undescended testicles, or evidence of any breed-related inherited defects.

- Ask to see veterinary records for the pup.

- Parasites, like roundworms, mites, and fleas, are not uncommon in puppies—they should not be deal breakers.

- The runt may be small because she is not assertive at feeding time; she usually catches up in size over time.

THE RIGHT START

Birth to take-home age: The right care early on can make a lifelong difference

As soon as a puppy is born, his body grows at a precipitous rate, his immune system ripens, and his personality takes shape. For this reason, his environment and care are critical.

There are many observations to make and questions to ask the breeder when you visit a litter of pups. First, was the dam fully vaccinated? And did your pup receive colostrum, the antibody-rich milk the dam produces during the first twenty-four to forty-eight hours after birth? Were puppy vaccinations initiated at six to eight weeks?

Was the nursing bitch fed a well-balanced commercial food? Was she supplemented with vitamins and extra protein? Was she a willing nurser or did she reject her pups?

Lessons from Mom

- A pup's mother is his first disciplinarian.

- The dam is typically protective and attentive toward her pups.

- She introduces the pups to impulse control by scolding them for annoying behaviors like nipping.

- A pup that is separated from his mother early misses out on a lot of these crucial early lessons.

Human Socialization

- The human socialization period begins around six weeks of age.

- Between six and twelve weeks, pups should have ample positive interaction with people.

- Positive human interaction includes gentle touch, cuddling, "happy talk," and playing.

- Aggressive games like tug-of-war should be avoided at this age, and gentle reprimand should not begin until after twelve weeks old.

Were procedures like tail docking and dewclaw removal done early (first week) and by a veterinarian? Was the litter kept in the breeder's home or in a kennel? A home is great, because the pups are exposed to the stuff of human life. If the pups were raised in a kennel, a reputable breeder will let them run around the facility and expose them to noises.

During the critical social period of five to seven weeks, did puppy remain with his dam and littermates? During this time, the pup should have had plenty of human handling, and been getting accustomed to baths, brushing, trims, and collars.

Becoming a Puppy

- It is very important for a pup's psychological health and personality development that he not be removed from his litter before eight or ten weeks of age.

- A pup's litter is a canine nursery school of sorts.

- From his littermates, puppy discovers how to be a dog. He learns to read and to convey canine social cues, like the dominant stance and the submissive bow.

- Puppy also gains positive social experiences while developing play skills.

What puppies learn in the first twelve weeks:

- Two weeks: Eyes start to open and pup starts to explore environment

- Three to four weeks: Becomes aware of self and others; weaning begins and pup learns to eat solids and drink water from bowl

- Four to eight weeks: Becomes independent

- Five to seven weeks: Begins socializing with littermates and people

- Eight to twelve weeks: Engages in human social play and can learn basic commands

PUPPY TEMPERAMENT TESTING

Tests and observations you can make to predict a puppy's adult temperament

Discrete personality traits characterize each breed. Yet every dog is an individual—one dog might be bold and inquisitive, another flighty. While not exact, temperament testing can be a good indicator of how your pup's disposition will shape itself.

Puppy temperament testing is used to size up a puppy along several different parameters, including dominance/submissiveness, independence, sociability, obedience, play drive, problem-solving aptitude, noise tolerance, trainability, and stability.

Stability, for instance, can be measured using the umbrella test. Here, an umbrella is opened in front of the puppy and his reaction is gauged. Does he dash off? Whimper? Stare

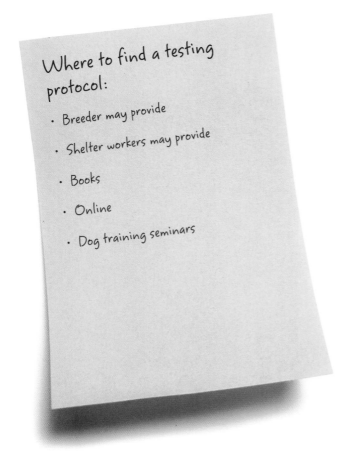

Where to find a testing protocol:

- Breeder may provide
- Shelter workers may provide
- Books
- Online
- Dog training seminars

Dominance/Submissiveness

- Lay puppy on her back (belly up) in your arms or on the floor or bed.

- While she is prone, rub her belly and gently tug her skin.

- If she resists touch or tries to right herself from this vulnerable position, she

probably has some degree of dominance; a submissive dog will generally lie still.

- A dominant dog is harder to manage, and is best placed with an experienced dog owner.

impassively? Lunge at it? It's better to have temperament testing administered by someone with whom your pup is not yet acquainted, such as a new dog trainer. Otherwise, the breeder or you can do it.

In general, it's better to take home a puppy who tests in the middle-of-the-road for most behavioral traits. But if you have a busy household, for example, maybe you should get a puppy that is confident and somewhat assertive. If you have small children, perhaps a less reactive, maybe even submissive, pup—with high noise tolerance!—would fit in best.

Retrieving

- Throw a ball, stick, or chew toy in front of your puppy and see if she retrieves it.

- The rapidity and intensity of her response, and whether she brings the object back to you, indicate the strength of her retrieval instinct.

- How eagerly puppy retrieves tells us something about her trainability and her play drive.

- High retrieval response may also suggest tendency to go after less desirable things, like spinning bicycle wheels and chipmunks.

MAKE IT EASY

If you videotape your puppy's temperament testing session(s), you can review it afterwards for subtleties you may have missed, and maybe even have an expert view it and give his assessment. Remember that the predictive value of this testing depends on many factors, including the particular test you choose, the tester, the testing conditions, and the puppy's mindset at the time of testing: Is she well rested? Hungry? Stressed? Full of pent-up verve?

Ideal conditions for temperament testing:

1. Forty-nine days old (or six to eight weeks)
2. Time of day when pup is alert
3. Test in quiet, neutral environment
4. Only people present: tester and scorer
5. Puppy does not know tester
6. Conduct/compare two or three testing sessions
7. NOT day of vaccinations/deworming/doctor visit
8. NOT immediately following feeding
9. NOT when puppy is hungry or agitated
10. NOT before puppy has gone to bathroom

READY, SET, GO

Pre-puppy preparations: What you must do to prepare for the new arrival

You want to have your infrastructure in place when puppy's paws cross your threshold. The most important ingredient for a smooth introduction is *time*.

Have your puppy's arrival coincide with a lull in your normal routine, when you have time to spend on orientation, training, cleanups, and good ol' TLC. Plan it for a time when you

have no out-of-town travel planned and are not expecting visitors or work crews at your home.

If you reside in a temperate climate zone, spring and summer are prime times to bring home a pup. Without the complications of snow and cold, you can better provide outdoor exercise and introduce your puppy to smells, sights, and

Contain Him

- Do not bring a puppy home without having a crate there ready for him.

- A valuable tool for housebreaking, the crate also provides confinement to keep him safe.

- Be sure the crate is clean and lined with a crate pad or a blanket.

- Situate the crate in an area of your home that has lots of activity but where you're bound to hear pup if he needs you when you're sleeping (your bedroom, perhaps).

Safety

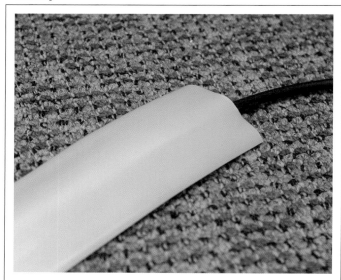

- Your puppy has three major weapons: needle-sharp teeth, swishing tail, and messy excretions.

- Puppies can get electrocuted if they chew electric cords. Tape electric cords to baseboards or keep them raised.

- To discourage puppy from chewing (nonporous) things that are off-limits, coat them with Grannick's Bitter Apple spray or Tabasco sauce.

- Use baby gates to wall off parts of the house where puppy could wreak havoc.

sounds of the neighborhood.

Have your barriers—baby gates and such— erected and anything that could endanger your puppy or that you hope to protect, like carpets, covered or out of the way.

The house should be stocked with supplies like carpet cleaner, stain remover, grooming tools, ID tags, collars, leashes, tethers, toys, and food/water bowls. Also, bring home a week's worth of the food that the seller has been feeding the puppy—if you are planning to use a different food long-term, you will need to do a gradual switch from the previous diet.

Be sure you have selected a veterinarian in advance, and schedule a first appointment for some time within forty-eight hours of puppy's arrival.

Outdoor Space

- Be sure there is a safe place for puppy to exercise on- or off-leash.

- Fenced yards and tennis courts (unless dogs are prohibited) are perfect for off-leash exercise.

- Yard fencing should be free of gaps along its length or between fence and ground. It should be high enough to contain puppy, and all gates should be securely latched. There should be a shaded area within the yard.

- Puppy should not be left in the yard unsupervised.

Family conference

- Have each family member select a role in puppy's care, such as the evening walk or dog food purchase.

- Choose training methods and uniform words so pup receives the same verbal cues from everyone. Will it be "heel" or "stay"? "Down" or "off"?

- Set puppy rules that EVERYONE agrees to follow, such as NO to feeding from the table, or YES to allowing puppy on couch.

- So as not to confuse puppy, try to agree on ONE name that everyone is happy with BEFORE he comes home.

KIDS & PUPPIES

It's just as important to train the kids as to train the new puppy

How children interact with puppies is a big deal because pups and kids cross paths a lot. According to the American Veterinary Medical Association (AVMA), nearly half of young parents have dogs. Moreover, pets are typically brought into the home when the oldest child is about eight years old.

Before you get a puppy, drill into your children's heads the idea of respecting that puppy. Notice the dents, scratches, and holes in your kids' toys. You do not want this to happen to your puppy.

Even children with the best intentions can hug a puppy too tightly. They can pick up the pup the wrong way, drop her, or fall on her. Be sure to teach your child about gentle handling. Monitor all interactions, especially in the beginning while puppy is still small and the child is still learning. Do not

Keep Everyone Safe

- Children develop empathy anywhere between five and seven years old.

- Children younger than this cannot be expected to care if they are harming puppy, inadvertently or on purpose.

- For the safety of both puppy and child, do not leave a young child and a puppy alone together unattended.

- No matter how cute, no matter what the breed, *every* dog has the potential to bite.

Children's Responsibilities

- Children under the age of thirteen are generally not mature enough to reliably take care of a dog.

- Give each child ten years and over a single puppy-related job, such as doing the feeding.

- Monitor the child's perfor-

mance of the task—even though the child "owns" the particular job, you as the adult are ultimately responsible for the puppy's welfare.

- Encourage compliance by creating a calendar of jobs and rotating them through the family.

let the child walk around with puppy in arms—he should be sitting quietly while holding puppy.

Teach your child to never strike or tease a puppy. Not only is this cruel and potentially dangerous, it can also hamper the puppy training messages you are trying to impart.

If the children play roughly, keep puppy out of the fray. And if their friends are over, supervise them closely around puppy.

If yours is a home free of children, look down the road at the possibility of children coming into your life during puppy's lifetime.

Meal-time Etiquette

- Test for food aggression by taking away puppy's food bowl while she is eating (a child should *never* perform this test).

- Help puppy see you are not going to steal her food: Take her bowl away briefly and then return it. Reposition it. Manipulate it while not removing it.

- Instruct children not to touch puppy or her food while she is eating until you are *very* sure she has no food-related aggression.

- If she is food aggressive, feed her in a closed room away from the children.

Tips for children and puppies:

- Have kids? Think twice about getting a protective breed or a delicate toy breed.

- Kids (and adults) should not feed puppy from table.

- Involve kids with puppy, from bathing to feeding, playing games to teaching tricks.

- Let children over eight years attend puppy training classes.

- Junior showmanship competition, which judges skillful dog handling is generally open to kids nine to eighteen.

SHOPPING 101: THE BASICS
Rev up your wallet and take a trip to your local pet emporium

The basic necessities for a dog—food and shelter—are something we dog lovers have gone far beyond. With our liver-flavored biscottis, doggie booties, and leopard-print fleece trundles, many of the items we buy our dogs reflect *our* human sensibilities more than actual *canine* needs.

According to the American Pet Products Association, there is unprecedented growth in the quantity and types of products available for pets. And we dog owners take full advantage of the canine consumer smorgasbord—the APPA estimates that the average owner spends over $600 a year on products (not including food and medication) for his dog.

Because of the plethora of items to be had, you can better tailor your purchases to your own puppy, your lifestyle, your taste, and your pocketbook.

If your puppy has an esophageal problem affecting swallowing, there are raised food and water dishes. If you plan to

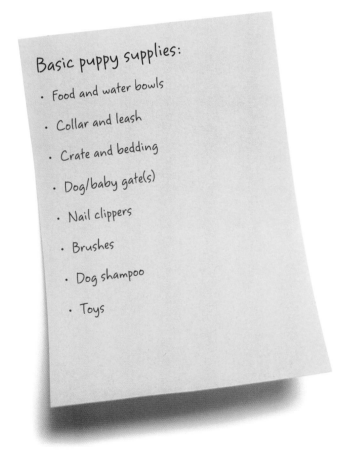

Basic puppy supplies:

- Food and water bowls
- Collar and leash
- Crate and bedding
- Dog/baby gate(s)
- Nail clippers
- Brushes
- Dog shampoo
- Toys

Measurements

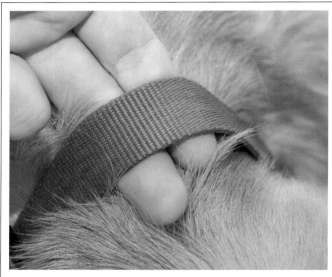

- Collars: Wrap a measuring tape around the center of puppy's neck and make sure you can slide two fingers underneath.

- Harnesses: Use neck size (as above) and girth. For girth, measure circumference of the rib cage about a half inch behind the front legs.

- Clothing can be sized by length, girth, and/or neck size.

- If your puppy is on the cusp between two sizes, go with the next size up.

take your puppy on auto outings, you can purchase a car harness, a cargo-area coverall, a backseat barrier, even motion sickness tablets.

Do you live on a busy street or plan to do a lot of nighttime walking with your puppy? Reflective collars and vests can be had. And to aid you during those trying days of housebreaking, you can buy a urine-off LED light that fluoresces on urine stains, as well as a variety of carpet stain removers and brushes.

Before puppy arrives, try to anticipate what items you will need. Talk to the breeder or whomever you are obtaining your puppy from and ask if there are items recommended for your breed, such as special grooming tools. Purchase the basics in advance of puppy's homecoming. After you spend some time with puppy at home, you may find your product needs to be different from what you'd anticipated. So save your receipts for possible returns and exchanges of any unused items.

Efficient Shopping

- The main outlets for pet products are mass merchandisers, grocery stores, pet shops, and pet supply superstores.

- Pet superstores offer a vast array of products with different features and varying price points.

- Purchase your basic puppy products before your puppy arrives home.

- For items like clothing, harnesses, and such, bring puppy to the store for proper fitting.

Online shopping tips:

- Check out dog-related Web sites you trust for product recommendations and advertisements.

- Survey the wide variety of product specs and brands.

- Learn more by reading customer reviews.

- Watch online videos demonstrating usage of many puppy products.

- Spend the time on price comparisons.

- Save mailing costs by researching online and then buying from a local pet supply emporium.

- Some Web sites offer online coupons.

- Spend the time you've saved shopping online playing with your puppy!

MEALTIME

Food, bowls, and cleanup: grocery shopping for your little omnivore

Think of how much growing a child does in her first fifteen years of life: That's how much growth a puppy experiences in her first year!

During this critical window of time, her body is developing rapidly. Her nutritional demands are greater now than ever. And the nutritional parameters are at their most stringent, in terms of amounts/percentages of proteins, fats, carbs, vitamins, minerals, and water.

Puppies require higher percentages of protein and a tighter calcium-phosphorus ratio. Be sure to supply the *right* nutritional components, and in the adequate *quantities* and *proportions*. The buzz term for this is *"complete and balanced."*

To give puppy the best shot at the right diet, feed her a commercial dog food labeled for puppies. Because of the specific nutritional demands, puppyhood is not the time to experiment with homemade diets.

Feeding schedule

- Scheduled meals versus free choice.

- Scheduled feeding advantages: scheduled pooping and weight control. Disadvantages: can predispose to food/air gulping and bloat in some dogs.

- Feed three to four times daily until puppy is six months old, then two times daily until puppy is a year old.

- Free-choice feeding means always keeping food in the bowl. This only works with a dry food diet. Advantages: Puppy paces herself; may decrease food obsession and gulping; no feeding schedule to maintain. Disadvantages: Excessive weight gain in some dogs.

Bowls

- Provide puppy with a food and a water bowl. Bowls should be made of stainless steel or sealed ceramic, rather than plastic, which can leach chemicals and are harder to clean.

- Raised bowls and specially designed slow-eating bowls—useful for larger breeds prone to gastric dilatation-volvulus (GDV) or "bloat"—can decrease air gulping that causes this serious stomach condition.

- Place bowls out of the fray, but remember that some dogs like to eat around people. A remote area of the kitchen may work well.

If puppy is a smaller breed, feed her puppy food until she is a year old; if she is a larger breed, do not switch her to adult maintenance food until she is a year and a half or so. If you are feeding a commercial puppy food, do not supplement with vitamins unless your veterinarian directs you to do so.

Choose a brand with an AAFCO nutritional claim. This statement is based on one of two methods: comparison with known nutritional requirements *or* feeding trials. The latter is the preferred method.

Body condition scores (BCS) range from 1 (emaciated) to 9 (obese). Aim for a BCS of between 4 and 5. For health reasons, slightly "ribby" (like the back of your hand) is better than "roly-poly."

When switching puppy from one food to another, do so gradually to avoid digestive problems: Blend in the new diet in increasing amounts over a week or so. Treats should compose no more than 10 percent of the diet. Fresh water should be available at all times.

Dietary Advice

- Consult your veterinarian regarding puppy nutrition.

- Consult your breeder for practical feeding tips.

- Dietary requirements do not vary between any specific similarly sized breeds.

- Large, fast growing breeds will have fewer orthopedic problems if fed a diet formulated for their needs.

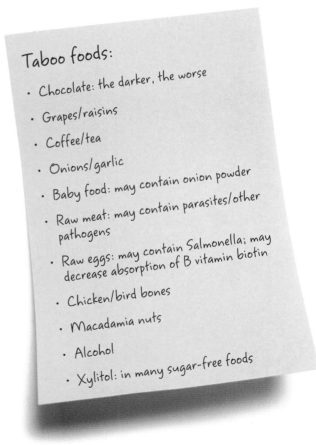

Taboo foods:
- Chocolate: the darker, the worse
- Grapes/raisins
- Coffee/tea
- Onions/garlic
- Baby food: may contain onion powder
- Raw meat: may contain parasites/other pathogens
- Raw eggs: may contain Salmonella; may decrease absorption of B vitamin biotin
- Chicken/bird bones
- Macadamia nuts
- Alcohol
- Xylitol: in many sugar-free foods

TOYS & CHEWIES

The dog toy aisle can boggle your mind, so find out which products are best

Chews and toys serve many purposes for puppies. They distract and relieve boredom; satisfy play drive and release pent-up energy; meet puppy's natural urge to chew; and serve as rewards sans calories!

For every canine craze, there is a dog toy to match. Many toys and chews are available specifically for puppies. Kong has teething sticks and binkies made of tough rubber that stand up to sharp puppy daggers. Nylabone has durable Teething Keys that many puppies enjoy chewing and clattering around. To lend cool soothing to teethers with sore gums, there are freezable chews.

When selecting toys for your puppy, go with sturdy

Choosing

- Dog toys and chews come in just about every material, from durable nylon to compressible rubber, firm plastic to tough rope.

- Your puppy will probably gravitate toward one type of toy, depending on whether he's a chomper, chewer, licker, chaser, tugger, ripper, or noise maker.

- Provide your puppy with an array of chews and toys, and see what type(s) he prefers. Save your receipts so you can return the ones he snubs.

- Rotate puppy's toys so he doesn't become bored.

Interactive/Enrichment Toys

- Many dog toys stimulate puppy's mind, wage interesting challenges, and/or provide fun for the two of you together.

- Rope tugs, balls, and Frisbees, by companies like Booda, can provide bonding activity for you and puppy.

- Manufacturers like Kong offer challenging toys, such as treat balls and puzzle cubes that puppy can roll to dispense kibble, as well as tough rubber tubes that you can fill with flavored Kong goop or peanut butter.

products. Avoid soft plastics and fiber- or styrofoam-filled toys. If you're on a tight budget, try old stuffed animals, but remove adhered parts, like eyes.

Size it right—not too big as to overextend your puppy's jaw while chewing, but not too small to be swallowed. Supervise your puppy in his early days of chewing. Remove chews and toys that puppy can break off large pieces from or shred.

And if you have more than one dog in your home, make sure the chews you've selected can stand up to the largest, toughest chewer.

Healthy Chewing

- Puppies have sensitive digestive tracts, and can experience diarrhea, vomiting, choking, or obstruction if they *ingest* what is meant only to be *chewed*.

- Pressed rawhide bones last longer than natural rawhide, and are less likely to shred and be swallowed.

Ingested pieces of rawhide can produce gastroenteritis.

- Natural chews, like cow hooves and deer antlers, resist splintering and appeal to many pups.

Toys for "super-chompers" to avoid:

- Toys with dangling or detachable parts (applies to all dogs)

- Toys filled with squeaks/rattles

- Shreddable toys (ropes and fabric)

- Stuffed toys

- Rawhides

PUPPY SUPPLIES

49

CRATES & BEDS

How to buy a crate your puppy will grow into, and smart bed-buying

To some, a crate might seem like a mechanism for canine incarceration, to others, extraneous indulgence. But if used correctly, a crate is as indispensable to your puppy training days (and beyond) as a leash and collar.

A "puppy container" of sorts, the crate separates pup from things (and people) she can chew on, shed on, or soil. It keeps puppy safe when you cannot be there to supervise her, and can also be used to secure puppy during travel. Plus, as she gets older, she's sure to seek out her crate willingly when she needs down-time.

According to the APPA, six out of ten owners have a dog crate or carrier of some type. Wire crates are great because

Types of Crates

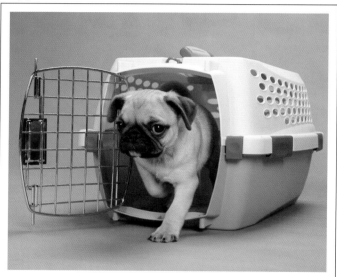

- Wire crates are standard. They have complete ventilation and visibility. Most have pan liners that can be removed and cleaned, and some have attachable food/water bowls.

- Travel crates are generally made of durable, light-weight plastic and have ventilation on all sides. For airline travel, buy a crate that is FAA approved.

- Other crate designs include lightweight, durable nylon; hardwood; cornerless geo-desic; and rolling (wheeled) crates.

- Crates run $100 to $200.

Pens

- You can use an adjustable pen to create play and sleep spaces for puppy.

- Pens can provide safety for puppy, as well as protection for your furniture, floor surfaces, and valuables during your puppy's chewing and housebreaking days.

- Pens can easily be moved from location to location, and can be situated indoors or out.

- Pens are available in metal, wood, and durable mesh. Most can be folded like accordions, for easy storage and transportation.

puppy can see out and you can see in. They're usually collapsible, for easy transport and storage. Some dogs chew the wire bars of their crate. This can result in broken teeth. If your pup chews on her crate, try switching to a different style of crate, perhaps a plastic one.

An adjunct to the crate is the dog bed. It can be used as padding in the crate, or to designate another spot for puppy to sleep. Your puppy's bed can be as simple as an old quilt or even the crate bottom separated from the top and lined with a mat. Or it can be quite elaborate.

Beds are available in fleece, plush polyester, odor- and water-resistant nylon, cabana- and beanbag-style, even chew-resistant faux suede. They come in earth-friendly materials, such as organic cotton, hemp, recycled sneaker mesh, and plant-based dyes, and different innards, like springs, orthopedic memory foam, cooling water-infused foam, and charcoal particles.

Dog beds run the gamut pricewise, from $30 to $500. Dog owners spent an average of $39 on dog beds in 2008, according to the APPA.

Matching Bed to Puppy

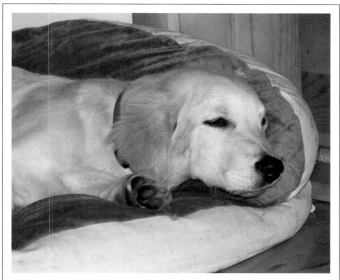

- "Leaners" are dogs that like to rest their chin or shoulders on raised surfaces. Beds for leaners feature armrest-like borders.

- "Nesters" tend to ball themselves up tightly when they sleep. Beds designed for nesters are round and encircled by a raised border.

- "Sprawlers" prefer to slumber all stretched-out. Flat, raft-like beds are perfect for sprawling.

- "Tunnelers" like to snooze while nestled in a cave-like enclosure. Tunneling beds look like fluffy pita pockets.

Measuring for Crates/Beds

- *Crates:* Measure puppy's height from floor to tip of shoulders.

- The crate should be high enough for pup to sit without hitting her head, and long enough for her to completely turn around.

- Avoid crates large enough

for pup to eliminate at one end and sleep cleanly at the other. If you purchase a crate to accommodate puppy's adult size, "puppy-size" it with crate dividers.

- *Beds:* Measure puppy from nose to tip of tail, and add twelve to fourteen inches for her to stretch.

51

TRAINING TOOLS

Every job well done requires proper tools, and puppy training is no different

The wide variety of training methods and the different situations in which your puppy will find herself warrant many training aids. Last year, according to the APPA, 59 percent of dog owners utilized training devices. Most commonly used were treats, training books/videos, professional dog training, clickers, and whistles.

Some dog owners like all the bells and whistles, literally. Others like to keep things simple. Whatever your style, you must prevent puppy's escape and control her movement. For this, a leash, and a collar are must-haves. Depending on your lifestyle, you may also want visible or electric fencing.

If you go electric, your puppy will need extra training (the

Positive Reinforcement Tools

- Edible treats are probably the best tools to reinforce desired behaviors.

- If you don't want your pockets full of crumbs and reeking of liver, keep treats in a plastic or canvas treat carrier, a fanny pack, or a Tupperware container.

- Next to food, playful interaction is probably the strongest impetus.

- Designate a play object for you and puppy to enjoy together. Keep it with you whenever you are with puppy. Take it out whenever puppy follows your commands.

Negative Reinforcement

- Training tools like squirt guns and spray bottles can negatively reinforce undesired behaviors, like barking, biting, chewing, and jumping on people.

- Shake a "shake can"—a can filled with coins—immediately when puppy displays an undesirable behavior.

- Vibration-triggered bark collars release a mild shock or a mist of citrus oil when puppy barks.

- Shock collars come with remote transmitters you can use to deliver a mild shock when puppy misbehaves.

electric fence company will instruct you on how to do this). Plan on having training flags bordering your property until training is complete. Also, you'll have to find a good dog trainer and register for puppy classes. Have your trainer, your breeder, shelter personnel, or other dog expert recommend a few puppy training books, guides, or DVDs.

Visit a pet superstore to see what other training devices you'd like to integrate. There, you'll find everything from basic whistles and clickers to pet pagers with which to communicate with puppy remotely.

Chew Chasers

- Grannick's Bitter Apple, available in spray, liquid, and gel, can be applied to objects and surfaces that you want to prevent puppy from chewing.

- A muzzle can also prevent or discourage chewing, as well as biting, barking, and licking.

- A shake can, squirt gun, or spray bottle can be used to deter chewing.

- These negative stimuli will be effective only if used to startle puppy while he is chewing.

Housetraining/elimination aids

- The crate tops the list. It is an indispensable housebreaking tool that will save your floors and carpets.

- No matter how diligent you are about crate training, keep a bottle of carpet cleaner, stain remover, and a good scrub brush on hand for accidents.

- Pee posts and indoor elimination mats/pads can be used to designate spots for eliminating.

- For puppies that eat their feces, coprophagia tablets can deter this behavior.

PUPPY SUPPLIES

THE BUDGET SHOPPER

Clever ways to cut costs and still get your puppy everything she needs

The difference between what you *want* to buy your dog and what your dog needs in order to thrive could be as great as the difference between a day at the spa bathing in mineral salts and a jump in the river.

If you have an "I'll-take-one-in-every-color"-sized wallet, then do take advantage of the smorgasbord of stuff available for dogs. But if you wish to budget a little, think about dogs in the wild, getting rained on, sleeping under bushes, and eating every second or third day. Now ask yourself: What does my puppy *need*?

If you answer this question honestly, you'll find plenty of places where you can economize. For instance, don't spend

Low-cost Substitutes

- Veterinary care tops the list of dog expenses. Save money at community vaccination days and low-cost spay-neuter clinics.

- Rather than buying a dog bed, let puppy sleep on old towels or pillowcases.

- Most dogs do not require professional grooming. If yours is one of these, bathe her with an outdoor hose or in the bathtub. If she needs clipping, buy a clipper and clip her yourself.

- If puppy soils the rug, clean it with laundry detergent solution rather than carpet spray.

Eating on the Cheap

- Food is the #2 dog-related monthly expense, averaging about $20 for a medium-sized dog (APPA).

- Cut food costs by mixing people-food leftovers (at 10 percent max) with commercial puppy food. Avoid high-fat table foods as well as the listed taboo foods.

- Rather than buying dog treats, which can be costly, bake them yourself using online recipes.

- Puppies have sensitive GI tracts. If diarrhea or vomiting occurs, discontinue table-food supplements and homemade treats.

$20 on dog bowls if you have a few durable metal or ceramic bowls collecting dust in your cabinet.

If you're on a tight budget, hopefully you have taken expenses into consideration before selecting a breed. Large breeds cost more to feed, medicate, and kennel, for instance. And some breeds require extensive grooming, which can be pricey. Managing certain breed-related health problems can also be financially burdensome.

Makeshift Toys

- Want to save money on toys? There are many ways to improvise.

- Fill a container with water. Add a few veggies, a ball, a short piece of rope, maybe a knotted sock. Freeze. Let puppy gnaw at the ice block until she has freed her treats.

- Tennis clubs regularly dispose of "dead" balls. Call around to see if you can get some free balls.

- Tie a rope through a tennis ball. Knot the end so the rope is secure. Use as a tug toy.

Economy traveler

- Travel-related costs are high on the list of dog-related expenditures.

- Reduce boarding expenses by bringing pup along on vacation. There are dog-friendly hotels all around the country.

- If you must leave puppy home, try to find a friend or relative to take care of her.

PUPPY SUPPLIES

PUPPY PROOFING YOUR HOME

Get on your hands and knees, and check your house through a puppy's eyes

The purpose of puppy proofing is two-fold: to protect puppy and to protect your possessions.

Puppy proofing should be done before bringing puppy home, although you will certainly augment your efforts with every chopped-up candle or carpet stain you find!

First thing's first: Keep puppy safe. This means removing or blocking off anything that can pose a danger to him (see below). Drop to your hands and knees for a puppy's-eye view of all the things there are to get into. Close doors or gate off rooms that are prohibited. Keep cabinets and drawers shut, and use baby-proof latches if you need to.

Toilet lids should be down to prevent potty drinking, or even

Protecting Your Possessions

- Crawl on the floor so you can get a puppy's-eye view of any potential hazards.

- Most pups prefer a particular type of object to chew. Many favor leather; some fancy wood, plastics, or even metals, like jewelry. Others like to disembowel pillows and stuffed animals.

- Place anything you covet out of puppy's reach.

- To protect stationary objects, coat accessible parts (i.e., table legs) with a repellant, such as Grannick's Bitter Apple spray or liquid pepper. Keep puppy off carpets until housebroken.

Keep Out!

- Some sections of your home are simply unsafe for puppy.

- Attics, basements, and garages often contain verboten items like valuables, sharp/pointy tools, tangled hoses and ropes, and stacked items that can tip over.

- Puppies are uncoordinated and at risk for tumbling down stairs.

- Be diligent in your use of doors and baby gates to block off areas of your home to which you do not want puppy to have (unsupervised) access.

drowning. Garbage cans should stay behind closed doors or be placed above puppy's level. And electrical cords— many puppies love to chew these, possibly leading to electrocution or fire—should be protected by duct taping them to the floor or covering them with rubber runners or PVC.

Keep small, ingestible items like toys, remote controls, pencils, paper clips, and books off the ground or low shelves. And if puppy gets hold of something he is not supposed to chew, take it away with a stern "No," and replace it with a readily available puppy chew toy.

Outdoor Safety

- Perhaps the biggest outdoor danger is vehicles on the street. Keep puppy out of traffic with a leash or secure fence. Beware: Some breeds, like beagles and terriers, will dig their way out!

- Keep puppy away from gardening tools, nails, and ropes, as well as areas treated with pesticides, herbicides, or fertilizers.

- Antifreeze and rat poison are both tasty and deadly—keep them out of puppy's reach.

- Block off unsupervised access to pools or ponds.

Don't forget about the other animals in your home. They also need to be protected from puppy, and vice versa. Until everyone is accustomed to one another, puppy should be kept separated from other animals unless you are there to monitor the interactions. And pocket pets like hamsters and turtles should be kept safely behind glass.

Keep litter boxes out of puppy's reach, and the yard free of animal feces, a delicacy for many puppies (coprophagia). Not only does it permit a gross habit, but it can also transmit parasites and other pathogens.

Indoor doggie dangers:

- Medications/vitamins

- Taboo foods

- Indoor cleaning products and bug sprays

- Electric and drapery cords

- Furniture that can entrap or fall

- Hazardous foods

- Toxic plants (i.e., azalea, rhododendron, poinsettia, foxglove, lily of the valley)

- Jewelry and coins (may contain toxic metals)

- Ingestible items (i.e., undergarments, toys, holiday tinsel, which can cause GI blockage)

MEET THE RESIDENT DOG
Dos and don'ts for successfully introducing a puppy to a resident dog

The thought of bringing a puppy into a home that already has a dog arouses anxiety in many owners. Yet one third of all dog owners have two or more dogs, which suggests that adding to a canine household must not be such a bad idea.

A puppy is another source of entertainment for your resident dog. The companionship a puppy provides is particularly valuable during those times when you are not at home or simply too busy to give your dog attention.

Expect growing pains in the relationship between two dogs. While puppy is not likely to be aggressive—such behavior does not typically become manifest until social maturity, somewhere between twelve and eighteen months—she will likely annoy your older dog with her whining, nipping, and boundless energy.

Allow your older dog to correct puppy. She'll probably do

The Introduction

- Have puppy and your older dog(s) meet—*one* at a time —in neutral territory, maybe at a park.

- Keep both dogs on a lead, and make sure the person holding the older dog can control her.

- Keep leads loose and allow the dogs to sniff each other, or even play. (Be ready to take up the slack at a moment's notice.) Give them "happy voice" positive reinforcement as they do so.

- Keep the first meeting brief.

Safety

- Do not allow puppy and a mature dog to spend time together unsupervised until you feel that their behavior together is stable. This may take months—be patient.

- Until then, separate them using crates and baby gates when you're not around. Use leashes and head col-

lars or muzzles to control their interactions. If interactions become overexuberant, reprimand with a stern "No" and separate them.

- Signs of aggression include staring, bared teeth, growling, rigid walking, pinned-back ears, raised hair, and mounting another dog.

this by mouthing or snapping at puppy, or through subtler cues like snarling or baring her teeth.

Remember, puppy has thick skin formed into loose, well-padded rolls that can likely withstand a tug here and there. So as long as no one gets hurt, a little discipline from your older dog is okay because it schools puppy about acceptable behavior and it teaches her dog lingo.

········· GREEN ● LIGHT ·············

A puppy could ultimately bring valued companionship to your older dog. And phasing in a new pup might sustain you as your elderly pet nears the end of his life.

Role Model

- Allow your older pets some latitude in "training" your new pup.

- Puppies tend to chew, bite, mouth, and jiggle their bodies around clumsily.

- This can be annoying to many mature dogs, who may correct the inappropriate behavior with a snarl or a snap.

- Let the discipline proceed, as long as it remains at a controlled level.

Bonding

- When a puppy enters the picture, your older dog will probably try to establish hierarchical rules.

- Working out differences is part of the dog-dog bonding experience. Monitor your dogs closely as they do so.

- Certain breeds are more prone to interdog aggression. These include Airedale terriers, Dalmatians, and spitz dogs.

- The resident dog might accept a puppy of the opposite gender more readily. Reward good dogs with your happy voice or treats.

MEET THE RESIDENT CAT

Your cat may be horrified by the new addition, but cats and dogs can coexist

The adversarial ties linking dogs and cats are legendary. Think Lady (as in "Tramp") and those two sinister Siamese cats. These are funny, sweeping generalizations of complex relationships that vary with the dispositions of the individual animals involved. But there is some truth in humor.

Cats are cats, in all their fluid poise, standoffishness, and sense of entitlement. Contrast the feline mystique with the traits we have bred into our dogs: Their *raison d'être* is to rain love on us, follow us everywhere, regale us with their slobbery affection, and be on-the-ready to play.

This huge dog-cat personality gap sets the stage for natural animosity. Therefore, many people believe they cannot get

The Introduction

- When introducing your new puppy to your cat, trim your cat's nails first so he can't rake them across puppy's eyes.

- Let the two animals share space without physical contact.

- This can be accomplished by wrapping kitty in a blanket, or placing him in his carrier or behind a baby gate.

- Alternatively, you can keep puppy crated or on a leash while your cat scopes him out.

Safety

- Make sure puppy and your resident cat have safe retreat from one another. For kitty, this might be a countertop or a shelf. For puppy, safe haven could be his crate.

- Confine puppy from time to time so your cat can safely roam the house.

- Do not allow puppy to chase your cat under any circumstances. Even if the puppy is just playing, it's probably one-sided play.

- In most cases, the puppy is bigger and stronger than the cat and can mangle him.

a dog if they have a cat. While some dogs cannot be trusted around cats, usually having a cat does not mean you should not introduce a puppy.

Bringing a puppy into a cat household is usually not as problematic as bringing a cat or kitten into a home that has an adult dog. The puppy will not likely hurt the cat on purpose. Once mature, puppy will be habituated to cats.

Depending on the size of your puppy, the cat will probably be the more delicate of the two. So monitor them, and make sure your cat always has a means of escape from puppy. And remember, puppy is also at risk: Cats have five weapons (four sets of razor-sharp claws and a mouth) to a dog's one.

While shielding puppy from harm, let your cat assert himself in order to lay ground rules. Sometimes it takes a paw swat to teach pup a lesson. Cats tend to covet the sanctity of their environment, and when this is interrupted by something like a new puppy, it can throw off even the most adaptable cat, making them retreat and hide. Over time, most cats adjust to the new dog.

Litter Box Issues

- Many dogs consider litter boxes to be gourmet restaurants.

- Not only is feces eating a disgusting habit, it can also facilitate transmission of parasites and other pathogens.

- Keep litter box out of puppy's reach by placing it up high or putting it in a separate room to which puppy does not have access.

- If you cannot block puppy from the litter box, limit his access to waste using either a covered litter box or a self-cleaning litter box.

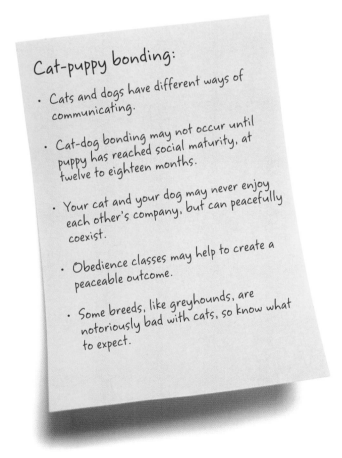

Cat-puppy bonding:

- Cats and dogs have different ways of communicating.

- Cat-dog bonding may not occur until puppy has reached social maturity, at twelve to eighteen months.

- Your cat and your dog may never enjoy each other's company, but can peacefully coexist.

- Obedience classes may help to create a peaceable outcome.

- Some breeds, like greyhounds, are notoriously bad with cats, so know what to expect.

WHAT'S YOUR PUPPY SAYING?

Your puppy is learning your language, but she's also communicating back at you

Dogs have a complex lingo based on body language, facial expressions, and breathing patterns, plus barks, growls, howls, yelps, yips, and whimpers.

Canine "words" are comprised of a rich alphabet of cues like tail position, ear angle, fur lift, and foot gait. So hardwired in our dogs' brains is this language that they exhibit it universally, regardless of breed, age, or country of origin. Once you master this language, you will become a more effective trainer and can forge a more meaningful bond with your puppy.

Puppies indicate contentment and willingness to engage by "smiling." The lips are relaxed and covering the teeth. The mouth is parted slightly. The eyes are alert. The tail is held

Submissiveness

- Hierarchy, important in the "pack" system of the canine world, is displayed through shows of dominance and submissiveness.

- The dog in your home will display gestures of dominance and submissiveness toward both animals and people.

- Signs of submissiveness include crouching down, rolling over to display belly, lowering head and neck, folding ears back, tucking tail between legs, and sometimes urinating.

- The submissive dog needs lots of reassurance from her owner.

Greeting Ritual

- The greeting ritual of dogs includes butt sniffing. This is a normal canine behavior and should not be reprimanded.

- A person greeting an unfamiliar pup should kneel down and extend one hand toward her, slightly below her mouth.

- To reduce the risk of being bitten, the palm should be down and the fingers folded under slightly.

- If puppy is shy, it is better to have her approach greeter than vice versa.

high and perhaps wagging.

An invitation to play might include quick yelps combined with the "play bow": forelimbs outstretched, head aimed forward and down, rump thrust in the air, and tail wagging.

Your puppy uses her tongue in many ways: to explore her environment, to show someone affection by licking their hand, or to indicate excitement or anxiety with rapid swipes of the tongue against open lips.

Dogs stomp their front feet out of excitement. They whimper to indicate pain, whine to solicit attention.

There are also minor individual and breed differences in communication. Hounds, for instance, are howlers and generally vocal. Chihuahuas—self-protective dogs—tend to curl their bodies and crawl when they want to hide.

So when trying to interpret what your puppy is trying to tell you, be sure to assess all of her body gestures and postures, as well as her vocalizations.

Confident Puppy

- A confident puppy usually "prances" with neck and tail erect, eyes alert, and ears directed forward.

- This is a good mindset for puppy to be in for training.

- Don't mistake shows of dominance for confidence.

- To instill confidence in puppy, set clear boundaries, correct misconduct as soon as it occurs, provide reasonable, noncorporal discipline, and be sure to praise good behavior.

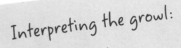

Interpreting the growl:

- Can be a threat

- Can be an invitation to play

- Exercise caution

- Consider context

- A low, steady growl is usually aggressive, particularly when hair stands up along back and neck.

- A dog usually would rather warn with a growl than resort to a bite.

- Over time, you'll learn what puppy's different growls mean.

SET BOUNDARIES

Consistency, kindness, and common-sense boundaries get your puppy off to a good start

Decide early on what you want from your puppy—and full-grown dog—and then construct rules for his behavior that will best produce the picture you have in your mind.

You might be envisioning your bed, with your dog curled up on the pillow. Or you find this image utterly horrifying. We all have distinct tolerance levels and sensibilities when

it comes to our doggie lifestyle. So as long as all involved—puppy as well as anyone coming in contact with him—thrive, there are no right or wrong answers.

Once you decide on the limitations, enforce them consistently. This means that if puppy is not allowed to bark at the parakeet today, he may not bark at the parakeet tomorrow.

Off-limits!

- Puppies tend to chew everything in their paths, including things that you would never expect.

- Do not allow puppy to chew items that could endanger him to ingest.

- If puppy so much as touches a forbidden item

with his teeth, immediately say "no" in a stern tone and discipline him appropriately.

- Scruff puppy and gently maneuver the item out of his mouth, or—for a stationary object, like a couch—maneuver his mouth off of the item.

Appropriate Teething

- Keep items that puppy can chew available at all times.

- If you are traveling or even sitting at an outdoor café with puppy, bring a few safe chewables with you.

- Give these items—preferably one at a time—to puppy during idle moments

to keep him from getting into trouble.

- If puppy chews on a banned item or a person, immediately correct the behavior by separating puppy from the object and handing him one of his chew toys.

Choose boundaries for puppy based on the expectations you would have for his adult self. If you don't want him to dig in the yard as an adult, then correct that behavior today, when he is a puppy.

Provide correction *immediately after* he commits the "crime" so he is not confused about what action is being censured. Correction should be neither cruel nor painful. The best corrective tools are ones that are attention-getting, and easily implemented, such as squirting puppy in the nose with a water gun or loudly rattling a can full of pennies.

Furry Piranha

- Puppy teeth—or deciduous teeth—grow in at about seven weeks of age.

- These teeth are gradually replaced by adult—or permanent—dentition between three and seven months old.

- Puppy teeth are sharp.

- Puppy will sink his teeth into just about anything to soothe his sore gums while teething. Once teething has ended, most dogs continue to chew for pleasure. By this time, he should know which items he can—and *cannot*—chew.

Ground rules begin in puppyhood:
- Which items he is allowed to chew
- What space comprises his "territory"
- Where he may go to the bathroom
- Where he may sleep
- What furniture, if any, he is permitted to be on
- Miscellaneous rules—licking, jumping, humping, begging for table scraps . . .

CRATED & CONTAINED

Games, food, and techniques can quickly acclimate your puppy to a crate

If you plan to use a crate to control puppy's meanderings and shape her behavior, you need to "sell" her on the crate. The goal of crate training is to make puppy feel comfortable in her crate, enter and exit the crate upon your command, and remain calm and quiet while crated.

Crate training is best begun early in the day, preferably around nap time. After puppy goes to the bathroom outside, place her in the crate, perhaps with a toy. Quickly exit the room, and do not let puppy out of the crate if she cries. Keep her in the crate for a few hours, and then immediately bring her outdoors to eliminate.

Habituate puppy to her crate with crate games. Throw a toy

Crate Location

- Situate the crate in a bustling area of your home so that puppy does not feel isolated.

- The crate should be located near an exterior door so pup can be let outside to relieve herself immediately after removal from crate.

- Be sure it's not a drafty spot or one that gets direct heat.

- If you plan to move the crate outside during the day, put it under an overhang.

Newbie in Crate

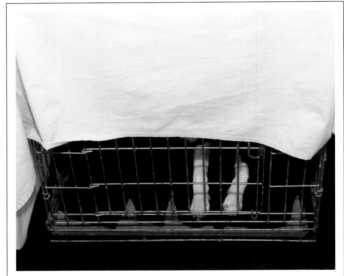

- During your puppy's early days, the crate might be best placed in your bedroom.

- You'll hear puppy if she needs to be attended to in the middle of the night, and she'll find comfort in your presence as she sleeps.

- When she snoozes, drape a blanket over her crate to block out light, noise, and bustle.

- Place a ticking clock and a warm water bottle inside to simulate the sound and feel of mom and littermates.

or treat to the back of the crate and give a consistent command, like "Go to your crate." Eventually, have her sit at the back of the crate with the door open. Reward her with a treat, and then let her exit after you issue a release command like "Out." Reward her when she exits.

Success means puppy bounds in and out of her crate without hesitation. Repeat games daily until puppy's movements in and out of her crate are consistently seamless. Once she can be trusted to roam the house unsupervised, leave the crate door open for her to enter and exit at will.

Comfort and Safety

- Lay a mat, cushion, or towels in the crate for comfort.

- If there are detachable food/water bowls, you can fill them once puppy is housebroken.

- Remove from pup's neck anything that might get caught on wire, like collars and tags.

- Do not leave a puppy under six months old in a crate for over four or five hours at a stretch.

Making Crate Fun

- Place a variety of toys, chews, and edible treats inside the crate.

- This will enhance the appeal of the crate.

- Since you are not always there to supervise pup when he's crated, avoid items like rawhides and toys containing squeakers, which pup can chew apart and choke on.

- Placing appealing objects inside the crate will nurture within your pup a positive attitude toward spending time there.

GOTTA GO

How long can a puppy hold it? When does he *need* to go? Here's the poop

Potty training your new puppy is the most important thing you can do for yourself as a dog owner. A puppy that soils your house is not going to be a good companion, period!

Owing to their meat-based, omnivorous diet, dogs have short digestive tracts. Puppies have even quicker GI transit time than adults, plus poor bladder sphincter control.

According to the APPA, 8 to 10 percent of dog owners report toilet habits to be a major drawback to having a dog. Because dogs start forming elimination habits around two months of age, puppyhood is the time to get toileting right.

Your dog is hardwired to squat and go—at will—as it moves. To twist his mind into pottying at designated times and places

Peeing and pooping: developmental stages

- Birth to three weeks: Dam stimulates pup to eliminate.

- Three to seven weeks: Puppy eliminates independently and randomly; starts developing bladder and bowel control.

- Around eight weeks: Puppy starts forming substrate/surface/location preferences for elimination.

- Four to six months: Males begin leg lifting to urinate.

- After first heat cycle: Females may not develop full bladder sphincter control until now.

- By fourteen to twenty weeks: Most pups can be housebroken!

Housebreaking Supplies

- Crates and leashes allow you to control where puppy eliminates.

- Training to pee and poop indoors? Stock litter pan/litter, newspapers, or leak-proof potty pads, available in washable and disposable ($20 to $30/100-pack) varieties.

- Attractant/repellant sprays and pet odor eliminators signal puppy where it's okay and not okay to eliminate, and cover up scents from inevitable accidents.

- Coprophagia tablets can deter puppies from eating stools.

is a project sure to tax your time, energy, and patience. To complicate things, there are individual and breed variations in housebreaking ease. For instance, puppies crated from day one are used to soiling where they sleep. So the crate may not be an effective housebreaking aid for them.

The breeds whose tasks are more basic—hounds, terriers, setters, pointers, and the cosmetic toys—are generally harder to housebreak. Dogs bred to display more complex skills, like herding and working breeds, tend to take to housetraining more quickly. Of course, there are individual exceptions.

MAKE IT EASY

To keep puppy's bladder from overfilling, provide him with water in small but frequent amounts, even in ice cube form on occasion.

Puppy "Holding" Patterns

- The maximum time between eliminations is give-or-take one hour for each month of age: For example, a three-month-old pup can "hold it" for about three hours.

- At eight weeks of age, puppy might urinate hourly and defecate four times a day.

- A six-month-old puppy needs to urinate three or four times a day and defecate once or twice daily.

- By eight or nine months, puppy can go eight to ten hours without soiling in the house.

Medical conditions hindering housebreaking:

- Urinary tract infection
- Urogenital/bladder malformation
- GI parasites (worms)
- GI bacterial/viral infection
- Dietary changes
- Anal sac disorder
- Neurological problem
- Behavioral issues (i.e., separation anxiety, submissive/excitement urination, urine marking)
- Certain medications

KEEP TO A SCHEDULE

Establishing a routine for walking and potty training is job number one for success

Our lives are governed by schedules. So, too, puppy's life—from play time to naps, feedings to potty time—must adhere to a tight roster. To keep potty time routine, work backwards: Schedule feedings. (You can feed free-choice after puppy is housebroken.) For a two- or three-month-old puppy, offer meals three times a day and take the bowl away after about fifteen minutes. Puppy's gastrocolic reflex, the wave of colonic contractions in response to signals sent by the stretch receptors in the stomach as it fills with food, will stimulate defecation within fifteen or twenty minutes after her meal. So be ready to take puppy out.

Each day, bring puppy outside to urinate or defecate six to

Consistency

- Consistency is the key to housebreaking.

- During training, take puppy to the designated elimination location at the same time intervals and to the same locations each day.

- Deny puppy the opportunity to have an "accident"

by crating her or keeping her leashed with you while indoors.

- Take her to the desired elimination location immediately after releasing her from the crate, if possible before her paws even touch the ground.

The Big Event

- Allow puppy to sniff and explore for ten or fifteen minutes before peeing or pooping.

- As she roots around for a spot to eliminate, encourage her with a chosen key phrase that you will use on a regular basis, such as "Do your business" or "Go potty."

- Do not engage with puppy or allow her to play or socialize with people or pets until she eliminates.

- Praise puppy and/or reward her with a treat or play time after she eliminates in desired location.

eight times. Always accompany her, so you can keep tabs on her eliminations. During housebreaking, keep yourself on the same schedule as puppy. To do this, do not introduce a new puppy into your household at a time when work or social obligations could interfere with your availability to her.

Once you begin housebreaking, keep everything else in puppy's life stable. If you have other dogs at home, keep them all on the same schedule. Puppy will learn housebreaking more quickly if she has an older dog to run through the routine with.

ZOOM

Activity and consciousness help to stimulate the bladder reflex. When sleeping at night, pups do not need to urinate as frequently.

Potty Signals

- Look for signs that puppy has to urinate or defecate.

- Signals include pacing, circling, sniffing and—if puppy is in a confined area she does not wish to soil—squirming and whining.

- Bring puppy outside to the designated "bathroom" area as soon as she indicates.

- Most puppies don't indicate their need to eliminate until after sixteen weeks of age.

- As housebreaking progresses, puppy can be taught advanced signaling, such as ringing a bell hung on the door.

When to take puppy out:

- First thing in the morning

- After waking from naps

- Fifteen to twenty minutes after eating

- Shortly after drinking a lot

- Following play/exercise

- Right before your bedtime

- Once overnight (puppies younger than ten weeks old)

- Any time puppy indicates she may need to eliminate

DON'T PUNISH, REWARD

Getting mad at him for pottying can have unintended consequences; train, don't complain!

If you feel your life lacks frustration, try teaching a puppy that the world is not his toilet. It ranks up there with trying to herd cats! But if you approach housebreaking systematically and with patience, it will happen eventually.

Every time puppy has a mishap, you are faced with the discipline dilemma. Avoid this dilemma by preventing the situation. Shadow your puppy every time he is out of his crate. Do not allow him to roam the house unsupervised. And when he goes out, accompany him so that you can applaud his outdoor evacuations. There will be days when you feel like you're making progress, and then your cozy socks turn warm and wet when you walk across the carpet.

Power of Prevention

- The issue of punishment never arises if puppy consistently "gets it right."

- Housebreaking can be a stressful time for puppy. Do him a favor by preventing him from having the opportunity to commit a housebreaking mishap.

- Prevent accidents through constant supervision, crating when you can't be there to supervise, and frequent visits to designated elimination areas.

- If puppy is signaling to eliminate indoors, pick him up immediately and bring him outside.

Encouragement

- Repeated encouragement and rewards are the keystones of housebreaking.

- Bring puppy to the desired potty area on leash or—if the area is confined/fenced—off leash. While there, repeat a chosen phrase, like "Time to potty" or "Go wee wee."

- Always speak in an encouraging tone of voice.

- Do not rush puppy. It may take fifteen minutes or more for him to urinate or defecate, but if you've timed it right, it will happen in due course.

Do you shove puppy's nose into the pee spot and say "Bad?" Many experts say correct the behavior only if you catch puppy in the act, not afterwards. But who's to say that puppy won't connect the urine smell to his past action and comprehend that urine does not belong indoors?

As a general rule, try to retain calm when housebreaking your puppy. Maximize positive reinforcement and minimize negative. Supervise and crate during unsupervised moments.

Finally, be *patient*—for many puppies, housebreaking is not cemented until around their first birthday.

Praise

- When puppy eliminates in an appropriate place, heap praise upon him.

- Hold praise until after elimination is complete to avoid distracting him.

- After puppy has gone to the bathroom, reward him with encouraging words spoken in a bright tone of voice, plus with a toy, edible treat, or play time.

- Praise should occur immediately after elimination. Do not wait until puppy has engaged in another behavior: He may become confused about the reason for the praise.

······· RED ● LIGHT ·······

Housebreaking should not be punitive or induce fear. Implement the tools of negative conditioning —like coin-filled "shake" cans and water-loaded spray bottles—to *minimize* startle effect. Many experts say to correct only if you catch puppy *in the act* of eliminating in verboten spots.

Scolding

- Benign interruption and correction is better than scolding, which can make puppy fearful of you or anxious about eliminating.

- If you catch puppy eliminating in a forbidden spot, try to interrupt the act with IMMEDIATE, MINIMAL negative reinforcement, like a sharp "no," a clap, or a foot stomp.

- Calmly scoop puppy up right away and bring him outside to continue eliminating. Praise him for correcting his action.

- Never correct puppy for housebreaking mistakes associated with abnormal urgency, such as diarrhea.

73

PAPER (& LITTER) TRAINING

Training for indoor elimination may be the route to take in some circumstances

Indoor potty training is controversial. Think hard before doing it, unless you are teaching your puppy to urinate and defecate indoors always and forever. Many experts say that paper and litter box training teaches puppy that it's okay to go to the bathroom in the house. This is true. Temporarily, we hope! Really, you are grafting puppy onto an elimination substrate—paper, padding, or litter—that you will gradually move outdoors and eventually do away with altogether.

Paper/litter training indoors versus straight outdoor training is really a personal choice. Paper training is a step-by-step schematic that probably draws out the entire housebreaking process a little longer. Peeling soggy newspapers off the

Litter Pans

- The pan should be three-sided or low enough for puppy to step into.

- Use shredded paper, wood chips, sand, or clay litter. If puppy ingests the litter, particularly clay, try switching to a different type. Supervise closely.

- The breeds most suited to litter pans are toys, since they excrete in lesser amounts.

- Litter pans don't work well for pubescent males, who usually can't contain their spray to the pan when they lift their leg to urinate.

Potty Pads and Newspaper

- Potty pads and newspapers can serve as training tools for outdoor elimination.

- To train for outdoor pot-tying, paper (three or four sheets thick) or pad the entire floor. Puppy learns to eliminate on paper/pads.

- Each day, reduce the size of the covered area. If puppy signals to eliminate, pick her up and put her on the paper.

- Over time, move the paper/padding toward an exterior door until puppy is eliminating outdoors on grass/soil/cement.

floor and stuffing them into the trash is no fun either.

Paper training, however, puts less pressure on puppy and you. If you've papered your entire floor, you're less likely to race home to let her out every two hours. And you'll probably give yourself a full night's sleep. Plus, it's a reasonable follow-up if your puppy's breeder started her off on paper training.

Hustling puppy outside every time she needs to eliminate requires vigilance, consistency, and a crate. But compared to paper training, it's a more direct route to achieving true outdoor toileting.

The Indoor Bathroom

- Newspapers and potty pads can be used for permanent indoor elimination.

- For regular use, potty pads work better than newspaper because their leak-proof backing protects floors and carpets.

- Indoor pottying, using paper, pads, or litter pan, can also be allowed on an as-needed basis.

- Allow yourself to set up for indoor elimination versus outdoor potty excursions when you cannot take puppy outdoors, like during inclement weather or schedule complications.

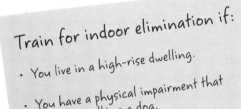

YELLOW LIGHT

Remember that potty pads are not biodegradable, and therefore are burdensome on the environment: Use them judiciously.

Train for indoor elimination if:

- You live in a high-rise dwelling.

- You have a physical impairment that prevents walking a dog.

- Your puppy has a physical impairment that warrants minimal activity.

- You live in inclement weather conditions.

- You have a toy breed and don't want to walk her.

- You cannot adhere to a regular dog-walking schedule.

75

CLEANUP & HYGIENE

Nobody enjoys mopping up puppy's mess, but it's necessary for everyone's health and sanity!

Puppies and messes go together. Their high inputs and seemingly higher outputs, combined with poor ability to control the latter, will have you cleaning constantly. Homes with puppies usually smell like puppies, no matter how much cleaning their owners do. So it's quite a task to stay ahead of the mess, but critical to do so not only to preserve the ambience of your household, but also for your health.

Puppies are worm factories. Most puppies, even those bred and whelped in excellent conditions, harbor worms early on. Puppies that have already been dewormed may still be infected. This makes cleanup all the more important. If you have other pets or small children, they can contract

Cleaning Supplies

- Use sturdy plastic bags to scoop stool, both indoors and outdoors. This is a great way to recycle your plastic grocery bags . . . but double them up first!

- Use carpet shampoos and enzymatic solvents to clean soiled rugs and neutralize pet odors.

- For carpet messes, use stiff scrub brushes to work in the cleaning solution.

- For wiping non-carpeted floors, keep handy plenty of paper towels, a water bucket, disinfectant solution, and a good mop.

Odor neutralizers:

- Important housebreaking tools

- Neutralize the odor of urine and feces

- Cut odors that attract dogs to the same spots for repeat offenses

- Available as pour-ons and sprays

- Examples include Nature's Miracle, Petzyme, Nilodor, and Outright

- Diluted vinegar can also be used to disinfect and deodorize floors (use cautiously on carpets)

worms—which are spread through fecal-oral transmission—from feces sitting on your floors or lawn.

Worms aside, many puppies like to consume feces. This can put the people in your household at risk for contracting infections from slobbery puppy kisses on the mouth.

Keeping a puppy household clean requires intense supervision, as puppies learn to leave deposits in hidden areas. It also requires vigilance, patience, and lots of cleaning product. Before you bring puppy home, stock up on disinfectants, deodorizers, mops, and such.

Flooring

- During housebreaking, confine puppy to easy-to-clean surfaces, such as linoleum.

- Avoid carpets and hardwood, which can rot when stained repeatedly, for puppies that are not housetrained.

- Use baby gates and pens to keep puppy on nonabsorbent surfaces.

- Block favorite potty spots with gates or furniture.

········· *RED ● LIGHT* ·········

Avoid ammonia-based solvents to clean up puppy accidents. Since ammonia is a major urine component, scouring with ammonia-based cleaners may "mark" the location as an acceptable indoor toilet.

Stool eating:

- "Coprophagia" is the scientific term for stool consumption.

- Stool eating is an unpleasant but not abnormal puppy behavior.

- Reasons for coprophagia include boredom, curiosity, anxiety, and mischief.

- Most puppies eventually outgrow this behavior.

- Prevent coprophagia by cleaning up bowel movements right away.

- Coprophagia tablets like Potty Mouth and Excel Deter work by making stool PARTICULARLY unpalatable.

VACCINATION ESSENTIALS

Vaccines are critical, but there is no "one size fits all" vaccination schedule for puppies

Because every puppy varies by health status and exposure risk, there is no one-size-fits-all vaccine protocol. Your veterinarian will customize a vaccine program specifically for your puppy.

The core vaccines that every puppy should have are rabies, distemper, hepatitis, and parvovirus; the last three are usually given in a shot combo that also includes parainfluenza virus.

The main non-core, or elective, vaccines are Lyme disease, kennel cough, lepto, and coronavirus. Vaccines may be elective if your pup has little risk of getting exposed to the disease, the illness is mild, the vaccine doesn't work well, or it frequently causes an allergic reaction or other illness.

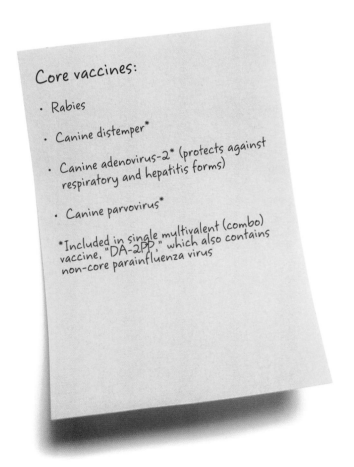

Core vaccines:

- Rabies

- Canine distemper*

- Canine adenovirus-2* (protects against respiratory and hepatitis forms)

- Canine parvovirus*

*Included in single multivalent (combo) vaccine, "DA-2PP," which also contains non-core parainfluenza virus

Vaccination Schedule

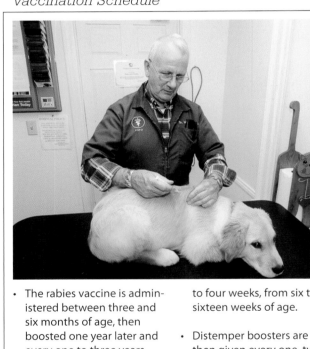

- The rabies vaccine is administered between three and six months of age, then boosted one year later and every one to three years after that for life, depending on state regulations.

- The distemper combo shot (DA-2PP) is given every two to four weeks, from six to sixteen weeks of age.

- Distemper boosters are then given every one, two, or three years, depending on the manufacturer's recommendations and veterinarian's procedures.

In some circumstances, your veterinarian may recommend an elective vaccine. If puppy will be used for hunting, for instance, leptospirosis and Lyme might be administered. If she is a Rottweiler, a breed especially prone to parvo, she may receive a monovalent parvovirus vaccine at five weeks.

Recent studies have shown that vaccines are effective for longer than one year. Many veterinarians have elected to re-vaccinate adult dogs every 2–3 years instead of annually.

········· RED ● LIGHT ·········

Vaccines can, *in rare instances*, cause an allergic reaction varying in severity from local/ facial swelling, hives, or low-grade fever to respiratory distress, plummeting blood pressure, fainting, vomiting, or diarrhea.

Other risks include development of autoimmune diseases, immunosuppression, transient infections, and vaccine-site tumors.

Rabies Vaccination

- Rabies virus causes an encephalitis that is universally fatal.

- Any *warm-blooded* animal can contract and transmit rabies. Birds, reptiles, amphibians, and fish do not harbor rabies virus.

- Rabies is present in almost every country, and in every U.S. state except Hawaii.

- Vaccination has brought the number of U.S. rabies cases in dogs from 8,384 (1946) to 79 (2006).

- Every state requires rabies vaccination in dogs.

Protect puppy's health:

- Puppies are born with some immunity to infectious diseases.

- This "maternal" immunity gradually declines after birth.

- Puppy can gain her own immunity through vaccines.

- Unvaccinated puppies are at risk for contracting certain infections.

- Puppy is not fully protected until a few weeks AFTER the vaccination series is complete.

- Keep puppy away from other dogs until a few weeks after administration of first two DA-2PP boosters, around twelve weeks old.

CREEPY CRITTERS

Team up with your veterinarian to protect puppy— and household—from worms and other parasites

Parasites thrive by robbing their hosts of precious resources, from nutrients to blood to tissue; in so doing, they inflict damage.

Of the parasites, fleas can be the most vexing because a female flea can lay up to fifty eggs a day; that's about 2,000 in her lifetime. So once puppy has a flea or two, the environment is most likely contaminated with eggs and larvae. The challenge of flea control is killing the fleas at different stages: egg, larva, and adult. The environment must be treated with chemicals, linens laundered, and floors vacuumed.

Puppy must simultaneously be treated with topical/oral medications that kill fleas and/or regulate their growth.

Intestinal worms

The four major intestinal worms of puppies are roundworms, hookworms, tapeworms, and whipworms.

- Over 90 percent of puppies under three months have roundworms.

- Roundworms and hookworms in puppies are usually acquired from mom in utero or through nursing.

- The typical "wormy" puppy is potbellied and thin, with dull hair coat, diarrhea, and vomiting.

- Dewormer pills are administered to puppies repeatedly starting at about two weeks of age. Several fecal exams are needed to confirm that puppy is worm-free.

Heartworms

- Heartworms are transmitted to dogs through mosquito bites.

- Larvae travel through the dog's bloodstream to the pulmonary vessels and right to the heart.

- Heartworm infection can cause coughing, sluggishness, fluid retention, fainting, and death.

- Heartworm prevention starts with annual/biennial testing, followed by preventive tablets (given six months or year-round). Puppies under six months need not be tested before starting heartworm pills.

Topical products kill and prevent fleas for four weeks or more, and can be used in puppies as young as eight weeks. A moderate flea infestation can rapidly cause anemia in a small puppy, so treatment must be prompt.

As with fleas, roundworms and hookworms can also deplete puppy. Hookworms eat away at intestinal lining, causing puppy to lose blood in his stool. Roundworms reside in the intestines, where they hijack puppy's nutrients.

Roundworms can lay 100,000 eggs a day, which pass in the feces and can contaminate the soil for years. Roundworms and hookworms can also cause dangerous disease in people.

Natural remedies have been used for the treatment of different canine parasites, like ticks, fleas, and biting flies, but their efficacy is questionable. Unfortunately, the only way to effectively treat parasites is with chemicals.

Because pesticides have potential adverse effects, especially in young animals, treatment should be done only under veterinary supervision.

Fleas

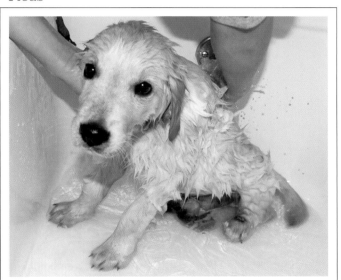

- Puppies can acquire fleas in any environment where dogs, cats, rodents, and wildlife dwell.

- Even a single flea can produce the itchy skin condition, flea allergy dermatitis (FAD), in a dog. Fleas can also transmit tapeworm infection and other diseases.

- A flea comb, which has tightly spaced teeth, can be used to locate and remove fleas.

- Oral and/or topical treatment can be used to break the flea life cycle in puppies.

Ticks and mites

- Ticks and mites are eight-legged parasites belonging to the arachnids, which also include spiders.

- Mites can burrow into puppy's skin. Puppies with mange exhibit itching, patchy hair loss, and inflamed skin.

- Ticks can transmit a variety of serious bacterial and protozoal infections to dogs and people.

- Perhaps the most dreaded tick-borne illness is Lyme disease, which causes arthritis/lameness in multiple joints, swollen lymph nodes, fever, and lethargy. The tick must be attached for at least eighteen hours before the causative bacterium can be transmitted.

SKIN PROBLEMS

Skin problems are easily treatable but can also indicate serious underlying disease

Because puppy's immune system is not yet mature, she is particularly prone to a number of skin diseases. One of these is demodectic mange, caused by the mite *Demodex canis*.

A normal canine skin inhabitant, this mite is transmitted from mom to puppy via close skin contact during nursing. Demodex does not cause major problems in mom because her mature immune system keeps it in check. But in puppy, it can run rampant, invading the hair follicles throughout the skin surface and causing general hair loss and irritation.

Demodectic mange can occur in any puppy, but certain breeds, like shar-peis and Dalmatians, are at increased risk. In fact, many breeds are predisposed to skin conditions.

Allergies

- Allergies are hypersensitivities to different substances, like parasite saliva, ingested foods, bacteria, medications/vaccines, chemicals contacting the skin, and environmental inhalants ("atopy"), like pollen, molds, and dust mites.

- Signs include itchy, reddened or darkened, thickened, crusty skin, patchy hair loss, and possible ear infections.

- The primary treatments are oral steroids, antihistamines, antibiotics, and medicated shampoos.

Skin Parasites

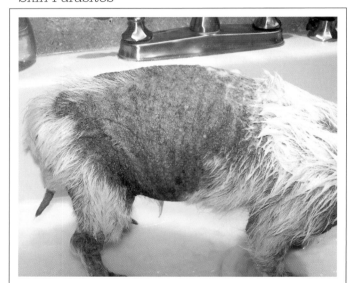

- Flea allergy dermatitis (FAD) is an extreme skin reaction to proteins in flea saliva. A single biting flea can cause FAD in a predisposed puppy.

- FAD results in redness, inflammation, crusting, itching, and patchy hair loss, typically over the tail base, lower back, inner thighs, and neck.

- Affected dogs are usually over six months of age.

- Mites cause "mange"—red, crusty patches usually on the face and ear margins. Itching varies depending on the mite species.

Schnauzers, for instance, are prone to acne-like waxy plugs known as "comedones." Samoyeds and poodles tend to develop *sebaceous adenitis,* a scaly condition involving damaged oil glands.

Breed aside, any puppy can develop a general "dermatitis" or skin inflammation. This can show up as a few isolated pus-filled cysts, or generally reddened, scabby skin with hair loss.

The common skin bacteria *Staphylococcus intermedius* and/or, less frequently, the yeast *Malassezia pachydermatis* can infect damaged skin and add to the misery.

Whatever the cause—parasites, allergies, low immunity, individual skin milieu—the smelly, inflammatory cycle of dermatitis is generally broken with an array of oral, topical, and injectable drugs that could include antibiotics, antifungals, antihistamines, and steroids.

But before your veterinarian treats any skin condition in your puppy, she will probably do some testing that may include smears, skin scrapings, biopsies, and blood work.

Ringworm

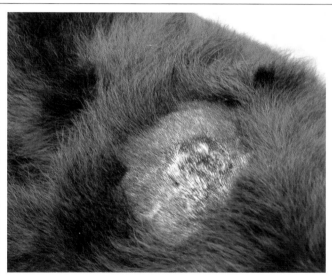

- Ringworm is actually not a worm but a fungal infection.

- Ringworm lesions are itchy round patches of reddened, scaly skin. The hairs are broken and/or missing.

- Puppies can acquire the fungi from the soil and/or directly from other animals, depending on fungal type.

- Ringworm is highly contagious (animal-animal, animal-person, person-person), and is treated with oral and topical antifungal medications.

Other puppy skin problems

- A cutaneous histiocytoma is a small, red, dome-shaped lump that generally appears on the head or feet.

- Occurring in young dogs about four months to four year of age, and peaking in incidence at about eighteen months, these tumors appear rapidly but usually go away on their own.

- Drug eruptions are itchy skin lesions that can show up as fluid-filled hives, facial swelling, flaky reddened skin, or acne-like pustules.

- Drug eruptions can occur hours to days after a vaccine or medication is given.

VOMITING & DIARRHEA
Puppies can leave messes at both ends. When it's serious and how to fix it

Puppy's gastrointestinal tract—a cauldron of digestive enzymes and absorptive cells extending from mouth to anus—is like a grenade ready to blow at the most minor disturbance. Because puppy's digestive system is maturing, it is more sensitive to things like dietary changes and anxiety. His body reacts quite readily by expelling gastric and malabsorbed intestinal contents in the form of vomit and diarrhea, respectively.

What's more, puppy's immune system is not yet fully competent to shield him from viral, bacterial, and protozoal infections that can set up shop in his gut. Also, puppy is pushing his developing digestive organs to the limit by ingesting

Causes of GI distress in puppies:

- Overeating/rapid eating/eating spoiled food

- Rapid dietary change

- Heavy exercise soon after eating

- Ingestion of non-food item leading to stomach irritation and/or obstruction

- Parasitic/viral/bacterial infection

- Pancreas, liver, kidney, or neurologic disease

- Anatomic malformation

- Medications/toxins

- Stress

Puppies at Risk

- Puppies are prone to gastrointestinal distress.

- Their stomach and intestines are sensitive to seemingly minor things like increased food consumption and dietary changes.

- Their developing immune systems cannot always fight GI invaders like canine parvovirus type 2 (CPV-2), coronavirus, canine distemper, and hepatitis.

- Puppies also suffer from their indiscriminate eating habits: Vomiting and diarrhea are normal reactions to consumption of things that do not belong.

anything he can fit into his mouth, food item or not.

Most cases of vomiting and diarrhea are uncomplicated. Acute gastritis (inflammation and irritation of the stomach lining) and enterocolitis (ditto, but for the intestines) typically resolve in three to five days, with little more than supportive care that includes rest, fasting, and possibly fasting followed by a bland diet.

However, sometimes a trip to the vet is in order. Vomiting and diarrhea rob a growing puppy of precious nutrients and tax his little body. Your once playful puppy is now holed up in a corner, sapped of energy. And after a few days of bringing up all he eats, his ribs have begun to show.

Be sure to bring a stool sample to your veterinarian's office so they can check for parasites and possibly parvo, a sometimes fatal disease that attacks puppy's rapidly dividing cells like the intestinal absorptive cells, causing profuse bloody diarrhea. Your veterinarian may also do a stool culture, blood work, and x-rays.

GI Healing

- Dietary restriction is the first step. For vomiting and/or diarrhea, withhold food for one day. If vomiting, withhold water too, but offer ice cubes.

- Gradually feed bland, digestible foods like white rice and ground beef boiled in small, frequent amounts.

- Your veterinarian may treat with antibiotics, GI protectants, antacids, antiemetics, motility modulators, and dewormers.

- Vomiting and diarrhea can strip the body of electrolytes. IV or subcutaneous fluids may be given to replace electrolytes.

It's an emergency when:

- Vomiting over three times daily

- Vomit contains red blood or looks like coffee grounds

- Unproductive vomiting

- Profuse, watery diarrhea

- Bloody or tarry diarrhea

- Vomiting or diarrhea of two days' duration

- Vomiting or diarrhea with other signs, like lethargy, dehydration, refusal to eat, fever, or abdominal pain

85

LAMENESS

Growing bones, joints, and muscles are susceptible to injury in boisterous puppies

The domestic dame, though she dines on kibble in the comfort of her home, retains the ability to leap into a herd of antelopes or twist and turn in the shadows of a fleeing rabbit. But as she develops, problems can come up that send her limping.

Osteochondritis dissicans (OCD) is a painful condition caused by deadened cartilage flaps that break off into the joint space. OCD occurs in large-breed puppies between four and eight months of age, generally in the shoulder, elbow, stifle (knee), or hock (ankle) joints.

Hypertrophic osteodystrophy (HOD) is an inflammatory condition involving the ends of the long bones in large-breed

Bone growth in puppies:

- Growth plates are the skeleton's bone factories.

- Growth plates are present at the end of the long bones.

- Growth plates are responsible for increasing the length.

- Growth plates close between six and thirteen months, depending on the bone.

- Growth plates may close later in large breeds.

- By six months of age, puppy has reached 75 percent of her adult size (height and length).

Canine Skeleton

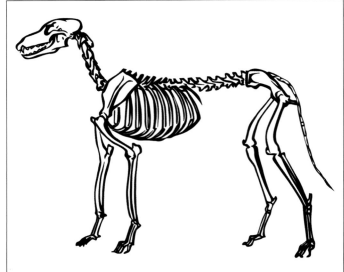

- Bones are mineralized tissue that remodel themselves throughout life.

- Bones support the body, protect internal organs, provide levers for muscle movement, store minerals, and produce blood cells.

- The dog has 320 bones, on average, excluding the tail.

- Dogs have a wider variety of bone size and shape than any other domesticated animal: Contrast the 42-inch Great Dane with the 4-inch toy yorkie, or the squatty, thick-boned basset hound with the tall, fine-boned greyhound.

puppies of two to eight months. Affected puppies experience joint pain, lethargy, fever, and weight loss, but the condition resolves on its own.

Similar signs are also seen in dogs with *panosteitis,* a painful disorder of the long bones of dogs six to eighteen months of age. The disease, which resolves spontaneously, is most common in German shepherds.

Young, large-breed puppies can have front-limb lameness due to *elbow dysplasia*. Here, a few of the bones of the elbow fail to fuse, resulting in joint pain.

Legg-Calve-Perthes causes hind limb lameness in affected puppies, primarily toy breeds like Yorkshire terriers, between five and eight months of age. It's caused by necrosis—or dying off—of the femur (leg) bone at the hip joint, usually from a loss of blood supply.

Hip dysplasia, or malformation of the hip joint, can be congenital. In more serious cases, it can cause young dogs to adopt a "bunny-hopping" gait or be chronically lame in the hind end, worsening with age.

Lameness First Aid

- If puppy begins limping, keep her quiet—perhaps with cage rest—so her injury does not worsen. Do not medicate, unless directed to do so by your veterinarian.

- See veterinarian if puppy is not bearing weight on limb for more than one hour, if lameness is mild but persists for more than two weeks, or if lameness shifts from leg to leg.

- See veterinarian if lameness is accompanied by other clinical signs, like lethargy, fever, or reluctance to eat.

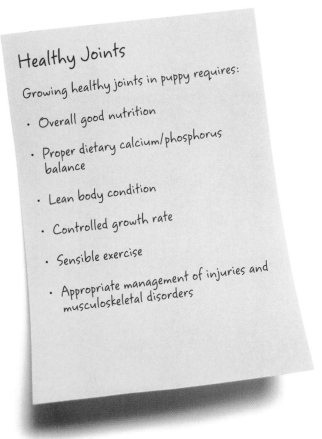

Healthy Joints

Growing healthy joints in puppy requires:

- Overall good nutrition

- Proper dietary calcium/phosphorus balance

- Lean body condition

- Controlled growth rate

- Sensible exercise

- Appropriate management of injuries and musculoskeletal disorders

DOWN THE HATCH

Help the medicine go down, in or on, using several simple techniques

A medication can only work if it's incorporated into the body appropriately, whether into the stomach, down the ear canal, in the eyes, or onto the skin.

Since 81 percent of U.S. dogs have taken at least one medication in the last year, dosing is a critical capability for the puppy owner.

In many cases, little skill is necessary, only strategy: Usually pills can be rolled into a moist, compressible treat, like peanut butter, cheese, or lunch meat.

Do not drop pills in puppy's regular food, because if he ever catches on to the ruse, he could develop an aversion to his staple diet.

Oral Tablets

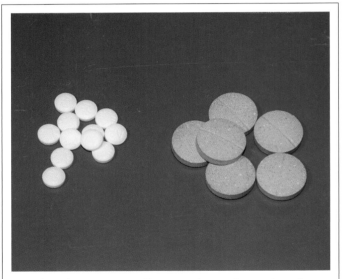

- Oral medications generally come in tablet, capsule, or liquid forms. Some, like Heartgard heartworm medication, are chewable and palatable.

- If your dosing regimen calls for one half or one quarter of a tablet, you can request that your veterinarian or pharmacist cut them for you.

- Whole tablets can easily be broken if they are scored.

- Alternatively, you can sever tablets with a pill cutter, which you can buy at the pharmacy, or with a one-sided razor blade.

Administering Oral Meds

- For liquids, fill dropper to designated line. Lift puppy's head slightly. Place dropper into side of mouth. Depress plunger/bulb.

- For tablets, straddle puppy from behind. Place left hand over puppy's muzzle (if right-handed). Lift puppy's head. The lower jaw should relax. With left hand, fold upper lips over teeth. With right hand, open lower jaw and drop pill(s) onto the rear base of tongue. Hold mouth closed until puppy swallows.

- Or use a pill shooter, a device used to inject pill into back of throat.

Rather, use a less familiar food, an occasional treat. Choose one with a strong flavor so puppy is less likely to taste or smell the hidden meds. And be sure the treat is small enough to be finished in a single gulp.

Those pups that meticulously pick their food apart to discard the tablet may need to be pilled directly.

Whether the pill is taken voluntarily in food or is manually dropped into the back of the throat, always observe puppy for a minute or two after you *think* he has swallowed it. If he spits the pill out, repeat the procedure.

Medicating Ears and Eyes

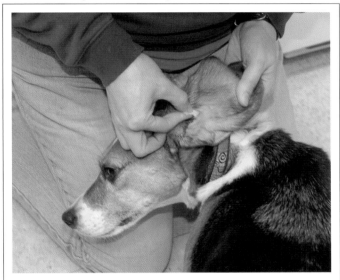

- Ear treatment is ideally a two-person job. One person steadies puppy's head, turning affected ear upward.

- Pour ear wash into ear canal. Gently massage base of ear for thirty seconds and then swab canal with rolled cotton.

- Instill medicated drops, ointment, or cream directly into canal and massage base of ears.

- For eyes, gently pull lower lid downward. Instill drops or ointment near corner of eye located closest to the nose. Gently massage closed lids to spread.

Applying Topicals

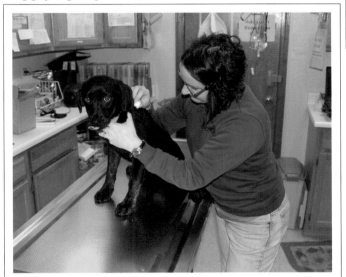

- For very hairy regions, clip around lesion if you think you can do so safely.

- Using sterile gauze, gently wipe away any debris, including gummed-up ointment from previous treatments.

- Instill or pat on ointment or cream as directed by your veterinarian. If you need to rub it in, wear gloves. Request a protective Elizabethan collar if puppy tries to lick treated area.

- Avoid applying topicals near eyes, mouth, and vagina unless your veterinarian has instructed.

WHEN IT'S AN EMERGENCY
When to wait until tomorrow and when to bring her in right away

Puppies are clumsy, curious, inexperienced, and infection-prone—they're likely to get hurt and eat things that they shouldn't. Have a plan in place should your puppy have a medical emergency. Canine emergencies are sometimes obvious, but sometimes, what constitutes an "emergency" requiring immediate care is not plainly apparent.

To properly diagnose an emergency, be able to recognize "normal." Start by assessing puppy's vital signs (you must do this on *your* puppy, because there are subtle individual variations of "normal").

Practice taking puppy's rectal temperature (normal basal temperature is 101 to 103 degrees Fahrenheit). Check her pulse by placing your index finger on the front inside of her hind leg, just above the knee. Monitor the pulse rate and

PUPPY CARE

Typical emergency conditions:

- Difficulty breathing
- Facial swelling/hives
- Fever >104.5
- Unproductive attempts to urinate/defecate/vomit
- Sudden/profuse/bloody vomiting/diarrhea
- Choking
- Ingestion of non-food item
- Ingestion of poison/certain medications
- Hit by car/fall
- Fracture/inability to use a limb
- Eye injury
- Fight with wild/unvaccinated animal

First-Aid Kit

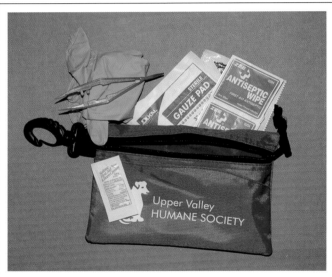

- To induce vomiting, stock hydrogen peroxide plus sixty-cc syringe/turkey baster. Have activated charcoal available to bind ingested toxins. Use when directed by your vet or animal poison control center.

- For wound care and stabilization, include bandages, gauze, disinfectant, and sterile saline squirt bottle.

- For transport, have a crate, blankets, and muzzle. Also scissors, tweezers, magnifying glass, penlight, rectal thermometer/lubricant, disposable gloves, styptic powders, Elizabethan collar, muzzle, and heating pad.

strength, both before and after exercise to note variations.

Note the normal color of puppy's gums. Press your finger on her gums and watch as the pressed area lightens. Release and count how many seconds it takes for the pink color to return. This measurement is less than three seconds in a healthy animal.

Watch puppy breathe, and note her normal respiratory rate and pattern, both before and after exercise. Note the appearance and feel of her abdomen, both before and after eating, and how she walks, noting any normal idiosyncrasies in gait.

In a potential emergency, be ready to first assess the ABCs: airway, breathing, and circulation. Are her airways clear? Is she breathing? Is her blood pumping?

Finally, know how your veterinarian handles emergencies: Is there an on-call doctor available around the clock? Do they share with other local practices? Do they refer to a regional emergency clinic during off-hours?

Obtaining Emergency Care

- Keep your veterinarian's phone number on hand, as well as his emergency number, if applicable.

- Also have handy the phone number of the closest twenty-four-hour veterinary emergency clinic, along with driving directions.

- Post the phone number of a twenty-four-hour animal poison control center.

- Have instant contact information available for a reliable person who can help you aid and transport your puppy, in the event of an emergency.

Emergency transport

- Protect yourself: When in pain or distress, even a docile dog may bite. Place a muzzle before examining or transporting puppy if no obvious facial injuries, choking, or respiratory distress.

- Try to stabilize and cushion injuries with wraps and towels. DO NOT GIVE ANY MEDICATIONS.

- Have another person help to transport puppy into the vehicle and ride with you to the veterinary clinic.

- If possible, lay puppy flat and keep her quiet and still during transport.

VETERINARY HEALTH INSURANCE

A rider against surprise health crises and routine care, pet health insurance can save you money

Veterinary health insurance was conceived in Europe some thirty years ago and hit U.S. shores around 1980. Pet health insurance is still in the starting gate in this country: Only 3 percent of owned U.S. dogs are insured. Compare this to England and Sweden, where, respectively, 20 percent and 49 percent of owners insure their pets.

There are seven or eight large pet insurance companies operating in the United States today. The oldest, California-based Veterinary Pet Insurance (VPI), claims 71 percent of the market, with about 472,000 active policies.

Pet insurance works differently from human medical insurance in several respects. The biggest disparity is that the pet

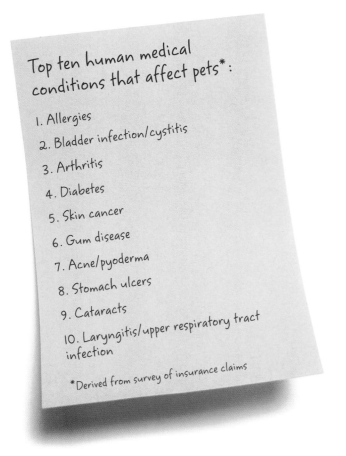

Top ten human medical conditions that affect pets*:

1. Allergies
2. Bladder infection/cystitis
3. Arthritis
4. Diabetes
5. Skin cancer
6. Gum disease
7. Acne/pyoderma
8. Stomach ulcers
9. Cataracts
10. Laryngitis/upper respiratory tract infection

*Derived from survey of insurance claims

Insurance Premiums

- Premiums are based on species and age (increase with age), as well as your state and chosen plan.

- Premiums average about $30/month for a basic plan covering illness and injury. Comprehensive plans that include preventive care cost more.

- Your premium amount may also be adjusted by the deductible level you select, potential breed surcharges, and multi-pet discounts.

- Most companies offer the option to pay the premium monthly or annually, with a discount for the latter.

owner pays the veterinarian in full and then submits his claim to the insurance company.

Depending on the company, reimbursements may be a flat percentage or they could involve a deductible, usually around $50 per incident or a couple hundred dollars annually. (The industry seems to be moving toward annual deductibles.)

Once the client meets the deductible, he is reimbursed 65 to 90 percent of eligible costs, which generally vary by geographical region. Most companies boast a fourteen-day reimbursement time.

Age limitations for insurance are usually around six weeks minimum and ten years maximum, so your puppy is probably eligible, but before you sign on, check the company's list of breed-related congenital and/or inherited disorders that are not covered.

Preexisting conditions are generally not covered, so if you are considering insurance, puppyhood is probably the time to do it.

Insurance Alternatives

- With no guarantee that veterinary insurance will save you dollars over the long haul, it's more a risk management tool than cost savings plan.

- Low-cost spay-neuter and vaccine clinics may be hosted by local shelters, veterinary offices, and your county.

- Membership to a discount program like Pet Assure grants you 25 percent savings from participating veterinarians for exams, shots, surgeries, hospitalization, and elective procedures.

Questions to ask when choosing insurance plan:

- What services will the plan cover?
- What are the exclusions?
- Is there a benefit schedule?
- Is there a flat percentage payout?
- What premiums and deductibles apply?
- Is there a surcharge for my breed?
- Are deductibles per-incident or annual?
- What is the claims-filing procedure?
- What is the turnaround time for reimbursements?
- Can I choose the veterinarian?
- Is the insurance company approved to do business in your state?

TEETHING SCHEDULE
Regardless of size or breed, all puppies teethe on a fairly consistent schedule

Teething—or cutting teeth—is one of the most significant physical events of your dog's life. During the teething process, she will erupt her puppy teeth, lose them, and have them replaced by a full set of permanent teeth.

A process that takes about twenty years in you and I completes itself in just six months in puppy. All told, her tooth count will go from none at birth to twenty-eight deciduous—or puppy—teeth, and finally to forty-two adult teeth.

For her mouth to get fast-tracked through this transformation, many physiological changes need to occur all at once.

The head and jaws are growing to make room for a full set of adult teeth. Simultaneously, the tooth roots and the body

A Changing Mouth

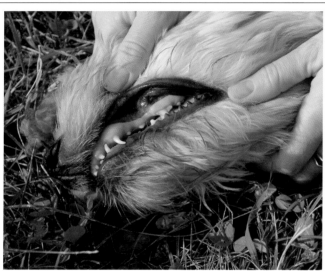

- Puppies are born edentulous, or without teeth. Tooth eruption begins at three or four weeks of age.

- Eruption begins up front, with the incisors, and works back toward the throat.

- All deciduous—or puppy—teeth are in place by about eight weeks.

- Between four and seven months of age, the deciduous teeth are replaced by permanent teeth: first incisors, then premolars, then canines, and finally molars.

Other Adolescent Changes

- A dog in the midst of teething—about six months of age—is, in human years, roughly equivalent to a five-year-old child.

- At this time, there is rapid growth of the long bones, and the head and jaws are remodeling to accommodate the permanent teeth.

- Cartilage development is evidenced by the changing position of the ears, between flopping and standing.

- Puppy fat starts to give way to leaner muscle.

of the puppy teeth—the dentin—are resorbing into the gums. What remains is the outer shell, or enamel. This "crown" becomes detached and either falls out of the mouth or gets swallowed.

As the new teeth are pushing through the gums, which have been busy with the resorptive process, they are causing abrasions and inflammation. In order to soothe her throbbing gums, puppy is besieged with the urge to chew. Enter the dog days of puppyhood!

Retained Puppy Teeth

- Occasionally, a puppy tooth fails to fall out when its permanent counterpart erupts.

- The permanent tooth usually erupts in front—or "noseward"—of the puppy tooth.

- Retained puppy teeth, more common in small breeds, can cause tooth overcrowding, impair normal socket development, and lead to buildup of food particles around teeth.

- Monitor puppy's developing dental arcade, and if you notice retained puppy teeth, consult with your vet.

Teething truisms:

- Large breeds generally erupt teeth earlier than small breeds.

- Puppy teeth are sharp.

- Puppy teeth are replaced by adult teeth.

- The entire teething process takes about six months.

- Teething is accompanied by an increased urge to chew.

TEETHING & CHEWING

95

HOW YOU CAN HELP

Teething hurts—what you can do to soothe your puppy and save your furniture

In addition to being an outlet for curiosity or tension, chewing is puppy's endeavor to find relief during the painful process of teething. As adult teeth push through, they tenderize the gums. Blood rushes in, bringing along agents of inflammation. As the gums throb, the nerve endings flood with neurochemicals that send pain messages along the nerve fibers.

When your arm gets socked with a baseball, you immediately grab and rub it. So, too, puppy applies pressure to sore gums by gnawing on something. If that "something" is the mahogany lamp you brought back from Thailand or the electrical cord that can electrocute puppy, or your son's building toys, which sharp puppy teeth can break into pieces that may

Chews to avoid

- Shun toys with bells or squeakers inside, or small parts attached—an enthusiastic chewer can easily dismember them and possibly choke.

- Avoid chews coated with paint or any other potentially toxic material.

- Stay away from toys that are replicas of household items (i.e., rubber remote control). This could confuse puppy.

- Discard toys and chews that have become worn out—puppy will likely shred it down to nothing if allowed.

Natural Chews

- There are many natural chews you can make yourself at home.

- Some, like frozen carrots and ice cubes filled with tempting treats such as hot dog bits, satisfy puppy's urge to chew while soothing his sore gums.

- A thick piece of rope makes a great chewing medium—pliable enough for puppy to sink his teeth into, yet firm enough to hold up to his pearly daggers.

- A ham bone or a solid stick works too, but monitor closely for breakage or splintering.

lodge in his esophagus, then chewing becomes a problem.

Most pups have a preferred class of chewables: One pup goes for pliable stuffed toys; another relishes tissues he can mush up and swallow. Hide belongings, at least temporarily, and provide puppy with various chew toys. Keep no more than three available at a time, so as not to confuse him. Rotate new toys in occasionally. If you think boredom or anxiety is a factor in puppy's chewing, provide comfort in your absence by leaving on the TV.

Synthetic Chews

- Look for toys made of durable materials like nylon, rubber, and tough plastic.

- Synthetic chews that are textured by ridges, pimples, or blunted spikes provide excellent massage for sore gums, as well as abrasion for dental health.

- Teething rings are also available in edible and non-edible varieties.

- The Chilly Bone canvas chew is great for teething. Just wet it, freeze it, and let puppy chill his gums while he chews.

Protecting Valuables

- Confine puppy, using crates and gates, if necessary. The kitchen makes a good "safe room," with chewable items on high counters and floors typically of linoleum/tile.

- Trash cans fascinate puppies. Keep cans tightly lidded or inaccessible, and free of odors.

- Keep all chewable objects from puppy's reach. Remember, his reach will expand as he grows. Provide appropriate chew toys.

- Coat stationary items, like crown molding and table legs, with chewing deterrents, such as Bitter Apple or Tabasco sauce.

PRIZE GUARDING

Your chewing monster may get possessive about her things—teach her you're not a threat

You're taken aback: As you approach your little puppy, you are greeted with a low rumble. *Couldn't be,* you think. *She would never growl at me.* You get closer, and the growling becomes louder, deeper, and more persistent. She's serious!

You lean in for a look, and you find a rawhide between puppy's paws. She's warning you that the bone—though you haven't the slightest interest in it—is *hers,* not *yours.* And if you get any closer, she just might bite you.

Though the whole concept of puppy possessiveness is sort of cute, prize guarding is potentially dangerous and must be curtailed. The "prize" can be anything from puppy's special toy to your socks. An associated problem—food-related

Problems with resource guarding:

- Termed "possession aggression" +/- "food-related aggression"

- This natural canine behavior can become problematic in a household.

- List of puppy's coveted objects can grow over time

- Hard to predict what thing(s) puppy will "own" next

- Potentially dangerous to anyone approaching coveted item(s)

- Puppy bites become stronger adult bites: Break her habit early!

Trading

- Trading games can habituate puppy to yielding prized possessions to you.

- While puppy is guarding a prize (item #1), approach her with two or three items—toys or edible treats—she may value even more.

- Offer item #2. If she drops item #1, remove it, praise her and promptly give her item #2. Shortly thereafter, return item #1 to her.

- Repeat regularly to teach puppy that giving up possessions can be a positive experience.

aggression—can involve whatever is in her food bowl.

Fortunately, there are ways to eliminate—or at least reduce—your puppy's impulse to protect her belongings. In one exercise, a string is tied to a favorite toy. If puppy growls when you near the toy, yank it away. Return the toy—with praise—when she stops growling.

Retrieving games, in addition to being fun, also hinge on showing puppy that although a toy is taken away, it's also given back.

Food-related Aggression

- Guarding behavior can involve food. If puppy guards food, employ some easy exercises to show her you're not a threat.

- Sit on the floor and place her food bowl on your lap. Let her eat out of the bowl, occasionally feeding her kibble by hand.

- With puppy eating from her food bowl, placed at its normal station, occasionally take bowl away, but give it back soon after.

- While puppy is eating kibble, approach and drop tasty treats into her bowl.

Comfort Zone

- Do retrieving games and take-and-return exercises frequently, using whatever nonedible or edible items your puppy has a tendency to guard.

- These exercises teach puppy that relinquishments needn't be permanent.

- Just because *you* may have built trust with puppy does not mean puppy trusts others near her possessions.

- Keep resources, like chews, adequately abundant, and keep feeding times regular so puppy does not perceive scarcity.

99

MOUTHY PUPPIES
Being mouthy is normal for puppies, but he can learn what's appropriate and what's forbidden

Olfaction—the sense of smell and, to some degree, taste—resides in the most primitive part of the brain. Just as children are tactile, leaving smudgy fingerprints everywhere, puppies explore their new world with their mouths.

Puppies might also mouth things in their quest to soothe the pain of teething or in an attempt to quell hunger pangs.

Behavioral reasons for oral exuberance include play and boredom. In more serious circumstances, puppies chew to relieve tension associated with problems like separation anxiety.

When the object of licking or biting is a person, you need to consider whether it is associated with a desire to interact,

Discouraging Mouthiness

- Remove all but one item in the object category your puppy prefers, such as remote controls.

- Spray the remote control with a taste deterrent, such as Bitter Apple.

- Ensure that any remote control within puppy's

reach is coated with the deterrent.

- This procedure also applies to your person. If your hands are the objects of puppy's mouthy habit, rub on some deterrent and then offer your hand to puppy. Eventually, he should stop mouthing you.

Reprimanding

- Biting a person, even playfully, is not acceptable. And overzealous licking is inappropriate and annoying.

- If puppy is mouthy, use the upper-lip-pressed-against-upper-teeth method to get him to release. (*Never* rip body part or object from puppy's mouth.)

- Now hold his empty mouth shut until he whimpers, and say "no." If he thinks it's a game, isolate him in a room for a few minutes.

- Whenever puppy gets mouthy, issue a negative stimulus with a squirt gun, shake can, or horn.

garner attention, or taste human skin. If the mouthing takes the form of biting, is it play behavior or is it aggression?

Puppy teeth are sharp and can really pierce and rip. But those puppy teeth will grow into adult teeth and jaws that have even greater force.

Whatever the reason for biting and mouthing, if it's excessive—beyond what is normal for a puppy—there are steps you can take to stop or prevent it. And biting a person, even in play, should never be tolerated.

Redirecting

- Sit on the floor with a forbidden object that puppy has chewed in the past.

- When puppy expresses interest in it, issue a stern "no" and then offer him an appropriate alternative chewable, a treat, or an invitation to play.

- Praise him when he chooses the acceptable alternative.

- Redirecting also applies to instances in which puppy spontaneously goes for one of your possessions or a part of a person's body.

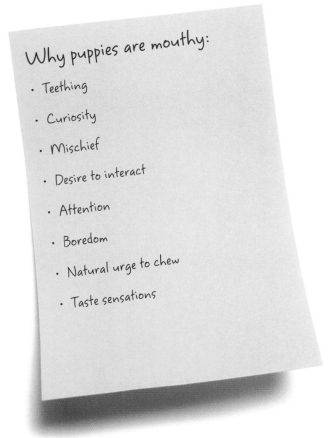

Why puppies are mouthy:

- Teething
- Curiosity
- Mischief
- Desire to interact
- Attention
- Boredom
- Natural urge to chew
- Taste sensations

TEETHING & CHEWING

STOP & DROP
Two possibly life-saving commands, and easy to teach through play

During the course of her life, puppy is likely to chew many things that do not belong in her mouth.

To recover a stolen article, you have a choice: You can rip the item out of her mouth, risking her teeth and gums, the item you are trying to reclaim, and your very sanity.

Or you can *calmly* issue the "drop it" command that you taught puppy during the heyday of her chewy adolescence.

Having puppy release an item on command is the safest and quickest way to reclaim anything, from a book to a hairbrush to your hand. But teaching the rapid recall requires patience, practice, and reward.

First, select a single verbal command that you will use consistently. It could be "Drop it!" "Leave it!" Or "Give it up!" . . . to name a few choices.

Make a game of releasing, using forbidden objects puppy likes. Resisting the urge to give chase, command puppy to

Forced Release

- Do not try to pry the object out of puppy's mouth.

- Although it's often easy to pull the object from puppy's mouth, it gets harder to do with an adult.

- Trying to yank the item out also increases the risk of your being bitten, loosening puppy's teeth, and damaging the object you are trying to salvage.

- To safely force release, place one hand over puppy's snout and press her upper lips inward over her upper teeth. The pinch will likely cause her to open her mouth, releasing the object.

Voluntary Release

- Cue "drop it" and offer a more enticing object/treat. Once puppy drops the item, praise her.

- If this fails, distract: Rattling your keys or knocking on a door will usually cause puppy to drop the item in anticipation.

- Or use taste appeal: Dab peanut butter on her nose— impossible for her to lick it off with a wallet in her mouth!

- Alternatively, leave the room and shut the door behind you. All alone, puppy will probably drop the object.

drop the item. If she does, reward her with a treat and heap the praise.

If she resists, repeat your order while offering an enticing toy or treat as a trade. If she obeys, treat her. If she still resists, follow one of the tactics below to entice her to voluntarily release or, if all else fails, to force release. Always reward compliance. And, most importantly, stay calm.

RED ● LIGHT

Never give chase to reclaim a valuable that puppy has taken from you. She might interpret it as a game, which could reinforce her negative behavior.

Testing

- Test and reinforce puppy's self-discipline by leashing her up and walking her past a favorite forbidden object.

- If she grasps the item, cue "drop it" and then follow one of the aforementioned voluntary release procedures.

- If she walks past the item without grasping it, praise her and then offer her a treat or play time.

- Repeat several times in sequence to reinforce the behavior. Practice this exercise daily until you notice a consistent change in puppy's behavior.

Rewarding

- When puppy releases an object, couple this desired behavior with a positive stimulus.

- Positive reinforcement should always start with praise—both verbal and tactile.

- Also tender a chew toy, a ball, an edible snack, or an invitation to play.

- Gradually increase the amount of time between relinquishment and reward. After desired behavior is achieved, stagger rewards so they accompany relinquishment *sometimes*, but not *every* time.

START HER OFF RIGHT

Types of foods, amounts, and feeding intervals that produce a fit, growing puppy

For puppy's first year, feed him a *commercial diet labeled for puppies (or growth)*. Now is not the time to experiment with homemade diets. Puppy foods have specially balanced levels of proteins, vitamins, minerals, and energy. They are highly digestible and palatable. And they come in small bites as well as large-breed formulations.

Ideal feeding amounts vary slightly from puppy to puppy, based on breed, age, activity level, and environmental temperature. Though you could calculate the average daily caloric requirement using a complicated mathematical formula, it's probably better to follow the feeding guidelines on the food package.

Feeding Amounts

Feeding intervals:

- Introduce moistened solid foods pre-weaning, at three to four weeks old.

- Puppy is eating only solids by about six weeks old.

- Feed three or four times a day until six months old.

- Feed twice daily until one year old.

- After one year, feed once or twice daily.

- If puppy has no weight or housebreaking issues at one year, you can do free-choice instead of scheduled feedings.

- Every commercial food has a unique nutrient profile, including caloric density. To compare any two foods, look at the "dry matter" (DM) nutrient levels which eliminate water from the analysis.

- Follow the feeding instructions posted on the label for recommended daily portions.

- Feed dry food at about one cup and wet food at about 1 can per ten pounds of body weight daily.

Feeding frequencies also vary with puppy's age. Young puppies must be fed every six to eight hours. By six months, feeding frequency can be reduced to twice daily.

Free-choice feeding can be implemented after a year if there are no problems with obesity or housebreaking. But it should not be done during puppy's first year because of the potential for rapid weight gain leading to health problems.

Dietary Transitions

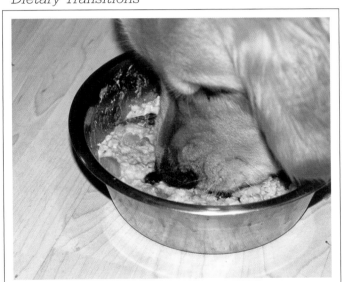

- Feed a commercial diet formulated for puppies for puppy's first year.

- At one year, switch puppy to adult maintenance food.

- For large breeds, many experts recommend not switching to adult food until a year-and-a-half.

- When switching to a new food, the transition should be done gradually over seven days. Mix new food with original food at 1:3 ratio. After a few days, mix half-and-half. Then 3:1. And finally, complete conversion to new food.

Food for thought:

- Make informed dietary choices.

- Compare pet food labels.

- Call food manufacturer/distributor customer information numbers with questions.

- Ask breeder for dietary recommendations.

- Check with your veterinarian BEFORE finalizing dietary decisions.

- Don't rely on Internet sources—no quality control of information.

- Consider your sources: Erroneous nutritional theories abound.

NUTRITIONAL BUILDING BLOCKS

Know which proteins, fats, carbohydrates, vitamins, and minerals puppy needs, and why

Like wild candids—who eat a variety of mushrooms, grasses, fruits, roots, and veggies—our domestic dogs are not strictly carnivores at all. They are omnivores: They eat everything!

As such, they need a *balance* of the key nutrients—proteins, fats, carbohydrates, vitamins, minerals, and water—from dietary meats, vegetables, and grains.

While proteins build body infrastructure, and fats and carbohydrates provide most of the energy to gas up the machine, vitamins and minerals maintain the immune system, blood clotting, metabolism, muscle function, bones, teeth, skin, and vision.

Vitamins E and C, beta carotene, and selenium are

Vitamins and minerals

- Vitamins are either fat-soluble (A, D, E, and K) or water-soluble (B-complex and C).

- The minerals are calcium, phosphate, potassium, sodium, magnesium, iron, zinc, copper, manganese, iodine, cobalt, and selenium.

- Calcium, primarily from bones and chicken meal, lamb meal, and fish meal, is the mineral needed in greatest amounts. It must be given in proper amount—and correct ratio—with phosphate, which comes mainly from muscle meat, eggs, and dairy products.

Proteins and Fats

- Proteins are nitrogen sources and primary building blocks of body tissues, enzymes, hormones, antibodies, and hemoglobin.

- Proteins are comprised of amino acids. There are ten "essential" amino acids dogs need from their diet; the others they make.

- Protein requirements are greater for puppies (20 to 32 percent DM) than mature dogs (15 to 30 percent DM).

- Dietary protein comes from lean muscle meat, meat by-products, chicken, eggs, soybean meal, and whole grains.

antioxidants that protect cells from free radical destruction and shield flavor freshness in food. Palatability, affected by food odor, texture, fat and water content, and temperature, is a key to nutrition, because it affects food consumption.

Fiber—as cellulose, soybean mill run, and beet pulp—aids in satiety and gut function.

Water, the most important nutrient, is required for all that happens within the body. Fresh water should be made available at all times.

While nutrient balance means *enough,* it also means *not too much.* Excess calories lead to obesity, which quintuples diabetes risk, nearly triples the occurrence of lameness, boosts the rate of skin problems by 50 percent, and leads to a threefold increase in mortality.

Excess dietary protein gets converted to fat and also burdens the kidneys. Abnormally high calcium has been shown to cause skeletal deformities in as many as half of oversupplemented large-breed dogs. Increased sodium levels can initiate or complicate heart and kidney failure. And high magnesium can lead to bladder stone formation.

Fats and Carbohydrates

- Fats deliver energy (9kcal/g), maintain cell membranes, promote neurological development and absorption of fat-soluble vitamins, and enhance food palatability. They include essential fatty acids.

- Dietary fats, from sources like egg, animal fat, fish oil, soybean oil, and flaxseed, maintain healthy skin and hair coat.

- Dogs have no requirements for carbohydrates, which are added to dog foods for energy (4 kcal/g), fiber, palatability, variety, and to facilitate baking.

Beware of dietary supplements:

- Supplements are available as vitamins, minerals, and joint fortifiers like chondroitin.

- Most commercial dog foods are complete and balanced for vitamins and minerals.

- Supplementing with vitamins and minerals can cause serious health problems.

- Excessive calcium can cause developmental bone and joint disease in puppies.

- Eight percent of dog owners used supplements in 2008, a decrease over last decade (APPA).

- Check with veterinarian before giving your puppy supplements.

UNDERSTANDING FOOD INGREDIENTS

Become an educated consumer by learning how to read dog food ingredient labels

When you pick up a bag or can of dog food, look for the phrase "complete and balanced" on the front. This means that the food has the full panel of nutrients, and in the correct relative amounts, to meet the requirements of the designated life stage.

For a puppy, look for a brand that is listed for either puppies or *all life stages*, which includes puppies.

Also look for the "guaranteed analysis," a chart situated usually on the side panel of bags and the back of cans. The guaranteed analysis gives the minimum percentages of crude protein and crude fat the product could contain, as well as maximums for crude fiber and moisture.

Ingredients in Kibble

INGREDIENTS:
Beef, Beef Meal, Cracked Pearled Barley, Brown Rice, Millet, Rice Br (preserved with mixed tocopherols), Ocean Fish Meal, Tomato Pom Natural Flavor, Salmon Oil (source of DHA), Choline Chloride, Taurine Root, Parsley Flakes, Pumpkin Meal, Almond Oil (preserved with mixe Sesame Oil (preserved with mixed tocopherols), Yucca Schidigera E Blueberries, Cranberries, Carrots, Broccoli, Vitamin E Supplement, Ir chelated source of iron), Zinc Proteinate (a chelated source of zinc), Copp chelated source of copper), Ferrous Sulfate, Zinc Sulfate, Copper Sul Iodide, Thiamine Mononitrate, Manganese Proteinate (a chelated source Manganous Oxide, Ascorbic Acid, Vitamin A Supplement, Biotin, Calciu Manganese Sulfate, Sodium Selenite, Pyridoxine Hydrochloride (vitam B12 Supplement, Riboflavin, Vitamin D Supplement, Folic Acid.

GUARANTEED ANALYSIS:
Crude Protein	22.00%
Crude Fat	12.00%
Crude Fiber	4.00%
Moisture	10.00%
DHA (Docosohexaenoic Acid)	0.05% *

*Not recognized as an essential nutrient by the AAFCO Dog Food N

CALORIE CONTENT (calculated):
Calories (ME)	387 kcal/cup

- Kibble, or dry food, is 3 to 11 percent water.

- The first ingredient in most kibble is corn, often viewed as a "filler" and a food allergen.

- In truth, corn delivers high quality protein, essential fatty acids, and antioxidants. It is highly digestible, and it rarely triggers food allergies.

- The more likely allergens in dog food are beef, dairy, wheat, lamb, chicken, egg, and soy, which account for 93 percent of food allergies.

"Meat" Terminology

- *Beef* (or *chicken* . . .) means food ingredients are at least 95 percent beef.

- *Beef dinner, platter, entrée, recipe,* or *formula* . . . means food contains at least 25 percent, but less than 95 percent, beef.

- *With beef* means food contains at least 3 percent, but less than 25 percent, beef.

- *Beef flavor* means food contains less than 3 percent beef, but enough beef for flavor to be recognized by pet.

Caloric content as well as percentages of key minerals, like calcium, are also listed. For large-breed puppies, avoid foods high in calories, or with calcium content in excess of 1.2 percent (dry matter basis).

Ingredients will be listed by weight. You'll see lots of grains, which, contrary to some reports, dogs can digest as prepared.

There is also meat, listed either as the meat itself, meat byproducts, meat meal, meat and bone meal, and or meat stock. The latter four non-rendered and rendered byproducts, though not something we would likely eat, are great sources of nutrition nonetheless.

Among the last ingredients are preservatives, which safeguard freshness and taste. Look for products containing all-natural preservatives like mixed tocopherols, which are forms of vitamin E.

Moist and Semi-moist Foods

- Moist foods are 60 to 87 percent water. They are packaged in cans or tins. Moist foods have high levels of meat and meat by-products, elevated concentrations of protein, phosphorus, sodium, and fat, and greater palatability, than semi-moist and dry foods.

- Semi-moist foods are 25 to 33 percent water. They are packaged in bags, packets, or tubular "chubs."

- Semi-moist foods typically contain meat meals and artificial flavors that provide a savory, quite palatable flavor.

Quality kibble has:
- Complete and balanced nutrition
- High digestibility
- Minimal or no additives
- Natural preservatives (i.e., mixed tocopherols)
- High palatability
- Quality ingredients and manufacturing

DIET CHOICES

There are many ways to feed your dog, and you can blend diets too

The pet food market consists of over 4,000 pet foods from over 250 different manufacturers. So much to choose from, it almost makes you want to cook puppy's food yourself.

Not so fast. Commercial formulations are regulated for the needs of specific canine life stages.

Dog food claims are regulated by the FDA. Their ingredients are policed by the U.S. Department of Agriculture (USDA). Further standards are sealed with an optional "merit badge"

by the Association of Animal Feed Control Officials (AAFCO), which is listed on food packages as an "AAFCO statement."

Puppy has stringent nutritional requirements critical to her future health—so during this important stage of her life, stick to foods designed by the experts for puppies or *all life stages*.

While foods labeled "premium" or "gourmet" needn't meet raised standards, they are generally pricier than the grocery

Raw/Processed Raw Diets

- Raw food— "B.A.R.F." (bones and raw food)—diets consist of uncooked whole carcasses, meat, bones, and organs.

- Raw food proponents believe these mimic what dogs have evolved to eat, and keep dogs healthier.

- Potential problems with BARF diets include oral abrasions, intestinal perforations, bacterial contamination, and social aggression.

- Processed raw food diets like Wysong and Honest Kitchen are an alternative to BARF diets.

Cooked Diets

- Cooked diets should consist of carbohydrate/fiber from cooked cereal grain, at least one animal-origin protein source, a fat source, minerals—(particularly calcium), and a multivitamin.

- The carbohydrate/protein ratio for dog foods should be 2:1 to 3:1.

- Because the parameters for puppy nutrition are so stringent, it is best to feed puppy complete and balanced commercial foods, rather than homemade diets.

store brands because they may have higher levels of quality assurance in the manufacturing process. However, premium and less expensive brands often utilize the same ingredient sources.

Some premium brands have championed the concept of prescription diets for medical conditions, as well as unique formulations for different life stages. Look for puppy dry food that has antioxidants shown to help build a healthy immune system in ninety days or large breed puppy dry formulas that have optimal calcium level and increased levels of omega-3 fatty acids and L-carnitine. Whether you feed dry, moist, or semi-moist food is your choice. Dry food is easiest and most economical, and some dry foods have proven benefits. Some people mix in wet food to increase dry food palatability. It's generally okay to mix table food in as well, as long as 90 percent of her diet consists of your puppy's commercial puppy food.

Meat Bones

- Meat bones are an excellent source of protein, phosphorus, and calcium for puppy. Meat bones also provide abrasion for healthy teeth.

- The safest meat bones are those that are less likely to splinter, such as ham hocks and large cattle joints.

- While puppy is chewing a meat bone, monitor to make sure that the bone is not splintering.

- Fresh meat bones can usually be obtained from the butcher.

Foods fed most often:

- Premium brands — 34%
  - Dry foods — 76%
  - Canned foods — 22%
  - Semi-moist foods — 7%

- Foods fortified with added vitamins and minerals — 29%

- Other — 15%

- Natural foods — 6%

- Organic foods — 2%

- Gourmet foods — 2%

- Raw foods — 1%

*Source: 2009/2010 American Pet Products Assn. National Pet Owners Survey Based on percent of dog owners to a multiple-response question.

111

TREATS
Assuming treats are even necessary, here's how to make healthful treat choices

What if you had to eat the same Rice-A-Roni dish every night? Wouldn't you need to jazz things up a bit with tasty treats like Doritos and M&Ms? Canine treats serve the same purpose, but . . . for dogs, not us! Treats can be used to break the monotony of puppy's static menu and can serve as both rewards in training and as bonding tools.

Treats can take the form of human food, such as meats, vegetables, cheese, even peanut butter in small amounts. But watch out for high-carb snacks, like crackers and potato chips, which are calorie-laden and break down to sugars that can cause dental disease in dogs.

Commercial treats come in many varieties. They are small

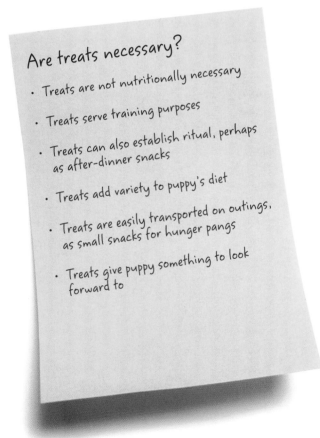

Are treats necessary?

- Treats are not nutritionally necessary

- Treats serve training purposes

- Treats can also establish ritual, perhaps as after-dinner snacks

- Treats add variety to puppy's diet

- Treats are easily transported on outings, as small snacks for hunger pangs

- Treats give puppy something to look forward to

Meat Treats

- Meat treats are very popular. Nearly 60 percent of owners who buy dog treats purchase meat treats.

- Meat treats advertise the primary meat, usually beef or chicken, on the front of the package. Depending on actual meat content, these treats may be high in protein and phosphorus.

- Human foods can also be used to satisfy puppy's taste for meat.

- Cut-up hot dogs (cooked or raw), beef jerky, and cooked liver are easy treats that puppies love.

enough to feed puppy easily, yet large enough that one at a time is adequate.

Many dog treats are, however, high in calories, calcium, and phosphate, all of which puppies—particularly large-breed—need in tightly controlled amounts and proportions.

A handful of treats can contain 40 percent of puppy's daily energy (caloric) requirement. A fifteen-pound puppy receiving two snacks daily can easily become 30 percent overweight in a year. Likewise, a growing puppy could double his calcium intake with daily snacks.

Always read nutrition labels on commercial canine snacks. Buy treats whose calcium and caloric contents are similar to those in puppy's food. Then subtract out comparable amounts of food to account for the treats.

Treats ideally should comprise no more than 10 percent of puppy's diet.

Low-cal Treats

- Giving several commercial dog treats a day can easily boost puppy's caloric intake to exceed his daily requirements.

- Most commercial dog treats are thirty or forty calories a piece—and some are as high as 250 calories each. Some brands even have light treats.

- A number of human foods can be used as treats that are friendly to puppy's taste buds and his waistline.

- These include popcorn, rice cakes, Cheerios, chopped carrots, and string cheese.

Commercial Treats

- There are many varieties of commercial treats.

- These include beef jerky strips, hard biscuits, soft treats molded into different food shapes (i.e., pretzel shapes), and pricier, freeze-dried snacks (i.e., liver).

- Commercial dog treats can be high in calcium, phosphorus, and calories. (Remember—puppies have narrow nutrient requirements, and excesses can harm them.)

- Some brands have treats formulated for various life stages, including puppies.

DANGEROUS FOODS & SUBSTANCES
A list of plants, foods, and other substances that can poison puppy

Poisonous substances fall into one of four categories: household chemicals, foods, plants, and medications. The top ten hazards to dogs (from the ASPCA Poison Control Center) are: ibuprofen, chocolate, ant and roachbaits, rodenticides, acetaminophen, cold medications with pseudoephedrine, thyroid hormones, bleach, fertilizer, and hydrocarbons. Other common hazards include ingestion of lead from pipes, putty or old paint; and zinc toxicity from eating pennies (1982 and newer), bolts/nuts, or zinc oxide ointment. Zinc destroys red blood cells, causing anemia, jaundice and bloody urine. And while 75 percent of poisonings are from ingestion, some toxins can damage victims by inhalation or skin contact.

Pets exposed to a toxin often have general physical signs: vomiting, diarrhea, muscle tremors, seizures, weakness, and delirium. Always contact a poison control center or your vet for advice before attempting to treat your pup. It may be

Taboo Foods

- Onions are a big no-no for dogs. Onion ingestion can cause red blood cell destruction, or hemolytic anemia.

- Also watch out for products like baby food that contain onion powder, as well as onion cousin, garlic.

- Coffee and tea cause restlessness, hyperventilation, and rapid heart rate.

- Macadamia nuts, grapes/raisins, alcohol, and the artificial sweetener xylitol can also be toxic to dogs.

Chocolate

- Chocolate contains two methylxanthines—theobromine and caffeine—that dogs don't tolerate well.

- Baking chocolate contains the highest dose of methylxanthine, with dark second and milk chocolate third.

- Clinical signs of chocolate toxicity, which range from hyperexcitability and GI upset to seizures and irregular heartbeat, depend on type of chocolate, amount consumed, and size of dog. Sixteen ounces of baking chocolate can kill a forty-pound dog.

essential to go right to the vet.

If your pup appears stable, first aid should prevent further exposure to or absorption of the toxin. For skin contact, wash puppy thoroughly with mild soap. If an ingested toxin is not corrosive and you catch it within 6 hours, you may be instructed to induce vomiting with syrup of ipecac or hydrogen peroxide. If you can't induce vomiting, you might give a GI protectant, such as milk, egg whites, baking soda paste, or milk of magnesia. Vets can remove stomach contents with a tube and then give activated charcoal to prevent more absorption. For some toxins, your vet may have a specific antidote: For example, ethanol—grain alcohol—is used to counteract ethylene glycol toxicity. Some rodenticides can stay in the body for weeks, requiring long term treatment with medications. So, when you bring puppy to the vet, take along any vomit, plus the suspected toxin, container, or label to help identify the source.

Toxic Chemicals

UPRIGHT POSITION. CLEAN UP SPILLS AT ONCE. Keep hands, face and childr... Drain Opener. Never use a plunger during or after use of Drain Opener because dr... drain did not clear properly. Do not reuse empty container. Rinse container and repla...

DANGER. CAN CAUSE BURNS ON CONTACT. INJURES EYE **MEMBRANES ON CONTACT. HARMFUL IF SWALLOWED. KEEP OUT** Do not use or mix Drain Opener with ammonia, toilet bowl cleaners, household ... because this product contains sodium hypochlorite (bleach). Mixtures may release h... eruption from drain. If gases are released, leave area immediately – ventilate if possib...

FIRST AID: EMERGENCY TREATMENT: IF IN EYES: Rinse immediately with cool running water. Remove any contact lenses and continue flushing with water for at least 15 minutes. Call a physician or poison control center promptly for treatment advice. **IF SWALLOWED DO NOT INDUCE VOMITING -** Rinse mouth thoroughly with cool running water, drink one to two glasses of water and call a physician or poison control center immediately. **IF ON SKIN OR CLOTHING:** Immediately remove rings and contaminated clothing, wash skin thoroughly with soap and water. Continually flush for 15 minutes. If irritation persists, call a physician. **Do not give anything by mouth to an unconscious person.**

CONTAINS: Sodium hypochlorite (bleach), sodium hydroxide, biodegradable surfactants, sodium silicate (corrosion inhibitor), surfactant. Contains no phosphorus.

ALWAYS INSURE CAP IS ON TIGHT

Distributed by: The Price Chopper, Inc.

- Over half of toxin *fatalities* involve pesticides, rodenticides, and antifreeze.

- *Pesticides,* which include ant poison, snail bait, fly sprays, and topically-applied flea products for pets, can cause vomiting, diarrhea, twitching, seizures, and death.

- Most *rodenticides*—or rat poisons—cause their victims to bleed to death.

- *Ethylene glycol,* or antifreeze, has a sweet taste that most pets love. As little as ½ cup of antifreeze can kill a dog within hours.

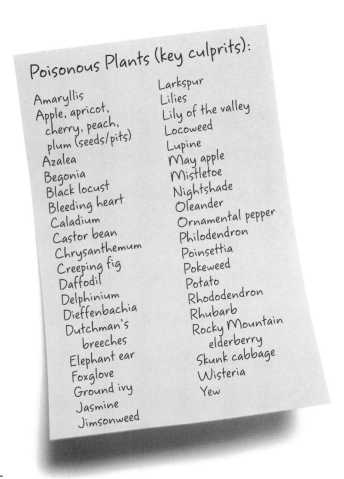

Poisonous Plants (key culprits):

Amaryllis
Apple, apricot, cherry, peach, plum (seeds/pits)
Azalea
Begonia
Black locust
Bleeding heart
Caladium
Castor bean
Chrysanthemum
Creeping fig
Daffodil
Delphinium
Dieffenbachia
Dutchman's breeches
Elephant ear
Foxglove
Ground ivy
Jasmine
Jimsonweed
Larkspur
Lilies
Lily of the valley
Locoweed
Lupine
May apple
Mistletoe
Nightshade
Oleander
Ornamental pepper
Philodendron
Poinsettia
Pokeweed
Potato
Rhododendron
Rhubarb
Rocky Mountain elderberry
Skunk cabbage
Wisteria
Yew

115

HARDWIRING OR ENGINEERING?

Every puppy has an innate temperament, but how to shape it is up to you

The process of socializing is what takes puppy from that anonymous furry mass you've brought home to a bona fide family member and participant in your human network and community at large. But molding puppy into a dog that will meet your expectations, from jogging buddy to children's playmate to therapy dog, is a project whose success depends on a number of factors. Every puppy has an individual personality, which is a complex aggregate of traits that vary on several scales. These include dominance/submissiveness, social attraction, play drive, touch/sight/sound sensitivity, overall reactivity, trainability, restraint, independence, and energy level.

Well-adjusted Dog

- A well-adjusted dog is not skittish and overreactive.

- Some breeds, such as the Jack Russell terrier, have been selected for high attentiveness, rapid response to sounds, smells and visual cues, and lightning-fast reflexes.

- Puppies that are reactive breeds can be desensitized, to some extent, through repeated and controlled exposure to stimuli.

- Vigilant training can produce self-control in puppy to minimize excessive reactions, like barking and chasing.

Training Yourself

- Research the idiosyncrasies of your preferred dog breed before selecting a puppy.

- Once you have committed to a particular breed, learn everything you can about that breed's temperament, behavioral tendencies, and intelligence.

- Tailor a training program, with the advice of your breeder and a trainer, to your puppy.

- While trying to mold puppy's behavior with your "nurture," be mindful of the "nature" limitations of his breed and individual makeup.

These innate traits are encoded in puppy's genetic script at birth, and largely before birth, when his breed was first created through successive matings aimed at harvesting specific attributes of body, mind, and soul. Your bold little Dachshund, bred to hunt the fierce badger, may welcome family time but maintain a "Keep out!" attitude toward visitors. Your basset hound, formulated to follow a scent and make independent decisions while doing so, is bound to be stubborn: Bear this in mind when you try to convince him that raiding the garbage is a bad idea.

Expect your catlike basenji to keep you on your toes as he calculates his next clever move to get his way. Your border collie? Affable and smart, he'll be a ball of nervous energy if you don't keep him gainfully employed.

So you see, your puppy is not a blank slate. Rather, he comes preprogrammed to behave in a certain way. But there's that nature-nurture concept that brings good news: You, as his owner, can modulate puppy's very being, to some extent, through the manner in which you train him, the way in which you socialize him, and the experiences you give him.

Doggie Diversity

- Expose puppy early on to what life has to offer: His later encounters with people, places, and experiences can be free of excessive fear or excitement.

- Introduce puppy to people who vary by age, gender, ethnicity, size, and appearance.

- Provide puppy with supervised exposure (once vaccinated) to local animals, perhaps cats, farm animals, and, certainly, other dogs.

- Get puppy accustomed to new places, different objects, and the sometimes jarring sounds of the world.

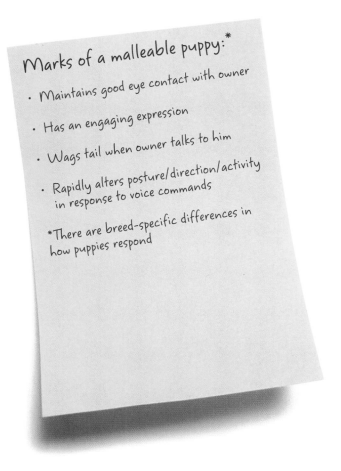

Marks of a malleable puppy:*

- Maintains good eye contact with owner

- Has an engaging expression

- Wags tail when owner talks to him

- Rapidly alters posture/direction/activity in response to voice commands

*There are breed-specific differences in how puppies respond

117

A SOCIAL BUTTERFLY

Encouraging your puppy to meet many different people helps her become a confident, stable adult

As your newest addition, puppy has left her canine world for formal induction into human society. She is now part of your world, which—unless you live on a deserted island—is likely filled with all manner of people.

Puppy needs to learn to interact properly with the people in her life. Healthy interaction with humans means neither shying away from people nor jumping on them, neither growling at them nor bathing them with her tongue. So too, puppy mustn't chew ankles or stare down your dinner guests in pursuit of table scraps. The only way to make puppy comfortable, confident, and mannerly around people is to provide her with opportunities to spend time with them.

Adults

- Puppy's major human socialization period is from about seven to fourteen weeks. During this time, puppy learns how to interact and bond with people, forms ideas about people to whom she is exposed, and generalizes those ideas to like people.

- At this time, puppy should be exposed to a wide range of people—young and old, big and small, male and female, and of various ethnicities and tongues.

- Try to keep all these early human interactions positive.

Children

- Between the ages of two and three months, puppy should be exposed to children of all ages.

- Children behave in a somewhat unpredictable manner, and their movements are often uncoordinated. This can be scary to puppy.

- All interactions between puppy and children under thirteen should be closely supervised.

- Because these first experiences can leave lasting impressions about children, do your best to keep all early meetings between puppy and kids positive.

How to habituate puppy to people? Once her vaccines are complete, take her with you everywhere you go, within the limits of social acceptability, of course.

Don't link greetings with a lot of fanfare. Rather, talk in a calm and friendly tone to the person whom puppy is greeting, and pair the greeting with positive reinforcement in the form of happy talk, edible treats, or a pat on the head.

Do not allow puppy to greet someone who you think might react with excessive excitement or fear, as this could cause anxiety for puppy.

Enforce mannerly conduct consistently and universally: For instance, jumping on people is not allowed. Not today. Not tomorrow. *Never.* And on *no one*.

Unfortunately, there will be times when it's necessary to discipline puppy for poor behavior around people. But always do so in a measured fashion, perhaps a firm "no" plus a tug on the collar. Remember, you don't want puppy to associate people with negative experiences like punishments.

Different Contexts

- Teach puppy through experience that humans can pop up in any situation.

- Expose puppy to people strolling in parks or (dog-friendly) stores; behind strollers or on roller skates; jogging on the street or delivering the mail; in daylight or dark.

- Let puppy investigate new people—politely, of course. Do so only with willing human participants.

- Keep these meetings positive by talking to both puppy and the other person in a happy tone.

Introductions

- Introductions between puppy and a new person should be non-threatening for all parties and done in a calm setting where there is little noise or distraction.

- If puppy is meeting a new person in the home, the visitor should be seated and puppy leash-walked into the room.

- Whatever the setting, the visitor should sit or kneel and slowly extend a palm-down hand for puppy to sniff, while talking to puppy in a friendly tone and/or offering treats.

119

SOCIALIZING OLDER PUPPIES
Once he's vaccinated, go exploring and introduce him to the big wide world

A newborn baby's gaze holds only newness. Everything he sees is a first. So, too, every sound, every odor and flavor, every texture . . . they're all new to him.

A puppy is no different. Even though a puppy is a precocious being—he runs, eats on his own, and plays—when compared to an infant of the same age, whatever he encounters holds some degree of novelty to him.

How puppies react to novel stimuli varies among individuals. One puppy might ricochet nervously off the car windows when you take him out for a ride; another may sleep. One pup might whimper and thrash as you try to walk him past a humming lawnmower; another may amble along ambivalently.

Physical Confidence

- Puppy's musculoskeletal system is developing, as are his reflexes.

- Let puppy encounter different surfaces, from blacktop to beach sand, pile carpet to piled snow.

- Test puppy's competence—under your close supervision—with reasonable physical demands, such as ascending and descending stairs, walking up ramps, jumping for balls, and paddling in water that does not come above his shoulders.

Puppy Class

- Enroll puppy in a training class around sixteen weeks of age.

- By this time, he should have the emotional and mental maturity for training. And he is probably protected against common transmissible viruses, his vaccination series complete.

- Puppy class gives puppy opportunities to interact with other dogs.

- Puppy class also teaches puppy self-control, as he is forced to obey the rules of proper conduct, enforced by his owner and teacher, and also by the other dogs in the class.

Whatever his breed or individual temperament, puppy needs to get "out there" as soon as he can do so safely.

Once he is fully immunized, help puppy to experience the world. This means taking him out, by car or on foot, and exposing him to the places, people, animals, and things that will be part of his life. This will not only teach him about—and help him navigate—his new world, but it will also build his confidence.

A Public Figure

- Bring puppy out in public at every possible opportunity. Try your neighborhood sidewalks, outdoor malls, and dog-friendly parks and beaches.

- Do not try to bring puppy into any food establishments, as this is prohibited by law.

- Keep puppy leashed in public, and bring along a water bottle, a portable water bowl, dog treats, plastic bags for picking up poop, a flashlight in case you're out after dark, and pepper spray or a walking stick to break up potential dog fights.

Auto Etiquette

- Assist puppy in the car. Remove the leash to prevent choking. Keep windows cracked no more than the width of puppy's muzzle.

- Protect seats with covers or blankets. To prevent heat stroke or hypothermia, do not leave puppy in your car unattended in extreme weather conditions.

- Puppy should *always* ride in the back seat. Use a crate or car harness to keep him stationary.

- On long trips, take bathroom and water breaks every two hours.

SOCIALIZING

DEALING WITH FEAR

Your puppy will have inevitable fears but will learn from you how to overcome them

Fear is an inevitable element in a dog's life. And that's not exactly a bad thing. Fear helped puppy's ancestors survive threats like saber-tooth cats. And fear could help puppy if she ever finds herself face-to-face with an irritated house cat. Whatever the object of puppy's fear, she will exhibit her trepidation through a classic set of reactions: crouching, shaking, urinating, piloerection, barking, aggression, and recoiling.

But fear is a wasted emotion if puppy cannot differentiate real threats from those that pose no danger. If puppy spooks every time the wall clock dings on the hour, or the lawn sprinkler goes on, then what's the upside?

Fear is a stressful reaction for both puppy and anyone

Fear-inducing Objects

- Objects of fear for a puppy can run the gamut and vary among puppies.

- Things that induce fear in dogs tend to have any of the following features: imposing size, odd shape, sound- or air-emitting, simulate person/ animal, spinning wheels, random/ sudden movements.

- Commonly feared objects include large stuffed animals, snowmen, hair dryers, lawnmowers, and bicycles.

- Various people and jarring sounds may also scare puppy.

Combating Fear

- If a fear is unfounded (fear of a harmless object), or excessive, it should be addressed.

- Never scold puppy for exhibiting fear—this will only add to the anxiety.

- Some desensitization to the object can be achieved through short periods of controlled exposure.

- During exposure, provide positive reinforcement: lots of "happy talk"; touch object; place dog treats on or near object and encourage puppy to approach object to get treats.

witnessing puppy's whimpers and attempts to flee from dreaded objects or people. Fears may develop throughout life, but the major "fear imprint" period occurs around two or three months of age. In other words, traumatic incidents that happen at this time can develop into lifelong phobias. But even an older puppy can become newly phobic of an object with which he has long been familiar and comfortable.

During puppy's early months, it is important to shield her, if possible, from scary experiences. While you probably will not anticipate the errant Frisbee, for example, that bonks her in the head, and you certainly cannot prevent the rumbling thunderstorm, you can minimize their impacts.

When the Frisbee hits, don't make a big deal about it. Show puppy the Frisbee. Let her sniff it. Toss it to her. And pair the Frisbee encounter with something pleasant, like a dog treat.

So, too, if the weather forecast calls for thunder, stay home with puppy during the storm. Bring her to an interior room, and keep the television on so as to cover up the rumbles. Distract her with play time, and comfort her with caresses and treats.

Building Comfort

- Puppy should be able to move about in her environment with assurance, rather than be hampered by fears.

- From a young age, expose puppy to the people, places, and objects that will be part of her life.

- If you live in Florida, for instance, don't worry about introducing puppy to snow, but do make sure she is comfortable with the rustle of palm trees.

- Puppies that are crated all the time may develop apprehensions to their world.

Fear periods:

- Fear is a normal part of puppy's emotional maturation.

- Traumatic events occurring during "fear imprint periods" can morph into lifetime phobias.

- Eight to eleven weeks: first fear imprint period

- Sixteen weeks to one year: puppy inquisitiveness peaks

- Sixteen to twenty weeks: second fear imprint period

SOCIALIZING

FIELD & STREAM

Teach puppy how to deal with everything Mother Nature has to offer, from beaches to woods

The outdoors holds endless opportunities for puppy to exercise, explore, and have fun. Whether you live in Manhattan or along the Appalachian Trail, whether puppy is a coiffed Maltese or an earthy bluetick coonhound, you should avail him of the wonders of the natural world.

The wilderness is one of the few places that welcomes both you and your dog, although it's important to always check signage at places like parks and public beaches to make sure dogs are allowed.

Exploring the wilderness is also a diversion that you and puppy can really enjoy in concert. Walking together, whether along a riverbank or a rocky hiking trail, is a good bonding

Adventure

- The Great Outdoors is likely within your reach, no matter where you live.

- Puppy will benefit from day trips to beaches, forests, deserts, mountains, and streams.

- Remember that puppy's sleep requirements are greater than those of a mature dog.

- If you will be out for a long time, be sure to take adequate rest breaks. Perhaps bring a blanket along for puppy to nap on.

Oceans, Lakes, Streams

- Puppies over three or four months can spend *supervised* time in water.

- Swimming is great exercise; many dogs love to fetch sticks and balls in the water. Puppies are born with the ability to swim, but some breeds are less adept at it. If you're unsure about your

puppy's swimming ability, keep him out of water above his shoulder.

- Be prepared: If puppy drinks outdoor water, he can contract the protozoan *Giardia*, which causes easily treatable diarrhea. Salt water ingestion causes short-term, profuse diarrhea.

experience for the two of you.

Puppy will also benefit from the changing scenery. Perhaps best of all, he will revel in the plethora of scents in Mother Nature's perfumeries.

Puppy's sense of smell is over 1,000 times more accurate than ours. So when puppy enters a bakery, he doesn't just smell cake. Rather, he smells the eggs, the flour, the butter. . . . So, too, he'll pick up endless scents—ones that you and I cannot smell—on a walk in the woods.

The variety of inclines and walking surfaces—craggy trails, beach sand, tangled underbrush, river rocks, ice—help to build his coordination and acclimate him to the world around him.

Once puppy has had his vaccine series, start thinking about places you can go together to enjoy the fresh air and bucolic scenery.

Bring key supplies, such as bottled water and a portable water dish, dog treats, and trail maps. And don't forget towels and a brush: Puppy will most likely coat himself in whatever is out there—beach sand, wood chips, mud, briars . . .

Weather Extremes

- Get puppy accustomed to all weather patterns that will be part of his life.

- Heat stroke is a risk for dogs, so avoid excessive heat. If you go out on a hot day, limit exercise and provide water.

- Excessive cold can cause hypothermia. If the temperature is below freezing, limit time outside. Keep puppy out of near-freezing water.

- Small dogs lose heat faster than large dogs. For small dogs, sweaters are a good idea in weather below forty degrees.

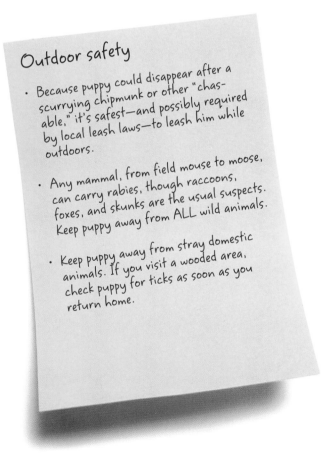

Outdoor safety

- Because puppy could disappear after a scurrying chipmunk or other "chasable," it's safest—and possibly required by local leash laws—to leash him while outdoors.

- Any mammal, from field mouse to moose, can carry rabies, though raccoons, foxes, and skunks are the usual suspects. Keep puppy away from ALL wild animals.

- Keep puppy away from stray domestic animals. If you visit a wooded area, check puppy for ticks as soon as you return home.

IT'S UP TO YOU

How you affirm, correct, and interact with a puppy will affect her behavior forever

A dog is only as good as her ability to live in symbiosis with you. The moment puppy enters your home, she starts to learn how to fit in peacefully with your life.

As puppy sponges up information about you and her new environment, you should be supplementing her with training. An untrained dog is a calamity.

Training teaches puppy where she ranks in the family hierarchy, and helps her comprehend and embrace human leadership. Training also helps bridge the interspecies language barrier by establishing a solid channel of communication between you and puppy.

Effective training helps you mold puppy's behavior so that

Talking to Puppy

- Establishing effective communication with puppy not only paves the way to bonding, but also sets the stage for training.

- Communication involves simple, consistent words to designate the important commands, people, places, and things in puppy's life.

- Your vocal tone and inflection color the messages you send to puppy, and impact puppy's response.

- Mind your body language: Puppy will probably read body language as closely as she will focus on vocal messages.

ABCs of Training

- Training can only be as effective as the bond between puppy and you is strong. Establishing a bond is the first step in training.

- Foundation training involves basics like name recognition, leash training, and simple manners.

- Consistency is key to making training stick. Rules must be enforced with unswerving regularity.

- When puppy fails to obey your rules, administer swift correction, followed by a reward once puppy corrects her action.

the bond between you and puppy becomes strengthened. It's also a potent self-improvement tool for puppy: Training teaches the dominant puppy to acquiesce to her owner, and it bestows a sense of confidence on the submissive puppy.

Dogs have a natural desire to please us, which is why they generally take so well to being trained. But in order to prime the canine pump for training, you'll need to provide a calm environment where, together, the two of you can build a bond.

No one knows for sure how many words a dog understands. One (published) study subject, a nine-year-old border collie, demonstrated an understanding of over 200 words. Research suggests that most dogs can understand up to 250 words.

At Ease

- While your rules should always be enforced, training sessions should be interspersed with pure bonding time.

- "Down time" together not only re-energizes training, but also helps you and puppy reconnect on an emotional level.

- Spend as much time with puppy as possible. Not only will you both enjoy it, but also it will build mutual trust.

- Quality time does not have to mean long hikes or sign language drills for puppy. It can mean "vegging" on the couch together.

Rules for interacting with puppy:
- Always use the same words with puppy
- Be a firm leader
- Enforce rules consistently
- Never punish
- If puppy misbehaves, guide puppy to correct behavior
- Reward puppy for exhibiting correct behavior

127

LAYING A FOUNDATION
Foundation training starts the minute puppy sets his four little paws in your house

The minute puppy enters your home, he begins to learn how to be a pet. At around three months, you can start to actively teach him the basics of good puppyship.

There are a handful of foundation skills that puppy should master early on: recognizing his name, walking on a leash, staying off the furniture (depending on your rules), and housebreaking. The other basics are chewing and begging. The first, chewing, is inevitable. But with time—and diligence on your part—he'll learn what he can and cannot chew.

As for begging, this is an introduced infraction—one that he is only likely to develop if you feed him from the table.

Puppies less than six months of age have very low

Training Sessions

- Training can begin at around three months of age.

- Puppies younger than six months have low concentration, so sessions should be kept to about fifteen minutes, once daily.

- Teach only one command at a time. Once puppy has mastered a command, you can go on to something else.

- Keep training concepts simple, and make sessions fun. Always end training sessions with play.

Reinforcing Foundation

- Basic training needn't only occur in formalized sessions.

- Fundamentals like leash walking, name recognition, and good manners should be refreshed as a matter of ritual. Reinforce the basics at every possible opportunity: Repeat puppy's name often. Leash him up often, even if you're strolling in the house. Give him mini-lessons on couch etiquette every time you see him eyeing your sectional.

- Be consistent in enforcing fundamentals. Flag puppy *every* time he breaks a particular rule.

concentration, so remedial training should be simple and fun, and sessions should be short.

Beyond this, know your breed so you are not completely taken aback when you start training puppy.

For instance, don't count on your graceful, athletic Afghan hound to follow your commands right away—he's a little headstrong and need lots of repetition and practice.

Basic training prepares puppy for serious obedience work, which you can then start him on at six to eight months old.

············· GREEN ● LIGHT ·············

Everything you do with puppy—from bonding to training—will be impacted by his breed. Research the trainability of your breed before you embark on teaching him. Some breeds require extra perseverance.

Name Game

- Choose puppy's name carefully. Everyone in the household should agree to the name, and commit to using it consistently.

- Dogs sometimes have preferences and aversions to certain sounds. If puppy displays distaste for his name, perhaps by not responding to it, consider changing it. But do this sooner rather than later.

- Repeat puppy's name often, always in a happy voice.

- If puppy turns toward you when you call his name, say "yes" or "good," and give him a treat.

The whole family must be on board:

- Dogs are creatures of habit. Learning requires predictable outcomes and uniform reinforcement.

- For these reasons, everyone in the household must know and enforce puppy's rules.

- Make sure all household members use the same enforcement tools and methodologies.

129

SAYING NO

There's more to correcting unwanted behavior than just saying "no" to a puppy

Your puppy is not a wolf cub and will not be roaming the wild. Rather, she will be residing in your home and, as such, will be part of human society.

Therefore, puppy must learn to live by your rules. Invariably, she will break them from time to time. So you must correct her, reinforce your lessons, and help her learn to help you, so

you can live together in harmony. Never meet puppy's infractions—whether chewing, biting, or urinating in the house—with punishment. This can create fear in puppy, and hamper the delicate bonding process between puppy and you.

Furthermore, punishment implies that puppy was wrong. Perhaps puppy failed to follow a command because you

Saying "No"

- Correct puppy only if you catch him in the act of disobeying. The correction should be immediate.

- Say "no" in a loud, firm tone of voice, free of anger, annoyance, and panic.

- How adamant your "no" should be varies by breed. If your dog is strong-willed, you may need to say it with greater emphasis in order to get his attention.

- Once corrected, do not prolong the "no" therapy or hold a grudge against puppy.

Doling Praise

- End every reprimand with praise, once puppy has corrected his behavior.

- First issue a verbal correction. When puppy looks at you, guide him to correct the behavior, perhaps releasing one of your possessions from his mouth, or ceasing jumping on a guest.

- Once puppy corrects his behavior, praise him, regardless of how many times you've had to correct him first.

- Praise comes in many forms: a verbal "good puppy," a tactile rub on the head, an edible treat, or an invitation to play.

failed to communicate it properly or because puppy is still learning.

When puppy behaves inappropriately, say "no" in a firm tone. Steer puppy to the correct behavior, be it getting down off the couch or ceasing to tug on the leash. Once puppy corrects her behavior, end on a good note with a treat and/or praise.

Remember, when training a puppy, your demands should be gentle but firm: A dictatorial voice or body language will not foster within puppy a desire to please you.

YELLOW ● LIGHT

Be prepared for frustrating moments with puppy. Puppies require more time and patience to learn new things than do their adult counterparts. So show tolerance with puppy, and control your temper.

"No" Situations

- Choose your battles: If you constantly say "no" to puppy, he will eventually tune it out.

- Some situations, however, should never be tolerated. One of these is aggression (toward people and animals).

- Use "no" clearly and consistently, whenever puppy fails to follow one of the foundation rules that you have taught him.

- When teaching puppy a new rule, it is important to reinforce training by flagging related transgressions with a definitive "no."

Types of No's

- There are several forms of "no" besides the verbal.

- Noise corrections, like loud horns, buzzers, and shake cans, provide enough of a startle to get puppy's attention.

- Physical corrections can be a knee tap or a leash tug, which only applies if puppy is leashed when he misbehaves. *Never* hit or raise your hand to a dog.

- Corrections, whatever the noxious stimuli, should always be accompanied by a verbal "no." They should be mild, nonviolent, and immediate.

131

BUILDING A BOND

Establish a bond of trust by becoming the "pack leader" and understanding your puppy

You must establish some governance over puppy in order to mold his behavior to your lifestyle. If you want to liken puppy's relationship with you and your family to relations within a pack of wild dogs or wolves—as is sort of tempting to do—you can draw a loose correlation.

A wolf pack is a unit of seven to fifteen animals, many interrelated, that have teamed up to survive and procreate. The pack's social hierarchy is based on age, experience, physical attributes, leadership qualities, and familial relationships.

The dominant, or "alpha," individuals control resources like food and shelter, and make decisions for the pack. The submissive individuals yield to the dominant.

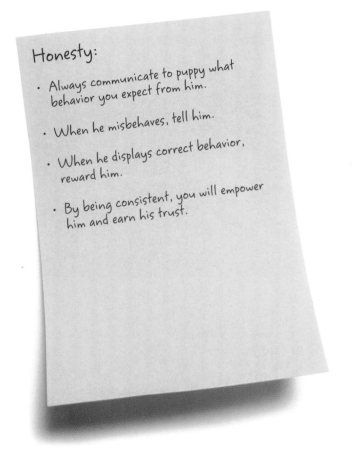

Honesty:

- Always communicate to puppy what behavior you expect from him.

- When he misbehaves, tell him.

- When he displays correct behavior, reward him.

- By being consistent, you will empower him and earn his trust.

Bonding Activities

- The main ingredient in bonding is time—the time that you spend with puppy.

- Include him in your day-to-day activities whenever possible.

- For instance, take him with you on your morning jog; let him accompany you as you run errands; bring him in the room with you when you fold laundry or cook dinner; hold him on your lap during TV time.

- Be sure to also schedule dedicated puppy time, perhaps walking puppy, playing with him, and training him.

The pack framework enables members to hunt cooperatively, protect their territory and each other, raise their young, and maintain social order.

Puppy will bring some of these hardwired canine social instincts into your home. As in the wild pack, puppy recognizes leaders and followers.

Your guidance will help puppy understand that you are the decision maker and that he is the adherent. By enforcing your decisions clearly, firmly, and consistently, you will gain puppy's trust.

Eye Contact

- Eye contact between puppy and you helps establish communication.

- If puppy looks you in the eyes as you speak to him, it indicates he is paying attention to you.

- Before giving a command, establish eye contact by saying puppy's name in a clear, firm voice.

- If your highly distractible puppy is reluctant to give you his full attention, hold a treat near your eyes as you say his name. Once your eyes meet, give the command. When he obeys, treat him.

Leadership:
- Dogs are naturally adapted to a hierarchical social system.
- There are leaders and followers.
- You, as owner, must command the leadership post.
- You can do this through diligent training.
- You must also earn puppy's trust.

133

CONSISTENCY IS KEY

Make sure you are not giving your dog conflicting messages or confusing commands

Dogs learn through consistency, and base their responses on the patterns they've experienced.

Puppy learns that when she hears your keys rattle, you are leaving the house. She understands that when the doorbell chimes, someone will enter the house soon.

You teach puppy through cause and effect. She does "A," you respond with "B." How puppy makes future choices depends on her understanding that "A" always evokes "B." Not today. Not sometimes. But *always*.

If you have decided, for instance, not to let puppy sleep on your bed, you must enforce this rule at all times. Not every day but Friday, the day you change your sheets, but *every* day.

PUPPY CARE

Body Language

- Puppy learns about her world through predictable and consistent signs and signals.

- Body language encompasses a major set of signals your puppy reads.

- Try to match your body language with the message you are trying to convey. For instance, if you ask puppy to sit, stand in front of her and point your finger toward the ground.

- Be consistent in your body language: Always supplement your words with hand signals and positional cues, and keep them uniform.

Wavering

- Once you have decided on expectations and limitations for puppy, you need to enforce them.

- It is paramount to enforce the rules *consistently*; this means that puppy must follow your rules today and *every* day.

- If you do not enforce your rules consistently, this will inhibit puppy's learning process.

- Random enforcement also causes puppy to be unsure of your expectations and his limitations, which is likely to cause her anxiety.

Puppy learns through predictable signals and responses: Inconsistency on your part sends puppy mixed signals. Certain actions should always be prohibited, and certain actions always encouraged. Furthermore, predictability gives puppy a sense of security and builds her confidence.

Before you lay down the laws for puppy, try to project into the future. You allow puppy up on the bed today, when she's small. But are you going to still want her on the bed when she reaches her adult weight of eighty pounds? Good luck trying to break her of the habit that you have helped cement.

Consistent Rewards

- Rewarding must be consistent.

- During training, reward puppy *every time* she displays desired behavior. Once puppy has adapted to a specific rule, such as exhibiting polite greetings, you needn't reward her every time she complies.

- When you reward puppy, *always* use vocal praise. Supplement this with edible rewards, toys, or play time, regularly at first, and then randomly. When puppy disobeys, use vocal correction. Once she corrects her behavior, reward her. Do this *consistently*.

YELLOW ● LIGHT

Random enforcement of your rules begets consistent confusion: So be vigilant about rules. Let's say you have a no-feeding-from-the-table policy, but tonight the meatloaf came out just right. You'll slip puppy a tiny morsel of it, tableside. Just this once. Congratulations—you've taken the first step toward creating a habitual beggar!

Keep language consistent:

- Help puppy build a vocabulary of words/phrases he understands.

- Consistency is the key to doing this.

- Always use the same words to designate things, people, places, and commands.

- Make choices carefully and adhere to them.

- For instance, will you use "no" or "stop"?

- "Down" or "off"?

- "Do your business" or "Go potty"?

- Make sure everyone in your household is using the same words/phrases with puppy.

135

LEASH ON LIFE
Harness your pup's energy and natural curiosity, and keep her safe and "at your command"

One of the "musts" of dog ownership is walking, hand-in-leash, in a relaxed, enjoyable, controlled fashion.

Even if you have a yard for puppy and no plans to include dog walking in your lifestyle, you must be able to leash puppy up for the inevitable trips to the vet and car outings.

Plan to train puppy to voice commands? No matter. If your municipality has dog leash laws—and most do—you will need to leash puppy when he is off your property.

When puppy arrives at your doorstep, he's gone through many changes already: He's stopped nursing, started teething, and left mom and sibs behind. He's been brought to a new home with new faces. And now someone is fastening a

Training Collars

- Choke collars, made of chain link, compress the neck when attached leash is pulled. Useful for large dogs, chokes should not be used in puppies under six months.

- Pronged collars are for dogs that are fractious and/or stronger than their owners.

- Electronic collars emit small shocks via remote control or automatically. Used in hard-to-train dogs over a year old.

- Head collars strap over the face. Effective in directing puppy where to go, head collars discourage puppy from tugging leash.

Leash Training

- First fit puppy with buckle collar that fits securely, with room to insert two fingers.

- Place collar when puppy is eating or otherwise distracted. He may scratch at it. Remove collar only when he is not displaying displeasure with it. Repeat.

- Once puppy is accustomed to collar, attach leash and let him drag it around indoors, under supervision. Offer treats, so he associates leash with good events.

- Next, pick up leash and encourage puppy to follow you, using happy talk and treats.

strap around his neck, and tugging him around.

For the safety and enjoyment of both you and puppy, you must acclimate puppy and have him walk on the leash, in a mannerly fashion, by your side. Consistency is an important part of leash walking. If you're right-handed, puppy should always walk on your left. Hold the leash loop in your right hand, thumb through loop. Gather up the slack and close your four remaining fingers over it. Grab the leash with your left hand, at your left thigh.

While walking, anticipate distractions that could send puppy lunging. Watch puppy's ears, eyes, tail, and hair along his dorsal midline for signs that he is ready to bolt.

If you're diligent, you can expect to have puppy leash trained within two or three weeks.

Pulling

- On leash, puppy should always walk beside you, not in front of or behind you.

- From the start, habituate puppy to a *loose* leash. Never pull puppy or let puppy pull you.

- If puppy pulls on leash, *stop* immediately. If necessary to get his attention, give a quick jerk on leash. Never keep walking when puppy is tugging on leash. Once puppy stops pulling, resume walking.

- To further refocus puppy on you, practice walking backwards and making sharp turns.

Last but Not Leash

- Check your growing puppy's collar weekly and replace as needed.

- Attach to collar an identification tag with your name and phone number.

- A six-foot-long, ⅝-inch leash is ideal for medium and large dogs, with greater width for extremely strong dogs and giant breeds, and narrower width for small dogs.

- Leashes come in braided/webbed nylon, waxed cotton, metal, and leather. Leather combines high durability, secure grip, and hand comfort.

137

COME

Right from the start, your puppy should understand that when you call, good things happen

Puppy is an independent entity, but you are her owner and her safeguard. She needs to learn how to be the yo-yo to your string, rushing back to your side the moment you utter the command, "come."

Most young puppies cling to their guardians out of a sense of security. Wherever you go, puppy will follow. But once she hits three or four months of age, her independence and her inquisitiveness start to kick in.

As puppy explores her surroundings, the radius that she is willing to travel expands. Suddenly, you find that you no longer have to worry about stepping on this little puppy who always seems to be underfoot. Instead, you're always looking

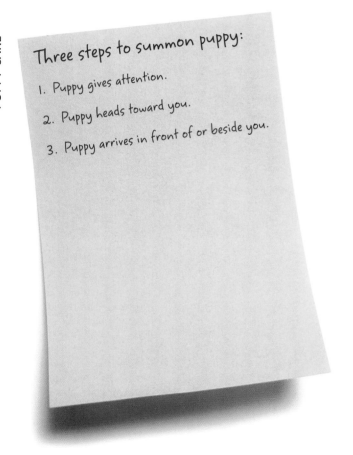

Three steps to summon puppy:

1. Puppy gives attention.

2. Puppy heads toward you.

3. Puppy arrives in front of or beside you.

Recall Training

- Begin training sessions when puppy is hungry. Start out with puppy on long lead, indoors, with few distractions.

- Give "sit" command. If puppy does not yet know sit command, gently press rear until she sits.

- Back up one to three feet. Stop. Say "come" and puppy's name in firm, happy tone, while waving edible treat or toy.

- Once she comes to you, give vocal praise and treat. If puppy does not come, tug leash while repeating command. Practice often.

for puppy, who is always wandering out yonder.

The instant recall is now critical. When you call puppy, she must come to you, even if she is engaged in something she finds pretty compelling.

"Come" is one of the most important commands you can teach puppy, one that you should start on early. It is worth the investment of your time, so plan to work on it until puppy has nailed it down. After this, reinforce it with sporadic practice sessions . . . it just might be the one command that saves her life.

Advanced Recall

- Once puppy is consistently responding to "come" command using procedure outlined above, start to change things up.

- Practice "come" command without leash as backup enforcement tool. You may need to resume leash temporarily if puppy does not respond off-leash.

- Increase distance from which you call puppy to come. Add distractions like noises, people, doors opening and closing, etc.

- Give edible treats randomly, rather than every time she comes to you.

Recall Games

- Recall games are fun, and great for relationship building.

- In back-and-forth recall between two people, puppy sits beside person A. Person B—about ten feet away, treat in hand—gives "come" command.

- Once puppy reaches person B, she is treated and asked to sit facing person A. Person A summons and then treats puppy. Or try hide-and-seek recall. Person A has puppy sit. Person B hides in another room and calls puppy. Puppy searches for person B, who treats puppy when she arrives.

SIT & STAY

The "sit" and "stay" commands enforce important skills for self-control and impressive manners

The sit and stay commands are the underpinnings of good puppy etiquette. Puppies are full of energy, and sometimes the only way to cut the furry frenzy is to order a "sit."

Placing puppy in the sit position helps puppy to compose himself and focus his attention on you. It's also a useful control mechanism during those times when puppy is misbehaving, such as when he is chewing on your table leg or jumping on your toddler.

Many trainers also recommend the sit-stay commands as tools to divert puppy's attention away from an unwanted distraction, such as a cat in the yard.

You can also immobilize puppy with the sit-stay for events

Uses of sit-stay:

- Avoid dangers (i.e., other dogs)
- At pedestrian stop lights
- Where stationary position required (i.e., vet's, groomer's, outdoor cafe)
- In presence of someone who fears dogs
- Auto travel
- Encourage cessation of misbehavior
- General discipline

Teaching "Sit"

- Have puppy heel at your left. Give "sit" command in firm tone, while pressing left hand on puppy's rear and holding up his chin with right hand.

- Resume walking, giving "heel" command for puppy to follow.

- Integrate hand signals for "sit," such as palm held over puppy.

- Eventually, puppy will sit in response to hand signals, and may learn to sit automatically when you stop. "Down" is taught in similar fashion, but by pulling sitting puppy's front legs out.

that require standstill, such as car trips and grooming appointments, as well as to keep him from running outside during those occasions when you have to keep an exterior door ajar. Keep in mind that the "sit" and the "stay" are, for training purposes, two entirely different commands. As such, they must be drilled individually before being blended together.

Of the two commands, puppy should be taught to sit first. And because puppy looks so nice and well behaved when he is sitting attentively, the next logical step is to try to keep him in that position. This is where the stay command comes into play. Just remember that you are dealing with a puppy: A puppy is all about energy, curiosity, and lack of restraint. In requesting that puppy "stay," you are asking for the antithesis of his very being.

A lot of patience and repetition is required before puppy finally masters the "stay" cue. How do you know when puppy has nailed it? When he remains seated—even in the presence of a cat or a squirrel or a hot roast beef—until you give the release command.

Teaching Stay

- With puppy on lead, place him in "sit." Say "stay" in firm tone, placing your flattened palm in front of his face. Step back; repeat "stay."

- If puppy rises, snap lead, walk toward him and repeat command. If necessary, keep your hands on puppy to enforce "stay" command.

- Initially, don't expect puppy to stay for more than twenty seconds. Circle, back away, and move left/right, repeating "stay" command before each move.

- Slowly increase distance from puppy and decrease vocal commands until he sits for three minutes.

Realistic Expectations

- Don't expect a puppy that is young or new to training to stay for more than a few seconds.

- In the early days of training, a ten- or twenty-second stay is a reasonable goal, but perhaps not achievable off-lead, if you back away from puppy, or if you add distractions.

- With practice, puppy should be sitting for at least three minutes on command.

- A completely trained puppy will remain seated until his handler releases him from that position.

MEETING & GREETING

From the impulsive jumper to the nervous piddler, your puppy can learn appropriate greeting behavior

With an excitable puppy, greetings can get messy. But no one wants to be assaulted by paws, fur, and slobbery tongue when they arrive at someone's house.

You must teach puppy early on how to receive any person—including you, her owner—who enters the house. Puppy should be asked to sit when she meets someone,

whether on the street or in the home.

If puppy leaps up, she should not be indulged with attention, but rather rebuffed. And if she sits, or even stands, she should be treated with a calm but friendly vocal greeting and gentle pat. Ideally, the visitor should stoop down to puppy's level, so puppy does not feel the need to jump.

Polite Greetings

- Practice sit-stay for greetings: Go out back door and come in front repeatedly during a training session.

- If a visitor approaches the house, place dog in sit position.

- Keep arrivals low-key by entering the house quietly

and not fussing over puppy. Have guests do the same.

- When greeting puppy, you and your house guests should quietly stoop to puppy's level so she does not feel the impulse to jump up to your level.

Handling Jumper

- Never reward puppy for jumping on you.

- If puppy jumps, retreat and ignore her for about fifteen minutes. Once she is calm, quietly greet her.

- If jumping persists, firmly say "no," "off," or "down." Everyone in household

should use same word.

- Use noxious stimuli if needed to break jump: quick leash tug (if leashed); startle (horn/water pistol); step forward into puppy to set her off-balance; squeeze paw to minimal discomfort; *gently* block jump with crossed arms, hips, or knee.

While there's little harm a tiny puppy can do jumping on you, it's important that you commit to a mannerly greeting style when puppy is young: You may not want her seventy-pound adult self hurling herself on you or your friends down the road.

Also, consistency is important. If you do not want your puppy to jump on other people, do not allow her to jump on you. In general, avoid rough play, as well. And make sure everyone who comes in contact with puppy adheres to these rules, at all times.

············· GREEN ● LIGHT ·············

If your puppy is an overexuberant greeter, and you are having a lot of people at your house, keep her away from the door at arrival time. Once your guests are situated, you can bring puppy out—on leash—to greet everyone.

Nervous Wetter

- Some dogs reflexively urinate in emotional situations. This is most common in female puppies under a year old, with a propensity in small breeds.

- Most nervous wetters are timid dogs, and are exhibiting submissive urination.

- Although nervous wetting often resolves as puppy matures, your vet should rule out underlying medical causes. Keep the wetter on an easy-to-clean floor at greeting times. Keep greetings subtle and free of fuss, raised voices, eye contact, or looming body postures. Never scold this behavior.

Low-key arrivals:

- Ignore puppy initially

- No eye contact

- No vocal contact

- No feedback if overexcited

- Wait ten or fifteen minutes before greeting

- Reward puppy for being calm, with attention or treat

- Make sure visitors follow this plan too

143

CLASSES

For seasoned and novice puppy owners alike, group classes are fun and available

Here's a simple fact of dog ownership: The quality of our experience with our dogs rides on good canine behavior. Unfortunately, puppies are blank slates that don't come with instructions. And they can be tough to figure out. Whatever your experience with dogs, you will benefit from working with a professional dog trainer.

Puppy training class is a great way to go because, unlike individual coaching, this form of instruction teaches puppy amid real life: other dogs and people. Most classes are about six weeks long, and run by private individuals, community organizations, or pet superstores. These classes, which puppies generally start at about four months of age, teach

Selecting Puppy Class

- Look for a class that is open to puppies of all sizes, breeds, and temperaments.

- Examine the trainer's credentials and talk to references, including local veterinarians.

- Visit the class without your dog so you can get a feel for the trainer's style.

- Is the trainer:dog ratio no more than 1:8? Is the facility clean, and preferably indoors? Is vaccination required prior to participation? Is the location relatively free of distractions, like human and auto traffic?

Go Prepared

- Never bring puppy to class hungry, although he should not be too full for treats. Make sure he has gone to the bathroom before class.

- For the first class, bring puppy's vaccine records, a six-foot leather or nylon leash, and whatever type of collar your instructor specifies.

- Bring along small, soft, tasty treats that puppy can easily eat without chewing, as well as water and a bowl.

- Don't forget a fanny pack to hold the treats, for easy access during class.

owners to teach their puppies the basics of canine behavior. A good training class will teach you how to socialize puppy and command his attention. It will also school the two of you in exercises like sit, stay, come, and mannerly leash walking.

Additionally, the instructor may offer coaching for behavioral challenges like jumping and digging. The class may also include drills for special situations, like conduct during the veterinary exam. Choose a class that implements *positive reinforcement* training techniques, and includes supervised off-leash playtime so the puppies can socialize.

Maximizing Class Experience

- Enroll in a training class when puppy is between thirteen and twenty weeks old, and at least two weeks after his last distemper combo vaccine.

- Have all your household members—including children over eight—attend the class, if possible.

- When choosing a spot in class, avoid positioning yourself and puppy near any aggressive, hyperactive, or otherwise distracting dogs.

- The classes are only beneficial if you take the lessons home with you: Do practice sessions daily.

Benefits of group classes:

- Owner learns instruction methods.

- Puppy trains amid distractions.

- Puppy interacts with other dogs.

- Puppy interacts with other people.

- Owner troubleshoots with trainer and other dog owners.

- Puppy gets to go on fun outing.

- Puppy and owner get to spend quality time together.

RETRAINING CHALLENGING TEENS

It's typical for your teenage pup to challenge authority and find her voice

Puppy adolescence begins around fourteen weeks. As with children, the juvenile period is a tough time for caretakers.

As the weeks wear on, you will no longer recognize puppy. Where is that delightful animal that plastered herself to your heels and delighted your friends with unmitigated affection?

Puppy is now super-sleuth, her nose into everything as she roots around exploring her world. Now nothing is sacred. If it seems interesting, then in the mouth it goes. Forget the pile of chew toys that she dutifully honed down as a little puppy: Your $900 violin is far better for gnawing.

You call puppy's name, and she hardly seems to hear. She's

Heat:

- Heat—or "estrus"—is the occurrence of ovulation.
- Time of fertility and sexual receptiveness
- Occurs in females, or "bitches"
- Sudden estrogen surge
- Some dogs become restless or aggressive.
- Others show no changes in temperament during heat.
- Additional signs: vulvar swelling, clear and/or bloody discharge, tail "flagging"
- First heat occurs at six to twelve months of age.
- Small dogs start at early end of spectrum, large dogs later.
- Dogs have an average of two heats yearly.

Behavioral Changes

- Adolescence begins around fourteen weeks and lasts until fourteen or fifteen months.

- Puppy displays independence as she investigates her environment. She may become stubborn and refuse to obey commands she has already learned. She

may also jump on people and chew inappropriately.

- She discriminates among people and dogs, showing fear and/or aggression toward certain individuals. Behavior and temperament usually stabilize by year two for small dogs, and by year three for large dogs.

busy looking around for her next dose of excitement. And she's starting to question the people and things she so happily cozied up to in the past.

As her hormones surge toward puberty, puppy becomes increasingly restless. Add in the fact that her body grows so quickly that she can no longer maneuver it. Hopefully you gave puppy ample exposure to people and other animals during the key socialization phase of three to twelve weeks. Build on this foundation now with continued socialization, classes, vigilant at-home training, and lots of patience.

Socialization

Adolescence can be a frustrating time for dog owners, and this is when many throw in the towel. In fact, studies have shown that six months is the age when dogs are at greatest risk of being relinquished to animal shelters.

- Puppies once friendly to every dog and person are now becoming unpredictable.

- Most owners segregate puppies at this time to keep them calm, making them further intolerant of other people and dogs.

- Fight the urge to isolate your feisty puppy at this critical juncture.

- Puppy needs intense socialization now: Take her for frequent walks, let her wrestle—supervised—with other dogs, and keep her in puppy class until at least one year of age.

Puberty in males:

- Starts around five months of age

- Onset of fertility

- Pursues intact females

- Becomes highly distractible

- Mounting and humping behavior begins

- May mount inappropriate objects, like couch or a person's leg

- By eight months, half of males lift their leg to urinate

- By thirteen months, half of males are urine marking

147

FINDING FOCUS
Tips and techniques for directing your teenage puppy's focus back on you

Puppy is born with his eyes shut, but they'll soon open. And during the first six months of his life, his eyes will also open *figuratively*.

Puppy is starting to really take notice of the people, places, and things around him. But as his world comes into clearer focus, he loses that focus on you, his owner.

This is a classic case of bad timing, because now, when you're trying to train puppy, is when you really need his attention. Focus is the key ingredient for training a puppy. Without focus, you can do nothing. With it, the possibilities are endless.

Fortunately, there are a number of means available for

Distractions

- Distractions, in the form of other people, animals, objects, smells, and sounds, are a part of life.

- As puppy matures, he becomes more attuned to his environment and more reactive to distractions.

- When he becomes easily distracted, he focuses less on your commands. A lot of the training that you thought was solidified now appears to have gone out the window.

- You must work hard to regain puppy's attention amid all the compelling stimuli.

Focusing Puppy

- Puppy is focusing on you when he looks at your face.

- Begin focus training sessions when puppy has not had contact with you for several hours, such as first thing in the morning. Have puppy sit. Then say his name, followed by a consistent word, like "focus," "look," or "listen."

- Maintain eye contact for five seconds; then reward him with praise and/ or treats. If he becomes distracted, repeat the command. Gradually demand his attention for longer periods of time, and amid distractions.

capturing puppy's attention amid all the distractions swirling around him. By using consistent commands spoken in a clear, firm tone, your words will start to burn into her consciousness.

You can also grab puppy's attention with training tools that emit sounds, such as whistles, clicks, and bells. And don't be afraid to use edible incentives. Most importantly, you need to be a diligent coach and hold regular focus-training sessions. If you want puppy to focus on you, you need to focus on him.

Motivators

- Sometimes you need a motivator to help you "grab" puppy's attention.

- Motivators like whistles and clickers can be effective in commanding puppy's attention.

- Food and edible treats can usually compel puppy, as long as he is not too full to eat.

- To harness eye contact, hold the treat next to your eye, say puppy's name, and then say "look." Hold puppy's gaze for a few seconds, and then praise and treat him.

Capricious puppy:

- Highly distractible

- No longer seems eager to please you

- Investigates smells

- Responds to every noise

- Chases moving objects

- Highly reactive

- Averts eyes when you try to get his attention

149

INTERDOG AGGRESSION

Your sweet puppy is suddenly becoming a thug with other dogs— now what?

You will be hard pressed to find a young puppy who is aggressive. But that changes as puppy approaches sexual maturity, around five or six months of age. As she scrutinizes her environment, she may become increasingly fearful, protective, and opinionated. Plus, her hormonal fluctuations make her reactive and more intense. Different varieties of aggression may boil to the surface—food-related, territorial, possessive, dominance, and, around the onset of social maturity between eighteen and twenty-four months, interdog aggression.

Most people find displays of dog-to-dog aggression disturbing. But these displays are, for the most part, benign. These episodes generally resolve without bloodshed. The

Interdog Aggression Displays

- Aggressive displays, particularly of the same sex, are common. They include threatening postures, stares, growls, and snaps.

- They can be generalized to all dogs in various circumstances, or targeted to certain dogs or situations, like access to the door, food bowl, or sleeping areas.

- This behavior sets in gradually between six and eighteen months of age.

- Interdog aggression contrasts starkly with the play behavior puppy engaged in with other puppies when she was younger.

Desensitize Safely

- Now is not the time to isolate puppy from other dogs. Rather, you need to do just the opposite.

- Take puppy on frequent walks around other dogs, as well as to dog parks and puppy classes.

- Always keep puppy leashed, but let her sniff other dogs.

- Let puppies snarl at each other and even nip to issue bite inhibition warnings. If things get too rough or injury seems imminent, quickly separate the dogs using leashes.

dogs are working out their hierarchical relationships. And what looks like biting is usually bite *inhibition*. Handle inter-dog aggression by socializing puppy with a wide variety of dogs. Supervise interactions closely and separate dogs if they inflict injury or don't resolve things with a reasonable amount of sniffing, mounting, growling, and mouthing.

Spaying and neutering generally take the edge off aggression. Behavior modification exercises must be done, as well. If you see aggressive tendencies developing in puppy, address them early, before they become learned behaviors.

Dogs in Household

- Intervene in ongoing status wars between dogs within the household.

- If challenger is younger and healthier, it is safest if you reinforce challenger's dominant status.

- Feed challenger first, greet her first, and give her a longer leash to walk ahead.

- If challenger continues to behave aggressively toward other dog, she is bullying. You'll need to protect and reinforce the status of the other dog.

- If challenger is older or more frail, make him defer.

Handling interdog aggression:

- Socialize puppy with dogs (and people) from early on (by eight weeks).

- Neuter/spay puppy.

- Reinforce earlier training lessons.

- Use praise when puppy follows your commands.

- Consider the situation serious if puppy injures another dog.

- Consult with a professional trainer if necessary.

SPAYING & NEUTERING
Spaying and neutering is important, but when you do it may be key

Your puppy, whether he or she is a he or a she, is marinating in a broth of hormones. As they rise toward puberty, these chemicals wreak havoc on puppy's behavior and your life.

By spaying or neutering your puppy, you remove the gonads—ovaries in her and testicles in him—that secrete those temperament-changing hormones, estrogen/progesterone, and testosterone.

"Altering" puppy will not turn tiny terror into precious pup, but it will remove the hormonal fluctuations that make puppy more reactive and distractible, and mute many sexual behaviors that are hard to live with.

Sterilization *does not* disrupt a dog's play drive or working ability, nor does it impact a dog's machismo or femininity.

In addition to eliminating the risk of pregnancy or siring, sterilization has health benefits. But it's not without potential long-term drawbacks.

Decision to Neuter

(Male) neutering/castration procedure:

- Medical term: orchiectomy
- Puppy receives preoperative checkup.
- Puppy placed under general anesthesia
- Small pre-scrotal incision made
- Puppy's testicles are surgically removed.
- Procedure takes about ten minutes (longer if testicles are undescended).
- Puppy observed for a few hours post-op, and goes home same day
- Puppy should be kept quiet for next few days.
- Puppy's sutures are removed in seven to ten days.

- Neutering removes the body's main testosterone source, and reduces sexual interest, mounting, roaming, urine marking, and interdog aggression. It eliminates chance of testicular cancer; reduces prostate infections and benign prostate enlargement; may boost risks of hypothyroidism and certain cancers.

- The testicles descend from puppy's abdominal cavity into his exterior scrotal sacs at six weeks. A "cryptorchid" dog's testicles fail to make this descent. Because retained testicles can twist or become cancerous, these dogs should be neutered.

Still, the risks associated with these routine surgeries—anesthetic complications, infections, wound rupture, and chewed-out sutures—are low, at under 4 percent.

While several states have proposed spay/neuter laws, none have them on the books. But most states mandate sterilization prior to adoption from a rescue. And several municipalities, such as Dallas and Los Angeles, have recently adopted sterilization ordinances aimed to reduce pet overpopulation.

While early neutering can prolong growth plate closure, leading to slightly longer bones, American Veterinary Medical Association (AVMA) research shows that young animals (as young as eight weeks) weather sterilization better than older ones.

Although there is some dispute, most experts agree that females should be spayed between six and twelve months, before the first heat, and aggressive males should be neutered at four to six months.

Decision to Spay

- Spaying removes body's main estrogen source; eliminates risk of uterine/ovarian cancers and uterine infections; reduces incidence of mammary cancer, particularly in dogs spayed before first heat.

- Spaying stops heat cycle and attendant behaviors, as well as estrus-related vaginal discharge. Many spayed dogs gain weight. Spaying before puberty may prevent weight gain.

- Spayed dogs are at higher risk for urinary incontinence, urinary tract infections, hypothyroidism, and certain cancers.

(Female) spay procedure:

- Medical term: ovariohysterectomy
- Puppy receives preoperative checkup.
- Puppy placed under general anesthesia
- Small abdominal incision made
- Puppy's ovaries, oviducts, uterine horns, and uterine body surgically removed
- Procedure takes twenty-or-so minutes (longer if in heat).
- Puppy observed for a few hours post-op, and goes home same day
- Puppy should be kept quiet for next few days.
- Puppy's sutures are removed in seven to ten days.

153

A WORD ON BREEDING

Breeding offers no health benefits, and the choice to breed should be carefully weighed

Birth is a major cause of death in dogs. This is because the great puppy factory that exists in our homes, kennels, puppy mills, and streets churns out more baby dogs than we can comfortably care for.

Communities struggle to manage the several million abandoned dogs that wash through our shelter system annually, but over half of these homeless animals are euthanized.

As a result of shelter sterilization policies and efforts by responsible breeders, veterinarians, and welfare groups to promote responsible pet ownership, three out of every four pet dogs are now spayed or castrated.

If you're considering breeding your dog, understand that

The Estrus Cycle

- The canine reproductive cycle lasts about seven months; most dogs go into heat twice yearly.

- In first stage, proestrus, eggs mature and estrogen climbs. Then in estrus or "heat" the eggs are released and the bitch may mate over this 5–21 day period;

clear to bloody vaginal discharge is secreted.

- Progesterone peaks during diestrus, which lasts two months if dog is pregnant and three months if not.

- For next few months, ovaries are in quiescent anestrus.

Managing Heat

- You can use doggie diapers to absorb vaginal discharges during heat.

- If you do not want your bitch impregnated, separate her from enthusiastic male suitors.

- Once two dogs copulate—or "tie"—it is virtually

impossible to separate them until mating is completed.

- A single litter can consist of puppies sired by several different fathers. While your dog is in heat, regulate her exposure to other dogs so you can control her matings.

there are no known health or behavioral benefits to a dog's whelping a litter.

Want to do it for the experience of producing puppies or to make money selling them? First, make sure the breeding dogs are healthy and free of genetic diseases and temperament problems.

Second, ensure that you can find good homes for all the puppies, which could number as high as a dozen.

Third, understand the costs—in both time and money—of breeding. If you own the bitch, you'll need to provide a high quality food during gestation, as well as a whelping area. You will also incur veterinary fees for routine check-ups during the pregnancy, plus emergency fees for any problems before or during delivery.

All told, it's cheaper to spay or neuter your dog than to whelp and maintain a litter of puppies. Plus, a number of community and rescue organizations offer low-cost sterilization, as well as national Spay Day USA discounts.

Gestation

- Gestation lasts sixty-one to sixty-three days in dogs.

- During gestation, bitch needs special nutrition and veterinary care. Your vet can usually palpate the puppies by about twenty-eight days.

- Litters consist of about six pups, with fewer in toy breeds and as many as fourteen in large breeds.

- Complications requiring extra care include infections and labor distress, or "dystocia." An emergency c-section can run upwards of $1,000 and can't always save mom and pup.

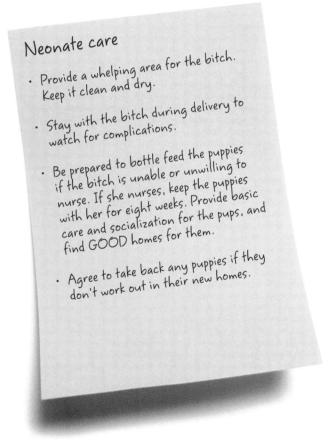

Neonate care

- Provide a whelping area for the bitch. Keep it clean and dry.

- Stay with the bitch during delivery to watch for complications.

- Be prepared to bottle feed the puppies if the bitch is unable or unwilling to nurse. If she nurses, keep the puppies with her for eight weeks. Provide basic care and socialization for the pups, and find GOOD homes for them.

- Agree to take back any puppies if they don't work out in their new homes.

AMBASSADOGS

Ensure you are a responsible owner and your dog a good ambassador for all dogs

With over 77 million pet dogs in the United States, more than one in every five American "citizens" is canine. From these numbers, it's obvious that the behavior of our dogs significantly impacts the quality of our society.

As a new owner, you have a social responsibility to produce a well-trained dog that is pleasant to be around.

You must also make sensible choices—like curbing puppy and keeping him leashed—that render him neither menace nor nuisance to those around him. There is, perhaps, no better way to alienate your friends than with a dog that jumps around, mouths, whimpers, squats at will, or otherwise misbehaves. Given the fact that nearly half of owners have large

PUPPY CARE

Physical Limitations

- Some dogs are poorly matched to certain situations, from a physical standpoint. You'll need to make adjustments or avoid such situations altogether.

- For instance, if puppy has long hair and/or sheds, think twice before bringing him into someone else's home. If you do bring puppy along, make sure he stays off the furniture.

- Ditto puppy drools.

- If puppy is klutzy, or has a long tail, keep him well controlled in places that contain breakables, such as outdoor restaurants.

Social Situations

- Habituate puppy to human interaction by giving him lots of touch and talking to him regularly.

- Expose puppy to varied social situations that include different people, places, and types of gatherings, like picnics, parades, and sporting events.

- Always keep puppy leashed when you take him off your property.

- If you bring puppy to someone's house, and he is not completely housebroken or is accustomed to getting on the furniture in your home, keep puppy leashed or seated on your lap.

dogs, these destructive behaviors are often magnified.

Want to be a good owner? Invest your time in training puppy so that you can control his behavior in any situation.

Finally, make socially responsible decisions concerning puppy: If you have no plans to breed puppy, sterilize him to quell sexual behaviors. Vaccinate puppy so he does not contract and spread disease. Muzzle him around people and dogs if he is prone to snapping. Also, follow leash laws. And confine puppy while on your property so he does not end up raiding the neighbor's trash cans, or worse.

Out in Public

- Check for dog restrictions before bringing puppy on outings.

- Don't put puppy in a situation he can't handle. For instance, if he's wiry and vocal, puppy might bark around a lot of people. So keep him out of crowds, or discourage barking by carrying him or putting him in a face halter.

- If puppy displays interdog aggression, think twice before bringing him around other dogs. Maintain a safe distance from other dogs, keep good leash control, distract puppy, and muzzle him if necessary.

Cleaning Up

- Do not let puppy urinate on other people's lawns without their permission: Urine can kill grass.

- Whenever you leave your property with puppy, be sure to bring along a poop bag to clean up.

- Poop bags come in biode-gradable and flushable varieties, and can be purchased at pet superstores and most grocery stores. You can also recycle plastic supermarket bags for this purpose.

- To prevent puppy from transmitting parasites to other dogs and people, deworm him as necessary.

ADVANCED MANNERS

VEHICLE ETIQUETTE
Most dogs love car rides; here's how to keep your puppy and your vehicle safe

For safety's sake, puppy must sit or lie quietly in the car. To ensure this, you can restrain her by harness or crate. If you do not wish to restrain puppy, at least restrict her from entering your space for minimal road distractions.

So never let puppy sit in the front seat (or in the back of a pickup truck). And equip your car with a gate or steel barrier to keep puppy from jumping up front.

Many dogs like wind in their faces—until a piece of flying road gravel lodges in puppy's cornea. So never let puppy ride with his head out the window, but it's okay to crack the window just enough for him to stick out the tip of his muzzle.

Encourage puppy to lie down by cushioning the floor or

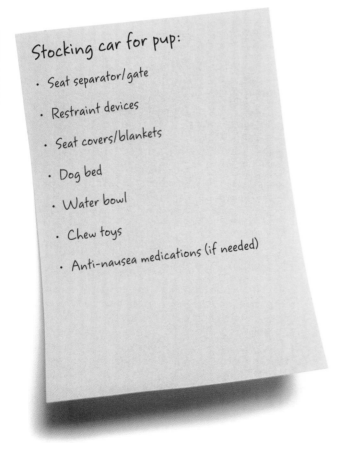

Stocking car for pup:

- Seat separator/gate
- Restraint devices
- Seat covers/blankets
- Dog bed
- Water bowl
- Chew toys
- Anti-nausea medications (if needed)

Ins and Outs

- If your car is high off ground, if you transport puppy by car often, and if puppy is too big to lift into your car, get a portable ramp.

- Remove puppy's leash as soon as you close car doors.

- For puppy's safety, she should not enter/exit your—or anyone else's—car without permission.

- Ask puppy to sit prior to entering and departing car. She cannot cross car threshold in either direction until cued. Prior to letting puppy exit car, attach her leash.

seat with a dog bed or soft blanket, and providing a chew toy. If puppy is lying down rather than staring out at the passing road, she is also less likely to become car sick.

When you introduce puppy to car trips, start out with short drives. As you increase trip lengths, stop for walks and water every hour or two.

Lastly, if you want puppy to display good auto etiquette, you must show the same: no jerky turns or erratic driving.

Restraint

- Upon impact in a 35-mph crash, a sixty-pound dog generates 2,700 pounds of force.

- Such impact could severely injure the dog, and turn her into a projectile that could harm other passengers.

- Despite the potential danger, 56 percent of dog owners do not secure their dogs in the car.

- Car crates provide full restraint, and fit into the back of most SUVs. Another option is a car harness that straps over the dog's chest and fastens to the seat belt.

Dog-friendly auto:

- Half of dog owners consider pet's needs when buying a car according to Business Week.

- Car features include extra cargo space, steel barriers between cargo and back seat, dirt-resistant fabric, and low entry height.

- Top-rated Honda Element SUV dog-friendly package includes stowable ramp, rear kennel, pet bed, seat covers, spill-resistant water bowl, and electric fan.

- Vehicles with best ratings for dog friendliness—Honda Element SUV; Mitsubishi Outlander SUV; Volvo xc90 SUV; Land Rover Range Rover Sport Supercharged; Toyota FJ Cruiser; Volkswagen Rabbit; Jeep Liberty; Saab 9-3 Aero SportCombi

CANINE BOOMERANG

Off leash, outside, no matter where, have your puppy come when called

Life is unpredictable, and distractions can come in many forms, often unannounced.

Puppy may run off, either toward a certain something, away from another thing, or in feverish search of . . . nothing in particular.

If puppy belongs to one of the more tenacious, strong-willed breeds, such as those in the hound and terrier groups, he is less likely to come bounding toward you when you call him. So enforcing the recall command with him will be more like hauling a cable versus pressing a button.

As puppy retreats from you, he enters a danger zone, where he can get lost or hurt, or injure others. So disaster prevention

Restrained Recall

- Here's how it works: Person A restrains puppy on leash and asks him to sit. Person B stands about ten feet away.

- Person B kneels in welcoming pose, perhaps arms outstretched.

- Person B summons puppy's attention, perhaps with hand signals. Once eye contact is made, Person B calls puppy in excited tone.

- Person A releases leash. Puppy is rewarded when he reaches Person B. The exercise is then repeated, but with puppy running in opposite direction, from Person B to Person A.

Practice Sessions

- Practice the "come" command three or four times a session, in a couple sessions daily.

- Practice indoors initially, in a quiet environment. Once puppy consistently obeys recall command indoors, move sessions outdoors, with puppy on leash.

- Eventually, move practice sessions to different locations and situations, and with distractions added in.

- Because your varying emotions may affect your tone of voice, it's important to practice the "come" command in different vocal tones.

is the main reason to train puppy to instantly come when you call him. Training a puppy in recall requires ample repetition. But it's a drill that puppy will enjoy, if you have taught him that when you summon, good things happen. Always positively reinforce the "come" command with vocal praise, other displays of enthusiasm and, of course, treats.

And if you ever encounter a situation where other enticements quash puppy's desire to dash to your side, never chase puppy down. (He's probably faster than you.) Instead, run in the other direction—he'll likely follow you.

ZOOM

Car versus dog collisions are the #1 cause of broken bones in pets. This is reason enough to teach your dog to stop on a dime and come to you when you call him.

Rewarding Recall

- Egg puppy on with vocal praise as soon as he starts moving toward you.

- Once puppy reaches you, shower him with copious pats, rubs, and hugs.

- While saying "Good dog!" in an upbeat tone, offer puppy an edible treat, a toy, or play time.

- Once puppy has mastered the recall command, you can stagger rewards. While vocal commendations should be consistent, incentives like treats should be dealt randomly.

Tips for successful recall:

- Use a long lead (>10 ft.) so you can enforce "come" command, should puppy refuse.

- Praise enthusiastically as soon as puppy advances toward you.

- Reward puppy for coming when called.

- Never summon puppy for a scolding.

ADVANCED MANNERS

MIMIC REAL LIFE

Start prepping your puppy with distractions to ensure a well-trained pet in public

Training a puppy without distractions is like teaching a sixteen-year-old to drive a car without showing him how to navigate about in traffic, by day or night, over hilly and flat terrain, and through snow, puddles, dirt, and whatnot.

Just like driving conditions, a day in the life of a dog is full of every interruption imaginable, some startling and some enticing. Most of them come out of left field and wrest puppy's attention from whatever you are trying to make her focus on.

When you start out training your new puppy, do so in a tranquil—even inert—atmosphere. A young puppy has a shorter attention span, and virtually everything is new.

The Canine Senses

- Puppy's field of vision is greater than yours (~240 degrees for dogs; 180 degrees for people), and so is her ability to see movement. So when you're out on a walk, she will react to the squirrel scampering behind you before you even see it.

- Puppy can hear higher-pitched sounds than you can, at up to 45,000 hertz (versus 23,000 hertz for people).

- Puppy's sense of smell is over 1,000 times stronger than yours, so her nose can set her focus astray.

Distracting Places

- Expose puppy to places featuring varying tempos of activity and sensory elements, from city streets to child-filled playgrounds to quiet nature trails.

- Puppy will probably never stop letting her nose lead the way, but as she visits these places more and more, they will overwhelm her focus less and less.

- Once she has demonstrated proficiency in basic commands at home, practice these in new settings. One day, you'll need puppy to sit or come to you at an outdoor mall or the beach.

Train indoors with doors closed and no other animals or people in the room. Electronic devices like TVs and radios should be turned off. Cellphones should be silenced. And any other environmental sounds should be minimized. Interesting objects that puppy could chew on should be removed.

Once puppy has demonstrated competency in basic commands like sit, down, stay, and come, it's time to throw in some reality. Take puppy outside, where distractions run the gamut, and are usually unannounced.

A portion of puppy's consciousness will undoubtedly be devoted to such intrusions. But with time, two things will happen. First, repeated exposure will desensitize puppy to the environmental stimuli that characterize her life. Second, puppy—as she matures—will become less distractible and better able to focus on single tasks for longer periods of time.

Puppy is not really "trained" until she demonstrates the required commands consistently, even when life gets in the way.

Introducing Distractions

- Distractions are sensory elements that invade the consciousness. They consume puppy's mental capacity, rendering him less able to focus on tasks at hand.

- Puppy must be able to obey commands amid distractions.

- So train among natural distractions, and introduce new ones. Amid the beeping oven timer and the aroma of pot roast, hold a treat next to your eye, say puppy's name, give a command, and reward her when she obeys. Repeat.

Distracting Training Tools

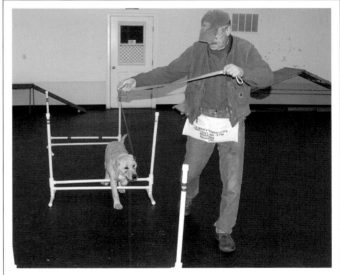

- Implement distractions during training, so puppy learns to focus on your vocal cues, facial expressions, and body language no matter what happens around her.

- Put chew toys around the room, and a full bowl of food.

- Wear a fanny pack, at puppy's nose level, full of treats. Demand puppy's attention; do not treat her if she begs or fails to follow commands.

- While training, distract puppy, perhaps by throwing a ball or walking another dog through the room.

THE CGC TEST

AKC's Canine Good Citizen test is open to all dogs and is more than just a certificate

The Canine Good Citizen (CGC) Program is sort of the honor roll of puppy behavior. Started by the American Kennel Club (AKC) in 1989, the CGC program emphasizes two things: responsible pet ownership and good dog manners. Dogs are given a ten-part test, administered by CGC–certified evaluators at events like dog shows and through participating dog clubs, veterinary hospitals, and community organizations like 4-H.

Prior to the test, the dog's owner must sign the Responsible Dog Owner's Pledge, which states his or her commitment to maintaining the dog's health, safety, and quality of life.

By encouraging responsible ownership and enticing owners to elevate their dogs to certain behavioral standards, the CGC

Pluses of CGC Certification

- The AKC maintains a database of all dogs with CGC certification.

- Some municipalities offer discounts on licenses for CGC–certified dogs. Some insurance companies recognize CGC certification, for underwriting purposes.

- CGC certification is an accomplishment to strive for and can instill a sense of pride within owners.

- The process of working toward certification helps to strengthen the bond between you and puppy.

Who Can Participate?

- CGC certification is open to any dog, purebred or mixed.

- There is no upper age limit for participants, but puppies must be old enough to have received all necessary immunizations.

- If the test is administered at an AKC show, the age requirements for the show apply, and testing may be restricted to show participants or purebred dogs.

- Because behavior and temperament can change over time, the AKC recommends that dogs certified as puppies be re-tested as adults.

PUPPY CARE

program has a positive impact on the community. It also aims to build greater public acceptance of dogs. In fact, thirty-four states have passed CGC resolutions. And several other countries have created their own versions of the program. The path to CGC certification can be a first step in training puppy, and can lead to participation in other AKC activities, like obedience, agility, tracking, and performance events.

Many owners start their puppies off in the AKC's S.T.A.R. program, an optional CGC precursor training regimen that teaches the basics to dogs under one year of age.

ZOOM

Some 40,000 dogs annually pass the AKC's ten-step Canine Good Citizen test.

Testing Day

- Bring a leash and a leather/fabric buckle or slip collar. Training collars are not permitted for testing.

- Owners must bring dog brush or comb to the test.

- Treats and toys may not be used as rewards during testing.

- Dogs are eliminated if they do not successfully complete any of the tasks, with the exception of item #10 (when test given outdoors). They may re-take the test on the same day, at the evaluator's discretion.

Ten items on CGC test:

1. Allow friendly stranger to approach.

2. Sit calmly to be petted.

3. Allow handling for grooming.

4. Heel on loose lead.

5. Walk calmly through crowd.

6. Sit and down on command.

7. Come when called.

8. Calmly greet another calm dog.

9. Handle distractions.

10. Behave in care of another person, with owner out of sight.

ADVANCED MANNERS

TEACHING THROUGH PLAY

Turn training into structured play time, and use puppy's innate drive to have fun

Good, clean fun can cultivate social aptitude while building motor skills and developing physique.

In nature, young animals learn key survival strategies through play. Predators, like cats, bears, and canids, play by using behaviors attendant to catching food: They chase, pounce, and wrestle.

Prey animals, on the other hand, like zebras and deer, develop escape skills through play: They run, leap, and kick.

Play also increases learning capacity in juvenile animals. Animals at play learn to assess the signals of their playmates, and to read and follow the rules, all while having fun.

Rats "laugh" in high-pitched chirps when they wrestle

Lead the Play

- Designate yourself leader of all play sessions. You, not puppy, should determine time, place, and type of play.

- Whatever form of play—fetching, chasing, or other—you should be the one to initiate and end play sessions.

- Allow adequate time to play, but end play while puppy is still having fun, before she has become tired and chosen to stop.

- When it's time to stop playing, remove toys from puppy's sight. Then distract her with food or alternate activity.

Playing Tug

- Some trainers frown on tug games as encouraging aggression. If puppy understands the playful context, and she is neither aggressive nor large enough to dislocate your arm during tugging, then this type of play is fine.

- Most dogs growl during tug games—these generally are playful, rather than aggressive, vocalizations.

- Soft, floppy, durable objects, like knotted socks and leather flaps, work well for tugging. Tug games are perfect opportunities to teach puppy the "drop it" command.

playfully with one another. Studies have shown that rats at play experience a rewarding release of endogenous opioids, or "happy chemicals."

So play, while fun, is serious. In fact, police K-9 units look for dogs with not only high "prey drive," but also "play drive." The more a dog likes to play, the more trainable she usually is.

Even the cadaver dog is playing a game while tracking the scent of death: She is looking for the hidden "treasure"—decaying tissue—signaling her master to its whereabouts.

Like the K-9 officer, you too can teach puppy, through play, commands like "find it" and "drop it." You can even teach her to "clean up toys" by turning the job into a retrieval game.

Determine what type of play your puppy enjoys. One dog might like retrieving while another relishes running. Help puppy develop reasonable expectations about play by compartmentalizing fun to a certain place or time of day. Keep playtime positive—no scolding. If puppy gets mouthy during play, startle her with a loud "Ouch!" And avoid games like Frisbee that involve jumping, which can overstress puppy's developing joints and bones.

Recall Games

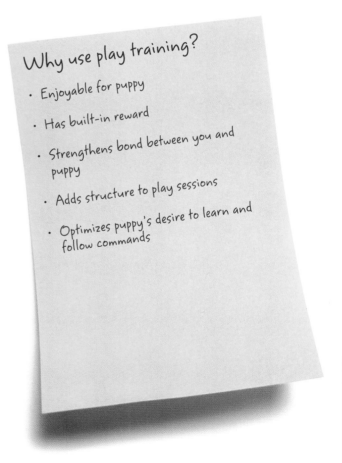

Why use play training?

- Enjoyable for puppy

- Has built-in reward

- Strengthens bond between you and puppy

- Adds structure to play sessions

- Optimizes puppy's desire to learn and follow commands

- Recall games are effective ways of teaching puppy "come" and "sit" commands.

- *Follow/chase:* Ask puppy to sit. Toss treat in front of her. Back up. Say "come." Let her advance toward you as she fetches treat. Repeat. Gradually move back farther and faster.

- *Ping pong* and *round robin:* Employ treats to lure puppy to run back and forth between two—or more—people, respectively.

- *Hide-and-seek:* Ask puppy to sit and stay. Hide nearby. Call puppy. When she finds you, give her a treat.

167

WALKING & HIKING

With some basic tools and tricks, your pup can become an unparalleled walking companion

The wolf roams some twenty miles in a day, often moving on foot for over eight hours daily. While our domestic dog needn't cover much ground to obtain a meal, he needs outdoor walks for a couple of reasons.

First, puppy must eliminate. Second, puppy must exercise. Third, and much higher on Maslow's hierarchy of needs, is fulfillment. Puppy needs opportunities to explore. This happens at the end of a leash.

Most dogs enjoy long walks, although there are individual and breed variations with respect to walking speed and duration, as well as type of terrain best for your puppy.

Some dogs love to ford mountain streams, jump fallen logs,

Benefits of walks

- Exercise
- Fresh air
- Potty time
- Socialize with other people and dogs
- Expand puppy's experiences
- Teach to obey in different places and situations
- Bonding time for you and puppy

Heel Command

- Teach puppy early on to "heel," or walk right next to you.

- If right-handed, the standard is to heel puppy on your left. But a safe alternative is to heel puppy on the grass side, with you on the street side.

- Heeling puppy helps you to walk him in a controlled manner, and is almost a must if walking two or more dogs simultaneously.

- On each walk, give puppy some loose-leash time to explore, during which he needn't heel.

and slosh through spongy mud. Others are better on flat, clean, "civilized" surfaces like pavement. And still others are best off being carried in a pocketbook!

To be sure, though, dog ownership will bring you places you otherwise wouldn't venture—into bushes, dunes, rock piles, wherever puppy's nose takes you both—and in all manner of weather. Taking puppy for walks is a great way to expose him to the world, and to teach him to obey you in different situations. Do let puppy choose which way to walk on occasion, but be careful not to let his exuberance lead the way.

Safety

- Be aware of moving cars in streets and driveways.

- Enforce traffic safety early on: Make puppy sit when you reach a street corner, and stay seated until you give the command to cross the street.

- Stick to safe terrain. If walking in an area with which you are unfamiliar—a new hiking trail, for instance—map your route first.

- On a hot day and/or for a long walk in an area with few water sources, bring bottled water.

Sniffing

- Dog's nose is like man's opposable thumb—that singular, stunning evolutionary gift the unendowed could never know.

- Most dogs follow their noses when out walking. Sniffing can inspire puppy to go to the bathroom.

- But too much sniffing and not enough walking can be frustrating.

- Keep puppy away from areas replete with animal scents. Walk backwards, puppy facing you. Hold puppy's gaze, call his name, and distract him with treats.

EXERCISE FOR PUPS

INDOOR GAMES

When the weather is frightful, play indoor games to exercise puppy's body and mind

Most zoos and laboratories devote ample resources to providing enrichment activities for their display and research animals. Without this, the animals' physical and mental health would most certainly decline.

In many regions, cold or rainy weather keeps our homes shuttered for months at a time, and the occupants—both human and canine—become like caged animals.

Dogs need exercise and to be kept busy. For growing puppies, little jolts of electricity wrapped in fur, multiply this need by a factor of . . . something big. When dogs become bored, they become anxious. And anxiety drives dogs to do stupid things, like spin habitually in circles, chase their tails, rip their

Fun indoor doggie activities:

- Hide-and-seek
- "Easter egg hunt," using dog treats
- "Shell game" (treats hidden under cups)
- Retrieve rolling ball
- Run up/down stairs for toy/treat
- "Catch" the glow (using flashlight/laser)
- Tug-of-war, wrestling
- Move to music.
- Puzzle toys, for puppy to disassemble
- Kong toys, from which puppy removes treats
- Blow bubbles for puppy to catch
- Treadmill walking
- Recall games
- Obedience commands

Hiding Games

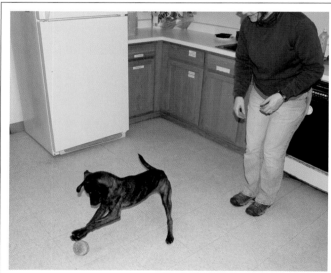

- Most dogs love the challenge of finding and retrieving hidden objects.

- Hide small edible treats around a room. Let puppy into room and command her to "find treats." Squeak toys placed under rugs work great, too.

- Put treats into some of the cups in a muffin pan. Place tennis ball over each cup. Watch puppy remove balls to find treats. An alternative is the "shell game."

- Play hide-and-seek. Throw a treat and run the other way. Hide. Call puppy to find you.

PUPPY CARE

170

fur out, chew your belongings, and whimper.

There are lots of indoor games you can play with puppy to entertain her while letting her exercise, even if you live in a small dwelling. Remember, the major thing puppy wants is you. And if you're there inside with puppy, and giving her concentrated doses of time via stimulating activities, she'll more than likely be happy. Have some games in mind, and a space designated for playing them. And consider a day in doggie day care, both to give puppy a change of scenery and to give you a break.

Indoor Exercise

- Exercise is mandatory for healthy dogs, especially energetic, growing puppies.

- For indoor exercise, play physical games that do not involve distance running, like wrestling (not too roughly), tug-of-war, and retrieving a ball rolled down a hallway.

- Have puppy run stairs to retrieve a toy you throw up/down. As an alternative, tie the toy to a rope pulley running along the banister. Pull rope so puppy chases toy up/down stairs.

Enriching the Indoors

- If puppy is cooped up inside, keep her from feeling isolated. Provide her with plenty of indoor human (and animal) companionship.

- Enrich the indoor environment with sensory stimuli from things like music and chew toys.

- Bring outdoor ambience inside. Let puppy access rooms with good outdoor views. Open shades. And whenever possible, crack windows for fresh breezes.

- If you have a screened-in porch, let puppy spend short amounts of time there.

EXERCISE FOR PUPS

171

EASY TRICKS

Teach puppy easy tricks to stimulate learning and impress friends and neighbors

Dog tricks are like the cherry atop an ice cream sundae—that extra dollop of fun that you can add to puppy's repertoire once he has learned some basic obedience commands.

Dogs can be taught to do almost anything. They can hold different positions: sit, lie down, play dead. They can make various motions: roll over, beg, spin, give paw.

They can perform tasks, such as retrieving and guarding. And they can accomplish physical feats, like jumping an obstacle, climbing a wall, even riding a wave on a surfboard!

These are all tricks that require teaching and repetition. But not *every* dog can—or wants to—perform *every* type of trick.

Trick Tricks

- Use short words to designate trick commands. For instance, say "through" instead of "walk through my legs."

- Break complicated tricks into discrete parts taught step-by-step. Practice tricks in short sessions that keep puppy wanting more. Rein-force with lots of repetition.

- Use treats for positive reinforcement. You can also use a *clicker,* which can be paired with treats to serve as a clear event marker that tells puppy he "did good." *Target sticks* are effective tools for directing puppy into certain trick positions.

Spin/Roll Over

- *Spin:* Hold treat over puppy's nose. Move it in circle around puppy, slowly enough so he can follow hand. When puppy follows hand in spinning motion, say "spin." Click/treat.

- Eventually, "spin" command and/or encircling hand motion will elicit spin.

- *Roll over:* Command puppy to lie down. With treat in hand near puppy's nose, make slow, vertical, encircl-ing motion with hand.

- When puppy rolls over to follow treat, say "roll over" and then click/treat.

For instance, your clunky English bulldog, with his constricted airways, isn't assembled to climb walls or spin circles. Your shih tzu probably wants no part of surfing—or swimming, for that matter. And your borzoi hound, though he can run down a cheetah if you asked him to, would likely not be motivated to retrieve the remote control for you, or to "speak" (bark) on command.

Any dog of any age, despite the popular adage, can be taught to do tricks. But do run puppy through some basic obedience schooling before adding tricks to his repertoire.

And consider his natural abilities, aptitudes, and preferences when selecting tricks.

Keep training simple. Practice one trick at a time, and start off with simple challenges with no distractions. Don't hold sessions right before puppy's meal time, immediately after puppy has finished eating, or when puppy is particularly energetic. And be sure to offer clear feedback during training sessions. Tricks are wonderful outlets for puppy's mental and physical energy. Plus, they nurture the bond between you and puppy, and are great confidence builders for puppy.

Shake Paw/Beg

- *Shake:* Ask puppy to sit. Grasp paw. Say "shake" or "paw." Click and treat. Repeat.

- Tap paw or ground to elicit puppy to lift paw. Eliminate treat. Introduce distractions. Use other paw. Add "high five" command (motion for paw and lift hand in air).

- *Beg:* Ask puppy to sit. Hold treat in air, slightly above his head. When he stands on hind legs, treat him. Support puppy's paws if necessary. Some dogs can't do this trick well, particularly chondrodystrophied breeds like bassets and Dachshunds.

Weave through Legs

- Leash puppy. Stand in front of him, your back facing him and your legs apart.

- Hold treat in front of you and call puppy. When he walks through your legs toward treat, say something like "weave" or "through." If puppy does not walk through your legs, use leash to guide him through.

- You can eventually build on this by having puppy weave in and out in different directions or through several people who are lined up.

- This trick works better with small dogs.

CHILDREN PLAYING WITH PUPPIES

Puppies and children are a natural combination, but teach everyone to play it safe

How many times have you heard someone gush: "My dog is so gentle, she even lets the kids pull her tail!" While it's great to have a mellow dog, every owner should rue such child-dog tail-pulling scenarios.

Children and puppies are energetic, clumsy, and unpredictable. Furthermore, children have quick, jerky movements and high-pitched voices, which can stimulate an already keyed-up puppy. So, too, puppy might confuse rough play with aggressive acts, and bite out of fear.

According to the American Medical Association, dog bites are the *second* leading cause of childhood injury, higher even than playground accidents! And most involve the family dog.

PUPPY CARE

Gentle Touch

- Puppies can confuse rough play with aggression, and act accordingly. Children should handle puppies gently, and avoid raucous, rough, or confrontational play.

- To offer a treat, child should place it in open palm, fingers outstretched.

- Child should pet puppy *under* the chin, rather than *over* the head, and should never lean over puppy, hug her, or stare into her eyes.

- Children should approach unfamiliar dogs slowly, with extended hand—palm down, fingers slightly curled under.

Teaching Puppy

- Training is a form of play that facilitates bonding between child and puppy, and teaches puppy to defer to child.

- Children eight and above should practice basic commands with puppy.

- Obedience commands also come in handy during play, particularly if child needs to settle rough play, or signal puppy that it's time to end play session.

- Commands like "sit," "stay," "come," and "settle" are simplistic and manageable enough for most older children.

174

This isn't surprising, in light of the fact that nearly half of all young parents have dogs (American Veterinary Medical Association). The family dog is usually brought into the home when the oldest child is eight. Children develop empathy between ages five and seven, so there are lots of children out there playing with puppies that they cannot grasp the concept of hurting.

Boisterous play can put both child and puppy in harm's way. Kids should be taught puppy's signs of fear, and how to play properly with them so training is not compromised.

Playing with Puppy

- Adult supervision is recommended for play between puppies and children ages thirteen and younger.

- During play, child and puppy may become over-exuberant, posing danger to one another.

- Play between child and puppy should consist mostly of nontactile activities, like fetch, hiding games, and dog tricks.

- A child should never run from puppy if puppy is giving chase. Rather, the child should stop and "stand like a tree."

No no's for kids and puppies:

- Chasing games

- Tugging games

- Riding puppy

- Smacking

- Teasing

- Pulling tail or other puppy body part

- Wrestling/roughhousing

- Rolling around on ground with puppy

- Using child's toys—versus puppy's toys—to play with puppy

- Surprising puppy during play

BATHING & BRUSHING

Get your puppy used to basic grooming by making it a gentle, interactive experience

Anyone who's had cats can attest to the hours they spend meticulously grooming themselves. No such luck with dogs. And puppies . . . they can get pretty gross!

Your breed of dog dictates the amount of time you will need to groom. It also determines whether you can do it yourself, or if professional grooming is warranted.

Dogs come in a variety of coats. Curly-coated breeds, like poodles and bichon frises, need intensive coat care, from daily brushing to regular professional grooming. But in the positive column, they don't shed. Flat-coated breeds, like long-haired Dachshunds and papillons, need occasional clipping; regular brushing reduces shedding, spreads the oils in

Brushing

- Groom after exercise, when puppy is tired. Keep treats on hand to make brushing a fun experience. If puppy won't stay still for brushing, put him on a table.

- Choose appropriate brushes for puppy's size and hair coat length/type. Brush gently.

- To remove mat hair, brush the ends and work inward. A dab of conditioner may help loosen hair. For stubborn mats, use clippers to avoid cutting the skin.

- Daily brushing is ideal, particularly if your breed sheds a lot or has an undercoat.

Preparing for Bath

- Purchase hypoallergenic dog shampoo. Dog shampoos are pH adjusted for canine skin, and have better "rinsability" than human shampoos. If dog shampoo is unavailable, use human baby shampoo or diluted dish soap. Brush puppy before bathing, to remove loose hair.

- If it's warm outside, you can bathe puppy outside using a garden hose.

- If it's cold, use an indoor tub and rubber hose or detachable showerhead. Place the rubber mat in tub. Close the bathroom door so puppy does not escape.

their skin, and shines their coats.

Wire-haired dogs, such as schnauzers and Scottish terriers, look best with professional grooming from time to time, as do long- and medium-haired breeds like Yorkies and German shepherds.

Short-haired breeds, like Dalmatians and boxers, need no professional grooming. Regular brushing removes loose hairs that are ready to be shed. And, like any dog, they should be bathed on an as-needed basis.

······· GREEN ● LIGHT ···············

How often you should bathe puppy varies from weekly to every two or three months, depending on his hair coat and lifestyle. Puppies that are long-coated, light in color, or have active, outdoor lifestyles would benefit from more frequent baths.

Washing

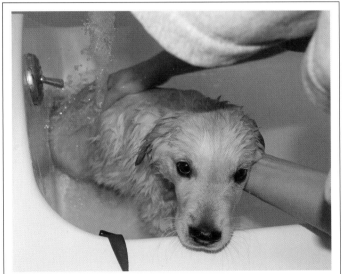

- Hose puppy using gentle spray. Acclimate puppy to water by starting at paws and working upwards. Keep nozzle close to fur so water does not splash in his face.

- Wet up to base of skull, while holding puppy's snout upwards so water does not drip into his face.

- Pour shampoo along puppy's spine—from neck to tail base, below neck, and along abdomen. Work up sudsy lather.

- Rinse well, in every nook and cranny. Shampoo residues can cause itching and allergic reactions.

Types of brushes:

- Natural bristle brush: universal grooming tool for regular use, available in soft, medium, and stiff bristle

- Pin brush: ball-pointed metal pins in variety of lengths, for long-coated breeds like shelties

- Undercoat rake: metal pins remove dead and shedding undercoat, as well as mats

- Shedding blade: metal "noose" with serrated edges, for removing dead hair in heavy-coated breeds

- Slicker brush: rectangular brush with short, bent, wire teeth set close together, for removing dead hair/tangles in medium-coated breeds

- Rubber brush: rubber teeth groom and polish short- or smooth-coated breeds

- Flea comb: closely-set teeth isolate and remove fleas

177

NAIL CARE
To clip or not? When to clip? How to clip safely? How to stop a bleed?

There is, perhaps, no sound quite as irritating as the "click—click—click" your puppy makes when her long nails hit the floor with each landing of her paw. Overgrown puppy nails also are great instruments for gouging wood floors, cabinets, even you!

Many dogs never need nail trims. Concrete is a wonderful nail file, and so puppies walked on sidewalks and streets usually have adequately short nails. Leash pullers, in particular, tend to chisel their nails along the ground, sometimes until they nearly bleed.

Furthermore, dog paws come in quite a variety, depending on breed. Airedales, Akitas, and keeshonds, for instance, have

PUPPY CARE

Paw Handling

- Some dogs are paw-shy for reasons that are often unclear, but probably multifactorial. These dogs tend to object to nail clipping.

- Prepare puppy for nail clipping down the road by acclimating her now to having her paws being touched and manipulated.

- When puppy is relaxed, touch her paws gently. Massage them, grasp each toe gingerly, and steady each nail as though positioning it for clipping.

- Pair these sessions with positive things, like happy talk and treats.

Cut to the Quick

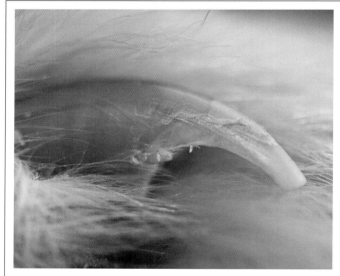

- The nail is comprised of a tough protein called keratin, deposited from nail bed throughout life.

- The nail vein, visible as a pink line about a centimeter long, runs through each nail. In dogs with black nails, this vein is not visible.

- Position digit with fingers to visualize nail and vein. Hold clippers, angled up at about 45 degrees to footpad.

- Cut just beyond end of vein, or "quick," without nipping it. For dark nails, take successive tiny nips to avoid vein.

compact catlike feet. Samoyeds and borzois have "hare" feet, with the center two toes elongated. The structure of your puppy's paws determines the degree of contact between her nail and the ground when she is walking, and thus the extent to which normal living keeps her nails filed.

If puppy's nails grow too long, they can become snagged in carpet, possibly even ripping down to the skin. In extreme cases, overlong nails can change the position of the paw and ultimately the posture of the legs. If their growth goes unchecked, the nails can curl under, sometimes even penetrating the paw pads.

For dogs that require regular nail trimming, intervals vary from dog to dog. Some need cuts every few months, others every few weeks. Check puppy's nails regularly. Trim when puppy is tired, perhaps after exercise. Choose a quiet, well lit spot. Lay puppy down, either on her side or on her stomach. With small dogs, it's sometimes easiest to seat them on your lap. After trimming, give puppy praise and treats to reinforce the positive nature of the nail trimming experience.

Types of Clippers

- Some clippers have blades, which must be changed when they dull; others have permanent tips.

- Electronic nail grinders, widely used in show ring, give nails clean edge. They do, however, require dog to sit still longer, and make sometimes scary noises.

- Clippers run $10 to $15. Electronic grinders run $15 to $70.

- Make sure handles have a good grip. Bladed or not, clippers should have sharp cutting edges. Clean regularly to make sure they don't stick during use.

Stopping the bleeding

- The nail vein will bleed profusely—but not fatally—if severed.

- Styptic stops bleeding by constricting the vein and sealing the wound. Styptics come in powders and sticks. Before clipping, get styptic ready. For powders, apply with wet Q-tips.

- To stop bleeds, grasp paw and press styptic into end of nail for three or four seconds. Twist to work particles into wound. If bleeding continues, repeat.

- Soap or baby powder are sometimes recommended to stop bleeding; these don't work well.

KEEPING TEETH PEARLY WHITE

Routine home dental care has important health benefits as puppy matures

If you've ever seen a toothless, seventeen-year-old miniature poodle that subsists on gruel, you can comprehend the importance of lifelong preventive dental care.

Dental disease begins as soon as a dog finishes his meal, when plaque starts to accumulate on the teeth.

Plaque leads to painful cavities, and over time, it morphs into tartar. Buildup of plaque and tartar may lead to gingivitis. Worse, the periodontal ligaments holding the teeth in the socket can become inflamed, a condition known as periodontitis. The unfortunate result: Teeth loosen and fall out.

Worse, dental disease can lead to infection that spreads to internal organs, like the heart and kidneys. Outward signs of

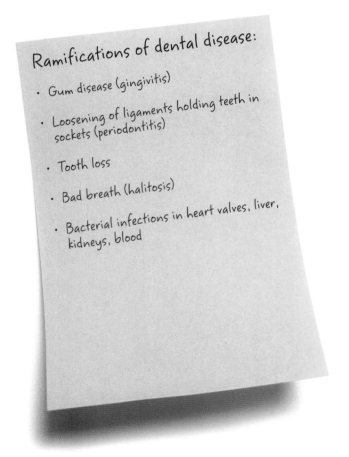

Ramifications of dental disease:

- Gum disease (gingivitis)
- Loosening of ligaments holding teeth in sockets (periodontitis)
- Tooth loss
- Bad breath (halitosis)
- Bacterial infections in heart valves, liver, kidneys, blood

Dental Products

- Keep a supply of human pediatric toothbrushes (soft) on hand.

- Toothpaste—made specifically for pets—is fluoride-free and comes in flavors like poultry. Most dogs love it.

- Antiseptic oral rinse is a useful adjunct to brushing, for dogs with dental disease and/or bad breath.

- Look for Veterinary Oral Health Council (VOHC) Seal of Acceptance, which certifies it meets certain standards for plaque control and tartar prevention.

dental disease are bad breath, bleeding gums, sensitive mouth, pawing at the mouth, reluctance to eat, and drooling.

Dogs are living longer. If you want puppy's teeth to go the distance, start brushing them daily, from an early age. Feed mostly dry food, since kibble provides some dental abrasion and gums up the teeth less than soft foods do. And don't feed puppy any human snacks, which are generally higher in fermentable sugars that eat away teeth. If tartar forms on your dog's teeth, you'll need to remove it with mechanical scaling. Also, have decayed teeth extracted or restored.

ZOOM

By age two, 80 percent of dogs have dental disease (Hill's Prescription Diets). By age five, 85 percent of dogs have periodontal disease (American Veterinary Dental Society).

Brushing Teeth

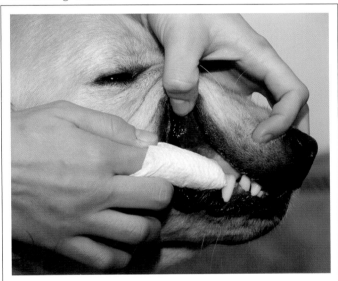

- Studies show that tooth brushing is the single greatest contributor to dental health in dogs.

- Brush daily. If daily brushing is not possible, then do so as often as possible.

- Begin brushing puppy's teeth early on, so he becomes accustomed to it.

- Using soft toothbrush, brush all tooth surfaces in a circular motion. Toothpaste is optional, but may induce better cooperation from puppy. Press toothpaste into bristles so puppy does not lick it off. (Do not use human toothpaste.)

Dental Chews

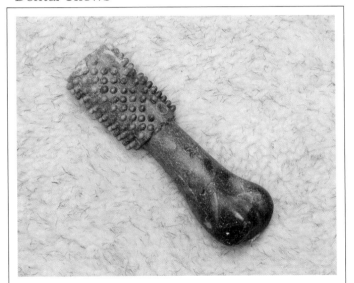

- Dental chew toys provide abrasion that helps keep plaque from accumulating, thereby reducing tartar. Effective chews are nubby, spiky, or rasping.

- Tough bones that are unlikely to splinter also deliver tooth abrasion, and most dogs like them.

- Dental rawhides, like C.E.T. chews, are infused with the antiseptic chlorhexidine, which kills bacteria and reduces tartar.

- Dental treats, like Pedigree's Dentabone and Dentastix, crumble into coarse pieces that scour teeth during chewing.

ALL ABOUT EARS

Routine ear care is necessary for some breeds, but any dog can get ear infections

Although a dog's ear canals are deep and well concealed, when they become infected, they reveal themselves with a fury.

You can smell an infected canine ear from across the room. Infected ears reek because they become loaded with rancid, waxy discharge, bacteria, and yeast.

An infected ear gets reddened and inflamed inside. As this happens, the swollen ear canal narrows, which further reduces air flow and provides a warm, moist bacteria nursery.

Inflamed ears are itchy, prompting the afflicted dog to shake her head continuously. If your dog has pendulous ears, like a golden retriever's, shaking them can break blood vessels. The

Ear Infection Causes

- The main inhabitants of normal ears are the yeast *Malassezia pachydermatis* and the bacterium *Staphylococcus intermedius*.

- These two microorganisms coexist in delicate balance. Ear infections occur when either grows out of control, or when conditions change,

allowing both to multiply.

- Conditions favorable to yeast and bacteria growth are moisture, altered pH, and inflammation secondary to allergies. A less common cause is ear mites, which produce inflammation and a crumbly black discharge.

Troublesome Ear Types

- Floppy ears, as seen in breeds like cocker spaniels and basset hounds, are particularly prone to ear infections.

- Because their ear canals have poor air flow, they tend to trap moisture.

- Dogs with hairy inner ear

flaps, like poodles and schnauzers, also have a problem with moisture, plus accumulations of dirt, food, and ear wax that draw bacteria and yeast.

- Dogs with erect ears, like German shepherds, are less commonly afflicted with ear infections.

frequent result: aural hematomas. These large blood blisters in the ear flap require drainage, and sometimes surgery.

Some dogs never have ear infections. Others experience them on a chronic basis throughout life. Dogs with floppy ears are more prone to moisture buildup and, consequently, infections. Ear infections also plague many dogs with allergies. Whatever the underlying cause, infections can be self-perpetuating. With each outbreak, the ear canals become more scarred and permanently thickened. Narrow ear canals mean greater susceptibility to further infection.

If puppy's ears become infected, bring her to the veterinarian right away. He will clean the ears, look inside the canals with an otoscope to make sure the eardrums are intact, and then put puppy on an ear ointment containing an antibiotic, an antifungal, and a steroid. An oral antibiotic may also be prescribed.

If puppy gets infections repeatedly, have your vet do ear swab cultures to identify the microorganisms and the medicines that will eradicate them.

Cleaning Ears

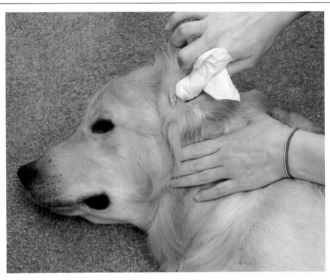

- Buy a bottle of ear wash. Ear wash typically contains agents like alcohol, and benzoic, lactic and salicylic acids, that clean, acidify, and deodorize.

- Hydrogen peroxide, vinegar-water solution (20 percent), or mineral oil will also do.

- Lift ear flap up. Fill ear canal with solution. Massage base of ear for thirty seconds. Stand back and let puppy shake. Swab out ear canal with cotton or gauze, and clean external ear folds.

- Maintenance cleaning is weekly (no more), and daily for problem ears.

Tips for ear health:

- Clean ears if waxy discharge builds up.

- Clean ears regularly (weekly) if problem ears.

- Keep ears dry.

- For hairy ears, pluck/trim fur from underside.

- Monitor ears for odor/discharge.

ODDS & ENDS
From nose tip to anal glands, keep your eye on your puppy's overall condition

You know when you're lookin' good. Your body is in fit condition. Your hair is shiny and you have a nice haircut.

When your body is thriving, your skin is clear and your color is healthy. Your nails are hard and you're keeping them manicured. Perhaps most importantly, you're sleeping well, and you have plenty of energy during the day.

Puppy, too, is either lookin' good—or not. And a lot of it has to do with your vigilance, as his owner.

Sure, there are the obvious things to look for: Is puppy too skinny? Too roly? And there are the more subtle things. How do her skin and hair coat look to you? A dull hair coat or flaky skin could indicate an incomplete or unbalanced diet.

Body condition

- A dog's weight is assessed by body condition score (BCS), ranging from one to nine (one being extremely emaciated and ten extremely obese).

- A BCS of four to five is usually considered ideal.

- From above, puppy's waistline should be apparent. From the side, he should have a slight abdominal "tuck." His ribs and bony prominences, like hips, should be palpable underneath a slight fat padding.

- Body condition can be tough to assess because it is in constant flux.

Skin

- The skin can manifest allergies, immune disorders, hormone problems, parasites, even kidney disease.

- Hydration status can be assessed by skin turgor: If you lift and release the skin over the neck, it should snap back.

- The skin should be intact all over. Abrasions should be investigated and treated by your veterinarian.

- Also consult your vet if puppy has hair loss, skin flaking/crusting, inflammation, hives, pustules, greasiness, or foul odor, or if you see puppy chewing his skin.

184

Beyond distinct physical markers, there's a certain *je ne sais quoi*—or I don't know what—that indicates how puppy is doing. These are subtle, and sometimes subjective, clues.

Does puppy *seem* happy and energetic? To borrow a term from veterinary medicine, is puppy *BAR*—bright, alert, and responsive? Are her sleep habits regular? Does she eat well? And look good overall?

It's important for you to stay on top of puppy's overall condition, from head to tail. Not only does her "look" indicate her underlying physical health, but it also captures your pride.

And puppy's appearance will certainly color the way your friends and family respond to her. If you walk down the street with a smelly, matted puppy with gnarled toenails and drool trickling from his jowls, people will clear a path.

So be a responsible owner and keep up on puppy's appearance. Watch his weight. Keep him groomed. And take care of everything from teeth to anus.

Anal Sacs

- The anal sacs secrete a foul-smelling fluid when puppy defecates. This fluid plays a role in marking behavior.

- These sacs can become impacted if they do not express naturally, as when dietary fiber is too low. Dogs with impacted anal sacs tend to scoot their bottoms along the ground.

- Express puppy's impacted sacs by inserting a gloved, lubricated finger into the anus. Apply outward pressure to each sac, located at five and seven o'clock. Stand back as they can squirt. Or, have them expressed at your vet's office.

The Head Shot

- Puppy's eyes should be clear and bright, with no off-color or excessive discharge.

- Puppy's nose should be free of mucousy run-offs. It doesn't matter whether his nose is wet or dry, warm or cold.

- Puppy's mouth should open and close completely, and his jaws should be even.

- Puppy's mucus membranes should be medium pink, unless pigmented brown/black.

DOGGIE FASHIONS

Beyond fashion: Dog coats and sweaters can have plenty of practical uses too

We've all seen the Chihuahua dressed in chinos, the poodle in the petticoat, even the hound in the hoodie. Decked-out doggie style means something very different today than years ago.

The earliest recorded use of dog clothing was in the Stone Age, 27,000 years ago. Archaeological evidence suggests that dogs were adorned in woven-basket caps, sashes, and belts to aid in procuring food and supplies for their owners.

In King Arthur's Great Britain, both horses and dogs were suited up in protective gear. And more recently, in United States history, military dogs have been clothed for various missions.

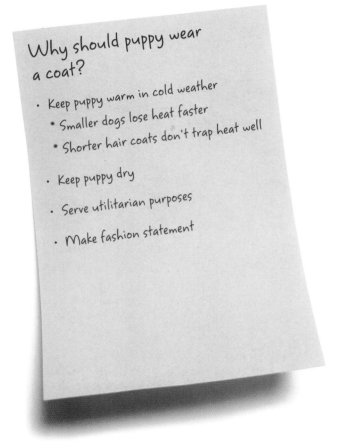

Why should puppy wear a coat?

- Keep puppy warm in cold weather
  * Smaller dogs lose heat faster
  * Shorter hair coats don't trap heat well

- Keep puppy dry

- Serve utilitarian purposes

- Make fashion statement

"Coating" Puppy

- If outdoor temperature is below about 40 degrees and puppy will be outdoors for a while, consider clothing her for warmth. Remember, small dogs lose heat faster.

- Keep a few coats or sweaters on hand, suitable for different purposes, such as warmth and rain protection.

- If you plan to clothe puppy on occasion, get her accustomed to clothing early on. She may walk hesitantly at first, but will eventually adjust.

Does your puppy need clothing, you ask? After all, her ancestors and her wild cousins survived inclement weather with only the fur on their backs. The answer is two-pronged.

A wild canid—a wolf, for instance—can shield itself from harsh winds by crawling into a cave. Plus, this same wolf has a thicker coat than your Boston terrier, which was selectively bred, and would likely not survive in the wild.

If your dog looks cold, she likely is. And remember, puppies, like older or infirm dogs, are extra susceptible to the cold. Plus, the smaller a dog, the faster it loses heat.

Clothes with Purpose

- For warmth, dog coats, and even snuggly turtleneck sweaters, are available in thermal lined, quilted, fleece, and corduroy fabrics.

- Coat should fit snugly, particularly around belly, for maximum warmth. To keep puppy dry, there are raincoats, hats, and galoshes. Plus, some coats and sweaters are lined with water-resistant material.

- Footwear is available, too. Though not usually necessary for mechanical paw protection or warmth, they can shield paws from harsh substances like de-icing crystals.

Safety Coats

- Neon garb lets puppy stand out around traffic and in other situations in which you want her to be visible.

- Reflective clothing—from coats to straps—makes puppy visible at night.

- Camouflage—some bulletproof—provides puppy with safety as well as anonymity for hunting trips, hikes in the woods, bird watching, etc.

- Coats made of flotation material provide warmth plus water safety, and are great for boat rides, beach walks and such.

187

MY PUPPY JUMPS UP!

Techniques for curbing the over-eager greeter, the wild jumper, and the nosey nudger

There is, perhaps, nothing quite so distasteful as being crashed into and jumped on by an excited dog. Sure, it was cute when puppy was a ten-pound wiggle worm, barely clearing your knees with each jump. But now the force of his jumps practically knocks you off your feet.

Prevention is the best medicine for jumping. Many new owners allow their puppies to leap up on them because it's pretty harmless. But that tiny puppy is going to get big. And as he grows, it won't be as easy when he hurls his weight into you.

And you're not going to like it when your grown-up puppy throws his muddy paws on your good suit, or unthreads your

Making Your Entrance

- Puppies often have the urge to jump up at greeting times.

- Keep your entrances to the house quiet and low-key so as not to overstimulate puppy.

- Refrain from making a lot of noise when you open the door. Avoid excited pronouncements like "I'm home!" and throwing your arms around puppy in excitement.

- If puppy is in his crate, wait until he is calm before letting him out. When you let him out, do so without fanfare.

Ignoring Puppy

- If puppy jumps on you at any time, do not make a fuss or give him attention.

- Reprimanding is a form of attention. A stern "no" will suffice.

- Next, turn your back to puppy and ignore him. Do not look at him or talk to him. Go about your business until puppy has stopped jumping and is calm.

- Once puppy is calm, reward him with your attention. Ask him to sit and then stoop down to greet him.

cashmere dress with his nails or worse, when puppy topples a small child or a frail elderly person.

Bad habits start early, and if you allow puppy to jump up on people, he will continue to do it even as he grows.

Puppy should never be permitted to jump up on anyone. Do not engage in play jumping. Never lift puppy onto your lap or feed him *in response to* his pawing or jumping on your leg. And make sure everyone in your home adheres to these restrictions.

If puppy is a chronic jumper, try to convert his ebullience into a more innocuous behavior, such as a spin.

As puppy bounds toward you with that "I'm going to jump you" look, have ready a treat that you know he can't resist. Once puppy reaches you, he will presumably turn toward the treat. When he does, move the treat around in a circle. As he follows it, praise him and say "Spin!"

Do this every time puppy dashes in your direction. Eventually, he will go into a spin when he sees you, rather than jumping up on you.

Proper Greetings

- Before greeting puppy, ask him to sit. If puppy is calm, stoop down to his level and pet him gently.

- Getting down to puppy's level generally removes the urge he feels to jump up to your level.

- Practice mock entrances with puppy by exiting the house, and entering a few minutes later.

- Stage entrances with friends, too, so puppy learns that a calm demeanor should be extended to any-one who enters the house.

Block Jumping

- There are a number of safe ways to terminate a jump.

- While saying "no" or "down," step toward puppy as he is jumping up on you. This will throw him off balance.

- Jut your hip, knee, or crossed arms into him, in a restrained manner to avoid injury. You can also squeeze his paw—as it meets your body—to elicit mild discomfort.

- If puppy is a chronic jumper, keep him leashed even in the house. When he jumps, tug his leash to forcibly halt him.

PROBLEM BARKING
From behavior modification to controversial debarking surgery: quiet the barking canine

Could dog's most powerful weapon be . . . her bark? Surprisingly, yes. Because a bark that is *loud* enough or *relentless* enough can be *enough* to drive a person crazy!

How can you silence the barking puppy? First, understand that barking is a usual way dogs communicate. Young puppies squeal to signal their desire to nurse. Older puppies yelp and cry when hurt. Adults growl, howl, whine, grunt, and bark.

Some barking is normal. But for a third of dog owners, the family pet barks too much. The best cure for barking is preventing it. What may be cute barking in a puppy is annoying in an adult. So nip barking in the bud now.

Provide Distractions

- If your puppy's barking is periodic, in short bursts, and elicits no complaints, then you needn't stop it.

- If your puppy's barking is pathologic or irritating people, try to mitigate it.

- When puppy barks, call his name and, without shouting, say a consistent word like "no" or "settle." Try to engage her in an activity, like a training exercise or a walk. Distract her with background noise, like TV or music.

- Reward puppy with subdued praise and a treat for quieting down.

Managing the Environment

- Sometimes there are environmental triggers for puppy's barking. Try to desensitize puppy to these environmental barking triggers.

- For instance, if puppy barks at bicycles, take her out on biking trails. This frequent exposure should reduce the effect that spinning wheels have on her.

- If the trigger is predictable, then try to avoid it. If the mailman comes at noon, bring puppy out for a walk at noon. To temporarily break the barking cycle, put puppy in a crate with a towel over it.

Never reward puppy for barking, but rather for quiet behavior. Talk calmly around puppy—if you're reactive, it could be contagious. If puppy barks when visitors arrive, keep her from charging the door.

Always respond to puppy within thirty seconds of the onset of barking. Find out why he is barking. If your puppy is an attention-seeking barker, ignore his barks. But if he appears to be barking for some pathologic reason, consult with a veterinary behaviorist.

ZOOM

The biggest barkers are beagles, Chihuahuas, some herding breeds, and several terriers, namely cairns, westies, schnauzers, fox terriers, and yorkies. The quietest breeds are Akitas, boxers, bulldogs, bull terriers, cavalier King Charles spaniels, chow chows, basenjis (which yodel rather than bark), Labrador retrievers, and Alaskan malamutes.

Desperate Measures

- In difficult cases, aversive stimuli can be necessary.

- Electronic, ultrasonic, and citronella bark collars emit, respectively, a shock, a high-pitched sound (inaudible to humans), and a noxious (to dogs) odor when the dog barks. Remote-control shock collars are also available, for selective shock delivery. Shock collars should not be used for barking related to separation anxiety or fear. In these cases, consider behavioral modification and medication. Debarking surgery usually softens puppy's bark, but should be used as a *last* resort.

Reasons for barking:
- Communication
- Alert/warning
- Attention seeking
- Excitement
- Boredom
- Loneliness/anxiety
- Startle
- Self-identification

191

DESTRUCTO-PUPPY

Overly destructive puppies are not bad but often acting out of anxiety or boredom

Between teeth and nails, puppies have some fifty little daggers they can use to cause destruction. Puppies chew things they shouldn't. Sometimes they scratch doors and hardwood floors. Or dig holes in the yard. For puppies, ruination sometimes feels good. Whether they are using mouth or paws, tearing things apart becomes self-perpetuating.

To harness your puppy's bad habits, try to determine why he destroys things. For instance, what has driven him to dig up your vegetable garden? Puppy could be digging to quell boredom, to create a safe hiding place for a valuable item, to uncover something he smells but cannot see, to create a cool resting spot, or to tunnel out of someplace.

Reasons for Chewing

- To relieve some of the pain associated with cutting teeth, puppies will chew on things, sometimes indiscriminately.

- Puppies teethe until seven months of age. But teething-related chewing can last until puppy is about ten months old.

- Puppies may also chew to exercise their jaw muscles, release energy, or relieve boredom or stress.

- Less commonly, puppies will chew as an attention-getting measure.

Supervision/Restraint

- If puppy has shown destructive behavior, supervise him at all times when you are home.

- Wherever you are in the house, bring puppy with you.

- Keep a leash on puppy, though you don't have to hold onto it. A dragging leash provides a means for quick restraint and reprimand, should puppy start to chew or scratch.

- If you cannot supervise puppy, crate him or keep him gated in a room that is relatively puppy-proofed, such as a kitchen.

If you want to stop puppy's digging in a certain area, block it off with gates. Or apply a noxious product to the site, such as Pet Organics No-Dig! spray. In a pinch, try scooping puppy's feces into the hole, then fill the rest with dirt—he'll likely leave the area alone.

If puppy keeps finding alternative places to dig, create a dig zone for him, perhaps in a shaded area. Till the soil there so it's nice and soft. Place some toys or treats there so puppy is drawn to the spot. As an alternative, fill a baby pool with sand and encourage him to dig there.

For inappropriate chewing, use the "drop it" command, provide alternative chew toys, and restrict access to your valuables.

Whatever the type of destruction puppy is causing, apply supervision, training, restraint methods, and, if necessary, aversive stimuli.

Banishing Boredom

- When puppy becomes bored, he's apt to try to make his own fun. Often, he does this by using his teeth and nails to cause destruction.

- In order to reduce the risk of puppy damaging your belongings and your dwelling, keep him occupied in constructive ways.

- Give him plenty of chew toys so he is less likely to gnaw on your belongings or engage in destructive behavior.

- Give puppy your attention. Sit with him. Talk to him. Play games with him.

Drain His Energy

- Though they sleep about twenty hours a day, puppies have an enormous amount of energy while awake.

- In order to prevent destructive behavior, you'll need to siphon off some of puppy's adrenaline with exercise.

- The best exercise for puppy combines running and fun. Play retrieving games, for instance. Also take puppy for plenty of walks.

- Avoid activities that place excessive stress on puppy's growing joints, such as climbing, lifting, and dragging.

SHE JUST WON'T LISTEN

If your puppy still misbehaves, roll up a newspaper and hit yourself over the head

Despite diligent training, puppy is clinging to her insurgent status: She seems determined to do things "her way." If you have truly followed the prescribed puppy training methods, you can probably chalk up some of puppy's disobedience to breed tendencies—certain breeds are simply more difficult to train.

You can't change puppy's hardwiring, but there are some things you can do to make her a bit more malleable. First, wrest puppy's attention from her scattered brain. Attention is the *sine qua non* of puppy training: *Without which, nothing!* Puppies are distractible; it's hard to hold their attention for more than a few seconds.

Why puppy might ignore you:

- Puppies are highly reactive to environmental stimuli.

- Some puppies are particularly distractible and filter out commands.

- Certain breeds are strong-willed and difficult to train.

- The home situation may be producing anxiety in puppy.

- You may not have trained puppy well.

- You may not be communicating your wishes to puppy adequately.

Handling the Frustration

- Getting toppled by a high-strung puppy, cleaning carpet stains, repairing chewed-up table legs, chasing a puppy-on-the-loose—day after day—can get frustrating.

- But expressing your frustration by yelling, using an angry/upset tone of voice, becoming physically animated, or—worst of all—physically harming puppy will make puppy anxious and further impede progress.

- Maintain a calm demeanor and voice and, when you need to, walk away for a few minutes.

Go for eye contact. Hold puppy's favorite treat near your eyes, and call her name in a clear, strong voice. Maintain puppy's attention for five seconds, and then give her the treat. If she becomes distracted, do not give her the treat. Rather, repeat her name, gain eye contact, and again count to five. Once puppy has given you eye contact for a full five seconds, praise her with lots of vocal fanfare and pats, and then treat her.

Practice this attention-getting exercise often. Once puppy understands that she should look at you *in anticipation* when you call her name, you can start issuing commands.

When you give puppy a command, speak in a clear, firm tone voice, using consistent language. Do not let frustration leach out into your voice, and certainly refrain from yelling at puppy—yelling only causes anxiety. Also, be careful not to "no" puppy too often—it loses its effect with overuse.

Be consistent in your expectations of puppy, supervise closely, and offer her immediate feedback for both successes and errors. If necessary, enlist the help of a veterinary behaviorist, private trainer, or puppy class.

Leashing Puppy

- If puppy still seems obedience-proof, despite your dedicated training, keep a leash on her in your presence.

- You don't need to hold onto the leash—let puppy drag it around. Just be sure you are there to monitor so that she doesn't get the leash caught on anything.

- With a leash dangling, there's something to grab if you need to get rapid restraint or mitigate a bad behavior.

- You can also give a quick snap on the leash to get puppy's attention.

Tips for handling the non-listener:

- Find better incentives for desired behavior.

- Go back to training basics.

- Enroll in training class.

- Enlist personal trainer.

AGGRESSION

Some puppy 'tude is normal, but some aggressive behavior requires professional intervention

Aggression is rarely seen in puppies, but may start to surface around sexual maturity (after six months) or social maturity (eighteen to twenty-four months). Aggression is manifest by biting, growling, and baring teeth, which can be *normal* puppy behaviors. Puppies love to play and are very mouthy. So a "bitey" puppy is not necessarily an aggressive puppy.

If you suspect aggression problems in puppy, consult your veterinarian, who can help you differentiate aggression from normal puppy behavior. Your vet will probably want to rule out physical causes of aggressive behavior, such as pain, seizures, and endocrine disease.

Once physical etiologies have been discarded, work with

Asserting Your Dominance

- For puppies with dominance aggression, reinforce your dominant status.

- Do so by not letting puppy sleep where you sleep. If puppy is in your spot on couch, ask him to move—or move him. For safety, consider muzzling him first.

- Let puppy watch you prepare his food. But don't feed him right away—make him wait.

- Make puppy sit before taking him for a walk or giving him a treat. Practice "drop it" command with puppy's toys.

Predatory Aggression

- Some dogs are prone to predatory aggression, and will attack small animals, like squirrels and cats.

- Though any dog can display predatory aggression, it is more common in breeds used for ratting and stalking large prey.

- Dogs with predatory aggression could pose an extra danger to babies and toddlers.

- Predatory aggression can generally be managed with close supervision and restraint, using aids like fences, leashes, muzzles, or a Gentle Leader Headcollar.

your veterinarian or a veterinary behaviorist to characterize the type of aggression. The main categories are dominance aggression, fear aggression, predatory aggression, territorial aggression, and interdog aggression.

Certain breeds are predisposed to certain *types* of aggression. Of the 4.7 million reported human dog bites a year in the United States, the top offenders are pit bulls, Rottweilers, German shepherds, Dobermans, Akitas, and chow chows.

Furthermore, "rage syndromes" have been characterized in certain breeds. "Springer rage," seen occasionally in English springer spaniels, is marked by sudden, unprovoked, extreme sparks of aggression, thought to result from decreased serotonin levels in the brain.

This said, any dog can have aggression problems. Furthermore, any dog, aggressive or not, can behave aggressively, *given the right situation*.

Aggression problems in dogs cannot really be cured, but rather the attendant behavior controlled. Environmental changes, such as avoidance and restraint, can be used to mitigate some kinds of aggression.

Intervention

- Characterize the type of aggression puppy has, if possible with the help of your veterinarian or a veterinary behaviorist.

- He or she can then tailor a behavioral modification program to the specific type of aggression.

- Medications such as selective serotonin reuptake inhibitors (SSRIs) and anti-anxiety drugs are sometimes used in conjunction with behavior modification to treat certain forms of aggression.

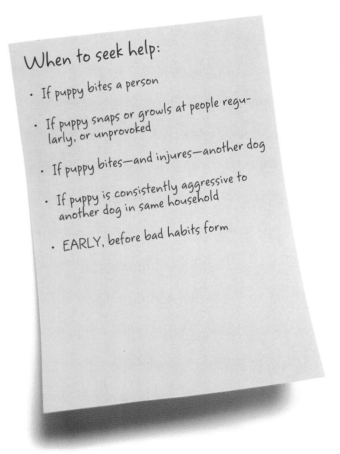

When to seek help:

- If puppy bites a person

- If puppy snaps or growls at people regularly, or unprovoked

- If puppy bites—and injures—another dog

- If puppy is consistently aggressive to another dog in same household

- EARLY, before bad habits form

VETS

Your veterinarian is a team member in puppy's well-being, so choose wisely

Your veterinarian will make a big difference in your dog-owning experience. Look for a veterinarian you'll likely be happy with over the long haul, because it's not good to switch around; it confuses the medical records, which can ultimately compromise puppy's health care. It's better for puppy to have the routine and predictability of a single practice.

Ask for veterinarian recommendations from people whose judgment you trust. Whom do they use? What were their experiences with the veterinarian and the office? Why do they like them? Is the office responsive with phone calls for test results or medical questions?

How about the veterinary technicians? They are vitally

Office/Staff/Policies

- Is the front office messy/disorganized? If so, how must things operate behind the scenes?

- Do hours of operation mesh with your schedule? If you work full-time, find a vet with evening and weekend hours. How are after-hours emergencies handled?

- Are they well staffed? Do appointments usually run on time? Do they send reminder cards for routine services like vaccinations and heartworm testing?

- Are the technicians certified veterinary technicians (CVTs)? (If so, that's a plus.)

Veterinarian's Credentials

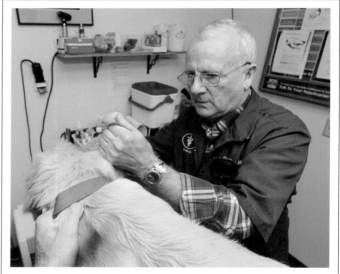

- Most veterinarians have *DVM* after their name. The equivalent *VMD* designation means they graduated from the University of Pennsylvania School of Veterinary Medicine. Most enter practice right after veterinary school. Some receive specialized training first.

- Years of experience can make a big difference in delivery of medical care.

- It's best if a few veterinarians staff the practice: In complicated cases, two—or more—sets of eyes, ears, and heads are better than one. Plus, it's good to have a choice of vets.

important to the delivery of medical care. They'll guide you in determining whether to bring puppy in for an appointment immediately or to address the problem at home. Plus, they often perform initial assessments when a sick animal walks in the door.

Visit the office. Ask about administrative policies, such as payment matters. Do they refer to a nearby clinic for after-hours emergencies, or do they have someone on call 24-7? Whatever practice you select, make sure it is in a location that is convenient to you, in case you ever need to get there *fast*.

Veterinarian's Demeanor

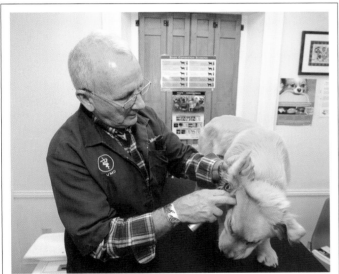

- Does he interact well with puppy? Is he polite with you? Is he gentle but confident with puppy?

- Does the veterinarian take a thorough history of puppy's problem? Does he take time to inspect scrupulously? Does he examine the whole puppy or just the "problem"

area, like an infected ear?

- Does the veterinarian seem to understand the problem, know the solution? Does the veterinarian communicate well with you, explaining things clearly and answering your questions in entirety?

············ GREEN ● LIGHT ············

What services does the veterinary practice offer in-house? When your dog needs an ultrasound or cardiac work-up, for instance, can it be performed there or must you be referred elsewhere? Some offices, though they may not have particular machinery or expertise, might have regular visits by a specialist, like a radiologist or cardiologist, who brings along portable equipment and performs specific examinations on site.

Where to get veterinarian recommendations:

- Other dog owners in your neighborhood

- Local humane society

- Groomers

- Pet shops

- State board of veterinary medicine (to inquire about status of vet's license, years licensed, and any disciplinary actions)

- State veterinary medical association (to obtain list of member veterinarians and their locations)

199

THE RIGHT TRAINER

There are trainers and there are *trainers;* find one who is knowledgeable and effective

The field of dog training is replete with false claims and hollow razzle-dazzle. Anyone can claim to be a "professional dog trainer." There are no licensure requirements, no mandatory certifications, and no tests to pass. Most trainers have entered the field through special schooling; online vocational programs in animal behavior; work in animal shelters or veterinary offices; or canine competition.

As you search for a trainer, you'll come across names with unrecognizable strings of initials after them. These generally are not university degrees, nor do they indicate expertise. Rather, they show that the holder paid a fee and took a course. This doesn't mean he is not a good dog trainer; these

Trainer Experience

- Experience is everything when it comes to dog trainers.

- Find out the length of time the person has been training dogs.

- Find out how, *exactly,* the person cut her teeth as a dog trainer. For instance,

  has she apprenticed under any reputable trainers?

- Inquire about any specialized experience the individual has, either with your *breed,* with your puppy's *specific problem* (i.e., separation anxiety, aggression) or with your *training objective* (i.e., hunting, agility).

Trainer Styles

- Every trainer has his or her own unique style.

- The preferable approach is positive reinforcement (rewards) instead of negative conditioning (punishments).

- The trainer might integrate additional tools as well, like

  physical manipulation (i.e., gently hand-forcing a sit).

- In marker training, command is matched to signal. The trainer may also advocate use of replacement behaviors (acceptable behavior, like sitting, is substituted for undesirable behavior, like barking).

letters show the person invested in classes, he probably takes his field seriously, and he likely knows more about dog training than does the average person.

Take a quality puppy training class. If you haven't made sufficient progress with puppy or if there is a serious behavior problem, then consider hiring a private trainer.

If there is a specific behavior problem, take puppy to the vet to rule out underlying medical conditions. Then ask your vet, groomer, and others for a few names of reputable trainers.

Classes

- Puppy classes are the gold standard. They are forums for puppy to socialize with others while being trained.

- Classes require puppy to pay attention and follow commands amid distractions. And they allow you to bounce ideas and strategies off other owners, and observe their approaches.

- Individual training is preferable to group sessions if you made little progress in puppy class, or if puppy has a specific problem, like aggression. Though costlier than classes, private lessons are also better if you have scheduling conflicts.

Lots of people label themselves "trainers" or "behaviorists," and charge $70 an hour to coach you and your dog. But calling oneself a trainer requires much more than a love for animals. And to come by the "behaviorist" title honestly, one must have completed graduate training in an area like animal behavior or zoology from an accredited university. Most *true* behaviorists are certified through the Animal Behavior Society and have the *CAAB* designation after their names.

How to select a trainer:

- Get recommendations from veterinarian or local humane society.

- Ask breeder, who might know a trainer who works well with your breed.

- Obtain member list from organizations like Association of Pet Dog Trainers (APDT).

- Contact a police K-9 unit. K-9 officers often make excellent trainers, and sometimes train on the side.

- Participate in message boards for particular dog-related activities.

- Always inquire about a trainer's credentials. Apprenticeships? Education? Years training?

- Ask around at dog competitions.

- Observe training session or view video of trainer at work.

FINDING EXPERTS

201

GROOMERS

A groomer can do more than just clip your dog; tease out a great groomer

If your dog is one that requires regular coiffing, your groomer will be a big part of your—and puppy's—life.

Choose your groomer carefully. Since grooming will become part of puppy's routine, pick one person or salon, and stick with them long term. This will make the grooming experience more predictable and less stressful for puppy.

There are essentially four types of grooming outlets: commercial salons; groomers operating within other businesses, like pet superstores, doggie day cares, and veterinary clinics; in-home groomers, often in rural areas; and mobile groomers—salons on wheels—especially popular among city dwellers.

Facility and Equipment

- Tour facility and observe cleanliness. Is dog odor low? Are floors swept regularly?

- Ask about flea control on premises. It's better to have a scruffy—flea-free—puppy than a coiffed pooch with even a single flea picked up at the salon.

- Is equipment kept in good condition? Is it cleaned between clients? Are blades sharpened regularly?

- There should be clean, comfortable, secured cages or quiet holding areas for dogs to rest before/after grooming.

Staff

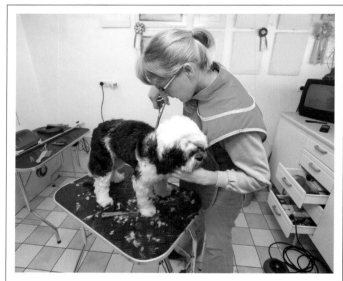

- The salon should be adequately staffed so dogs are never left alone.

- A dog in a tub, another on a table, and another under the dryer—with one groomer trying to do it all—is a scenario where dogs get injured.

- Interview prospective groomers about their training and experience. Apprenticeships? Number of years grooming dogs?

- Does groomer hold certifications, either for general grooming or grooming specific to your breed?

Services offered typically include bathing, blow drying and brushing, nail trims, tooth brushing, and anal sac expressing. Extra services, like hand stripping and show grooming, can be harder to find. Looking for a good groomer? Your breeder may be familiar with local groomers experienced with your breed. Ask for recommendations at your veterinary office.

Then interview the groomer about his or her expertise and office policies. Tour the facility. Check the company out with the Better Business Bureau. And, before you leave puppy there, be sure the groomer knows about all health conditions.

FINDING EXPERTS

Policies and Procedures

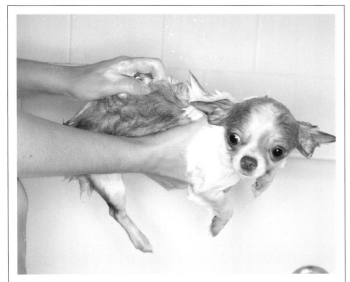

- Are hours of operation compatible with your schedule? If grooming is complete before you are able to pick up puppy, can she stay there for a few hours?

- How organized is the office? Do they send appointment reminders? Provide written pet service reports?

- Do they have a veterinarian on stand-by, should an accident occur?

- Will the groomer let you have a say in styling preference or will she only cut to breed standard?

Safety

- Grooming tables should be structurally sound and dogs securely restrained during grooming.

- Grooming areas should be well lit, not just for precise grooming, but also to avoid accidents caused by stray blades and such.

- Supervision should be excellent, especially at tables and drying stations, where dogs could fall or become overheated.

- Water should be available to dogs in holding areas. Closed-circuit cameras are a plus.

DAY CARE & KENNELS
A tired puppy is a good puppy (usually!), and the right day care can help

Dogs—puppies, in particular—need regular supervision and care. But life gets in the way sometimes. We go to work or go on vacation. When left alone, even for the work day, a dog can get into trouble. Dogs with separation anxiety suffer—and can be particularly destructive—when an owner leaves even for a few hours.

Doggie day cares and kennels keep puppy safe and occupied while we work or are out of town, or if we need to evacuate puppy from the house for another reason. Doggie day cares, run as large commercial facilities as well as in private homes, operate conceptually like child day cares. For $15 to $35 a day (multi-dog discounts may apply), depending on

PUPPY CARE

Facility

- Ask to tour facility.

- Facility should be clean. Some dog odor is unavoidable, but it should not be overwhelming.

- Are there indoor *and* outdoor play areas? Do play areas offer variety, like climbing structures,

tunnels, and different toys? Are there areas to segregate dogs by size, age, and temperament when playing? Are there comfortable sleeping spots where dogs can get quiet time?

- Is facility equipped with safety devices, like fire alarms and video cameras?

Supervision

- The staff:dog ratio should be adequate, so each dog is given ample attention and supervision. If there are too many dogs, safety and care could be compromised.

- Do staffers have much experience with dogs? Do they seem enthusiastic about their job?

- Do staffers attend dogs during activities, like play time and lunch?

- For kennels—and day cares that offer sleepovers—there should be someone on site through the night.

geographical area and options available, your puppy gets a structured and varied day of activities.

Most day cares offer play time, which may include games like hide-and-seek, tag, and fetch. The dogs can romp together in exercise pens. Some day cares have movie time—of the *Lassie* genre, of course!—and naps set to classical music. Meals, plus individual attention, are served up as well.

Larger commercial operations might offer extra services too, like grooming, training, routine veterinary care, even pick-up and drop-off taxi service.

Doggie day cares are great for socializing puppy to other dogs and people. To find a good day care or kennel, ask around at the dog park, vet's office, or groomer's. Your local humane society may even operate one.

Some day care facilities have five- or six-month age minimums, so your young puppy might not qualify.

Be sure to tour the day care or kennel first. Observe other dogs. Watch the dogs at play time. And make good use of your time away from puppy, so you are available to him when he returns home.

Daily Schedule

- There should be a daily schedule so that the dogs know what to expect when they are there.

- Schedules usually include time slots for drop-off and pick-up, play, individual attention, exercise, rest, and meal.

- If your feeding schedule differs from theirs, will they keep puppy on his own schedule?

- If something unforeseen comes up in your own schedule, can they keep puppy overnight?

Qualities of a good day care or kennel:

- Clean facility, not too noisy or overcrowded
- Dogs seems happy
- Adequately staffed
- Good flea control program for facility
- Nearby vet can be called for medical emergency
- Require dogs to be vaccinated and parasite-free
- Require dogs over six months to be sterilized
- Have a sick policy requiring pups to stay home if ill (day care)
- Screen temperament before accepting dog
- Separate dogs by size and temperament

PET SITTERS & DOG WALKERS
Home visits while you're working or vacationing can relieve puppy's boredom and give him potty breaks

Research shows that when we travel, most of us have family, friends, and neighbors come to our homes to care for our dogs. Many of us leave our dogs at friends' or relatives' homes instead. And a large proportion of us bring our dogs along when we travel. But what to do if we want puppy to stay home, and no friend is available to watch her?

Pet sitters to the rescue! Pet sitters, as well as dog walkers are widely available today. For $10 to $20/visit, a dog walker can fill the gaps in your daytime availability during this critical juncture when puppy needs to be walked every few hours.

If you're going to be away for longer than an afternoon consider a pet sitter. Pet sitters usually come to your home,

The Person

- Ideally, select someone whom you know, or whom a trusted friend knows.

- The individual should be a dog owner and/or experienced pet sitter, and have worked with puppies before.

- The person should appear to have common sense. Pose a few questions to the person and see how he answers. Also, use your sixth sense to gauge this.

- Invite the prospective pet sitter over to meet puppy. Observe her interaction with puppy. Is the person friendly?

The Schedule

- Leave a written schedule for pet sitter, so she knows exactly what is expected.

- State hours you want the sitter at home with puppy, and make sure sitter can comply with puppy's feed/exercise/bathroom schedule, which could include walks in middle of night.

- It's best for dogs, and particularly puppies, not to be left alone at night. See if sitter can stay overnight.

- If pet sitter is unable to stay overnight, ask if he or she would be willing to take puppy home with them.

although some prefer to watch dogs in their own homes. Having puppy remain in your home offers several advantages. First, puppy remains in her own environment. She has no travel stress, and is not exposed to the germs that sometimes float around kennels and other dogs' homes.

Contact a pet sitters' organization for names of pet sitters near you, or get referrals from your vet's office, local humane society, or trusted friends. In-home dog boarding networks can supply names in many metropolitan areas.

Before embarking on a long trip, put the sitter through a dry run with a shorter jaunt, maybe an overnight. Show her puppy's walking route and key spots around your property, like where she goes potty. Instruct sitter on safety issues and brief her on puppy's favorite vices.

Make sure puppy is wearing ID tags. Put her food, toys, and other supplies in one easily accessible spot. Provide sitter with emergency numbers, as well as letter of financial responsibility, should puppy need emergency medical care. And give your neighbors an extra house key.

Additional Responsibilities

- One of the benefits of hiring a pet sitter to come to your home—versus putting puppy in a kennel—is that someone is watching your dwelling in your absence.

- The pet sitter is there to report a water leak and deter a burglar.

- This person can do added jobs while there, such as put burglar alarm on and feed fish.

- Make a list of small tasks you would like performed, and demonstrate how to do them.

Pet sitter must:

- Be available to maintain puppy's schedule and stay with puppy for desired hours.

- Have backup in case he gets sick, has car trouble, etc.

- Be able to drive car or obtain transportation in case of puppy medical emergency.

- Be willing to do everything you do with puppy, such as throw a ball, brush her, or let her sit on your lap during TV time.

- Be willing to perform extra needed jobs, like bringing in mail and watering plants.

- Be insured and/or bonded.

- *Accreditation from a pet sitter organization, like Pet Sitters International, is not a must, but a plus.

OTHER PET SERVICES

From veterinary acupuncturists to dog whisperers, alternative procedures abound, but do proceed with caution

The practice of animal acupuncture goes back as much as 5,000 years, but it really developed in China during the T'ang Dynasty, from A.D. 900 to A.D. 600, spread to Europe in the seventeenth century, and entered American veterinary medicine in the early 1970s.

Acupuncture is a large part of complementary and alternative veterinary medicine (CAVM). Also known as holistic veterinary medicine, CAVM incorporates a wide variety of natural therapies, from environmental to psychological to nutritional, that treat the whole animal. Holistic treatments for animals also include chiropractic, physical therapy, massage, and herbal medicine, to name a few. They have been

Acupuncture

- Acupuncture is the insertion of fine needles into specific points ("acupoints") on the body.

- The goal is to restore flow of qi (chi), or life force, that has become out of balance due to the body's diseased state.

- It may also promote release of neurochemicals—like endorphins, enkephalins, and serotonin—relieve muscle spasms, and stimulate weakened nerves.

- The treatments, which take anywhere from ten seconds to thirty minutes, are typically done weekly or biweekly.

Chiropractic and Massage

- Misalignments of spinal vertebrae disrupt nerves radiating from the spinal cord, resulting in pain, tingling, and weakness. Chiropractic is manipulation of vertebral column to realign spine, thereby relieving symptoms.

- Massage incorporates vari-

ous techniques to relieve pain, improve immune function, and boost circulation.

- Put puppy in good hands, literally. These procedures should be performed only under veterinary direction.

used to treat all sorts of ailments, like hip dysplasia, disc herniation, kidney disease, intestinal problems, and skin infections.

In 2001, the American Veterinary Medical Association (AVMA) formally recognized CAVM. Today, hundreds of veterinarians practice some form of holistic medicine, mostly in conjunction with conventional medicine. CAVM is unregulated in many states. In others, only licensed veterinarians can administer these treatments. Check your state's Veterinary Practice Act to see who may dispense these treatments, and contact holistic veterinary associations for lists of license holders.

Herbs and More

- Over one hundred Chinese and Western herbs are used with variable efficacy to treat different canine conditions.

- In addition to herbs, the list of holistic therapies is almost as endless as the available materials and techniques out there.

- These include aromatherapy, ozone therapy, energy therapy, and Bach flower remedies. There are even animal psychics. They'll interpret puppy's thoughts and feelings in minutes through the telephone wires. Be careful what you choose, and use common sense!

Do not arrange alternative treatments for puppy without your veterinarian's request or assent. If you are interested in pursuing holistic therapies for a specific problem puppy is having, you can arrange a consultation with a vet who is well-versed in alternative medicine. To find a vet near you who practices alternative therapies obtain a membership list from an organization like the American Holistic Veterinary Medical Association.

FINDING EXPERTS

CAVM caveats:

- Many hands reach into the $34 billion U.S. pet industry pot.

- Holistic medicine—CAVM—accounts for a small portion of these dollars.

- Holistic therapies should not replace consideration of conventional treatments.

- Pursue these only under direction of veterinarian who uses conventional practices.

- The practice of CAVM does not require licenses, although many states mandate veterinary involvement.

- Herbal remedies are not FDA regulated.

- For CAVM therapies, scrutinize credentials and beware of claims.

WHY TRAIN TO COMPETE?

Getting involved in dog events can boost your dog skills and your social life

Now you've got your puppy. She's got her supplies, her shots, and her food. She's trained to be a house dog, and if you ever need any extra help, you know who can groom her and babysit her when you go away. Ho hum . . . what next?!

Looks like you're ready to turn it up a notch, puppy style. With over 21,000 AKC–sanctioned events a year, there's a whole world of canine competition out there just waiting for you and puppy to join, once she's at least six months old. You can choose from traditional dog shows (where looks matter), obedience trials, and performance events.

Showing began in this country with a group of gentlemen who met regularly at a Manhattan bar to crow about their

Types of shows

- There are several types of competitions for dogs.

- Most popular is the traditional "dog show." Here, purebreeds are judged on conformation, or adherence to their BREED STANDARD (defined breed characteristics).

- In companion events, dog-handler teams are judged in obedience and agility routines. In performance events, dogs display the innate abilities for which their breed is known.

- Events are also split between formal shows and informal competitions.

Performance Shows

- In performance events, dogs display skills for which originally bred, and earn points toward championships.

- Field trials and hunting tests are for hounds and sporting dogs (retrievers, spaniels, and pointers) to demonstrate tracking and hunting skills in the field.

- Herding (herding breeds), earthdog (dachshunds and small terriers), lure coursing (sighthounds), coonhound and working dog sport (working breeds like Rottweiler) events allow respective breeds to showcase natural instincts.

hunting dogs' talents and their own shooting accomplish-ments. They formed a club devoted to the sport of purebred dogs, and named it after their favorite hotel, the Westminster. The club held its first namesake show the following year.

The realm of dog shows has changed over the years. What was once a sport of the wealthy—and pure of breed—is now open to people and dogs from all walks of life. Most companion-style events welcome mixed breeds. Plus, there are over 5,000 dog clubs in the country, most either breed-based or event-based, that host classes and dog shows.

If you would like to compete with puppy, register her with the AKC or other dog registry. Vaccinate her and join a train-ing class and/or a training club. Learn the AKC showing regu-lations and attend dog shows. And start off with informal, no-points shows . . . at least until you and puppy get your paws wet!

Show Handlers

- For human participants, part of the fun and chal-lenge of dog shows is displaying dog handling skills in ring or field.

- Handling one's own dog also provides a bond-ing opportunity for both. Some owners prefer to hire professional handlers, for whom they generally pay travel expenses, plus fees to train and show dogs.

- Handlers must be over eighteen for most shows, though some general events allow youths. There are also junior handling events for children as young as two.

Canine Participants

- Most events are open to purebred dogs only.

- Some are all-breed and others are specialty shows, open only to certain breeds.

- As of April 2010, mixed breeds may participate in obedience, agility, and rally AKC events. Mixes can also take part in shows run by organizations like Mixed Breed Dog Clubs of America.

- For most shows, canine par-ticipants must be at least six months old (herding trials, nine months old; agility events, one year old).

CONFORMATION

Enter your dog in canine "beauty pageants" to see if he's got the right stuff

Dog shows are competitive displays of conformation. They are platforms for evaluating how a dog was constructed, from ground up, and nose to tail. The show judge compares what is before him to the breed standard, which is sort of an ingredient list for how to make a perfect dog of said breed.

The breed standard might include, in the AKC's words, the "'hippo' muzzle shape" of the Chinese shar-pei, the "mahogany markings and taper-style tail" of the tiny Manchester terrier, or the "driving action" of the Pembroke Welsh corgi's hind legs.

These breed standards are written by experts and put together by different AKC-sanctioned breed clubs. For international dog shows, breed standards are written by the

Competition

- Most AKC events are conformation shows, in which dogs are judged on external characteristics.

- Conformation events are divided into specialty shows (individual breeds); group shows (breed groups); and all-breed shows, open to all eligible purebreds.

- There are six different classes: puppy, twelve-to-eighteen month, novice, bred-by-exhibitor, American-bred, and open. In most shows, dogs earn points toward championships. To become an AKC champion, a dog must earn fifteen points under three different judges.

Breed Groups

- There are seven breed groups into which dogs are divided for the purpose of conformation shows.

- The groups are terriers, hounds, herding, working, sporting, non-sporting, and toy breeds.

- Each group contains constituent breeds. The toy group, for instance, includes the Chihuahua, the Maltese, the Pomeranian, the Japanese Chin, and others.

- In an all-breed show, the seven winners of each group compete against each other for Best in Show title.

Fédération Cynologique Internationale, which has eighty-four member countries and sponsors shows around the world.

Dog shows are wildly popular in the United States. In fact, the annual Westminster Dog Show—which is the oldest continuously held sporting event in the United States next to the Kentucky Derby—has over five million TV viewers.

Some shows, like Westminster, are "benched." At benched shows, the dogs—when not in the ring—are on display in designated areas, where attendees can get closer looks and meet the owners.

Judging

- Each dog is judged by how it measures up to the "ideal" specimen for its breed. The judge eyes everything from coat markings to tail carriage, gait to overt disposition.

- The dogs move around ring at requested gaits, and then each dog is called individually to be judged.

- The judge examines each dog head to toe, lifting lips, feeling coat, and so forth.

- While judge's final assessment is slightly subjective in assessing the positives, he rules out dogs with clear faults, like cleft palate.

Best in Show

- An all-breed show is a process of elimination ending in the coveted Best in Show title.

- In the largest shows, as many as 4,000 entrants are whittled down to a single winner.

- Male dogs and bitches do not compete against one another. Rather, a Winners Bitch and a Winners Dog are chosen.

- Next, Best in Breed is chosen. The breeds then compete for Best in Group title, and these seven dogs go neck-and-neck for Best in Show.

COMPETITION

BREED GROUP SPORTS

From earthdog to herding to lure coursing, find a fitting sport for your breed

Sporting events are sort of the ultimate celebrations of true breed differences, like the bearded collie's skill at herding sheep on rough, rocky ground; the fearless Skye terrier's penchant for diving into holes in pursuit of otters and badgers; or the powerful Alaskan malamute's capacity to pull a sled across an eternal frozen tundra.

Performance trials come in great variety and are designed to flaunt the skills for which different breeds were created long ago. In a sense, what canine sporting events are doing is paying homage to the origins of each breed.

These events are also great fun for the owners, the spectators, and the dogs themselves. The adrenaline rush that

Field Trials and Hunting Tests

- In field trials and hunting tests, dogs showcase specific hunting skills for which they were bred.

- Depending on breed, they are asked to trail rabbits, mark location of downed birds, and flush and retrieve on land and water.

- In field trials, beagles, basset hounds, dachshunds, pointing breeds, retrievers, and spaniels all compete separately for titles of Field Champion and Amateur Field Champion. In hunting tests, pointers, retrievers, and spaniels compete for titles of Junior, Senior, and Master Hunter.

Lure Coursing

- Lure coursing is exciting and fast-paced, sort of the downhill skiing of canine sports.

- In lure coursing, dogs bred to hunt fleet-footed prey, like hares, gazelles, and lions, show off their chasing prowess by running down artificial lures, sometimes

- over great distances.

- Dogs are scored on their speed, endurance, enthusiasm, and ability to follow a lure in an open field.

- Eligible breeds include sighthounds like whippets, Afghan hounds and Salukis, and Rhodesian ridgebacks.

a borzoi has as she zigzags across a field chasing a lure is apparent in her long, springy stride and her "What's next?!" expression. So, too, is the excitement of a border collie at a Frisbee tournament, salivating in anticipation, eyes so intent they seem ready to inhale the flying disc.

Canine sporting events come in a variety of forms. There are field trials and hunting tests for breeds that hunt rodents and birds; lure coursing events for dogs that chase down large game; herding trials for dogs bred to direct livestock from place to place; earthdog events for smaller breeds—dachshunds and terriers— that tunnel through the ground in pursuit of a scent; and coonhound trials for the handful of hounds that hunt raccoons by sending them up trees and then baying below.

Various other events demonstrate key canine traits like strength, speed, endurance, tenacity, and ability to anticipate and react fast. Dog sledding, Frisbee, and flyball are just a few of these.

Participants earn points and titles in performance events, which are held through numerous AKC–sanctioned clubs.

Herding and Working Dogs

- In herding tests and trials, herding breeds demonstrate their skills at steering livestock under the direction of a handler.

- Herding breeds include the border collie, the Australian cattle dog, the Belgian malinois, the puli, and the Old English sheepdog.

- Herding trails test abilities on a variety of livestock, generally cattle, sheep, goats, and ducks.

- A range of different courses are used in herding trails, to gauge dogs' skills on several types of terrain.

Earthdogs and Coonhounds

- In earthdog events, canine competitors display their talents at following underground scents. The dogs must roam distances to locate dens, and navigate tunnels of increasing complexity.

- Earthdog tests are for breeds that "go to ground"

for prey like foxes and badgers. These are small terriers, like Norfolk terriers, Cairns, West Highland Whites ("westies"), and Jack Russells.

- Coonhound trials assess the hunting skills of coonhounds, bred to track, tree raccoons and opossums.

AGILITY, OBEDIENCE & MORE
Canine contests can be fun—even exhilarating—for both dog and handler

Companion events are all about the dog-handler unit. They recognize that a dog weaving between poles is not simply about a dog weaving between poles.

So, too, a dog retrieving on the flat isn't just about that dog's ability to retrieve. And a dog's demonstration of scent tracking goes well beyond his nose.

These canine trials are significant not just because they demonstrate a canine ability but because the dog's actions are elicited by good communication between handler and dog.

In agility and tracking, greater emphasis is placed on the result: How quickly does the dog clear the course? Does he

Companion Events

- Companion events judge not only the dog's performance in certain tasks, but also how well dog and handler work together.

- The four companion events are obedience, rally, agility, and tracking.

- Dogs must be at least six months old—and intact or sterilized—to compete in companion events.

- As of April 2010, mixed-breed dogs may compete at companion events that are stand-alone (not combined with conformation classes for AKC–registered breeds).

Agility

- The dogs run obstacle courses containing jumps, tunnels, bridges, weave poles, and such.

- Handler guides dog—off-leash—through course. Handler cannot touch dog or obstacles, or use treats to reward dog.

- Scoring is by amount of time it takes to finish course, and whether dog accrues faults, for instance, for refusing to jump obstacle, displacing bar, or missing contact zone. Agility events are open to all breeds, and sometimes mixes, but dogs must be at least a year old to compete.

take the obstacles in sequence? Does he locate all the items along the track?

In obedience and rally, it's more about following direction. Depending on the skill level of the obedience class, dogs must demonstrate their usefulness by being well behaved in public and obeying commands.

In rally, which combines elements of obedience and agility, dogs must perform minor athletic feats on command. Depending on the expertise level of the rally class, this is done either on- or off-leash.

Companion events showcase the essence of what makes dog "man's best friend"—his willingness to take direction from his human. Back in the 1870s, agility performances began as pure entertainment at the famous Crufts dog show in England. The Kennel Club of England soon organized agility as an official event. Obedience trials sprung up in the United States in the late 1930s. Rally hit the scene in 2000, and became an official AKC–scored event five years later.

Obedience

- Dogs demonstrate ability to follow handler's verbal commands and hand signals directing them to perform different tasks.

- In novice obedience classes, dogs heel, stand for exam, and stay on command.

- Open classes are more ani-mated, as handlers direct dogs to do things like jump fences and run figure eights on command.

- In utility classes, dogs must perform even more complicated jobs, like scent discrimination, in response to hand signals.

Rally and Tracking

- In rally events, dog and handler navigate a course with ten to twenty signs cueing different exercises to complete, like "halt-pivot-halt."

- Blending obedience and agility in terms of team-work, rally differs in that it requires no fancy footwork, and teams can move at their own pace.

- Also, rally emphasizes excellent communication between handler and dog.

- In tracking trials, dogs that hunt by scent must stay on track while finding articles dropped along trail.

JUNIOR DOG HANDLING
Kids compete with dogs, including mixed breeds, in several venues for fun and ribbons

If you've ever observed children engaging in an activity that is typically within the domain of adults you can surely understand the appeal of junior dog handling. The purpose of junior showmanship is to allow the young handler to display how he interacts with the dog and with the judge.

Junior handlers also acquaint themselves with show ring procedures, learn showing techniques specific to their breed, hone grooming skills, and develop knowledge of the dog as a subspecies, from canine history to anatomy.

A youngster in the show ring must exhibit ability to pay attention, focusing on the judge (and the dog), rather than on chit-chat and other distractions. Through showing, the

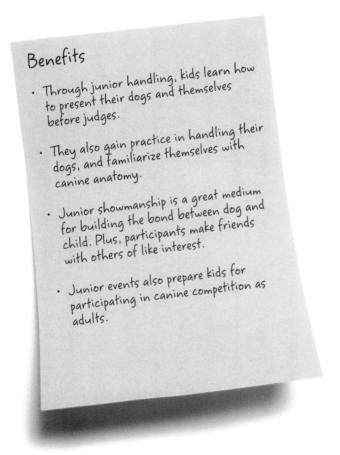

Benefits

- Through junior handling, kids learn how to present their dogs and themselves before judges.

- They also gain practice in handling their dogs, and familiarize themselves with canine anatomy.

- Junior showmanship is a great medium for building the bond between dog and child. Plus, participants make friends with others of like interest.

- Junior events also prepare kids for participating in canine competition as adults.

Eligibility

- There are junior showman-ship events for children of all ages, even "pee wee" classes for kids as young as four.

- AKC and 4-H junior dog shows are limited to young-sters ages nine to eighteen.

- Kids are usually segregated by age. At AKC shows, the groups are: juniors (nine to twelve), interim (twelve to fifteen), and seniors (fifteen to eighteen).

- Children should only par-ticipate in showing if they have the maturity, compre-hension skills, and attention span to follow directions.

child handler develops good sportsmanship. He also learns to work in symbiosis with an animal, and the bond between the two strengthens.

The benefits of allowing kids into the show ring were recognized long ago. The first junior showmanship event was staged in 1932 by the Westbury Kennel Club in Long Island. The following year, the Westminster Kennel Club added a children's handling class. And finally, in 1971, the AKC embraced junior showmanship.

Today, junior showmanship classes are part of all the major kennel clubs, namely the United Kennel Club, Kennel Club (UK), Canadian Kennel Club, and the worldwide Fédération Cynologique Internationale. And some organizations allow junior handlers to participate in the regular classes alongside adults.

Kids can also become involved in showing dogs through 4-H. Originally developed as an outlet for children of farm families to display livestock, 4-H is now a youth development organization.

Canine Participants

- Because it is not the dog being judged in junior handling events, but rather the handler, the dog does not have to be an exceptional specimen.

- The dog should, however, be well behaved, and predictable, even in the novice hands of the average child.

- The dog should be well matched size-, strength-, and temperament-wise to the child handler. A strong, energetic mastiff, for instance, will probably drag the typical ten-year-old around the ring.

- Some events are open to mixed breeds.

Judging criteria

- The child is judged on his ability to present himself and his breed to judge, as well as skill at handling and communicating with dog.

- This means following directions when leading dog around ring and when displaying dog to judge for table examination.

- Also, did handler show respect to judge? Did he make eye contact with judge? Dress appropriately? Correctly answer any questions judge may have asked about breed or canine anatomy?

WHAT'S IN A NAME?

Playing the name game is fun, but choose puppy's label carefully

One of the more enjoyable decisions you will make with regard to puppy is assigning him a name.

The name you select is very important because you will be calling that name for the rest of puppy's life. All told, you will likely utter this word over 20,000 times! Better make sure it's one you want to say . . . and one you want to hear.

It's also critical that you can articulate the name easily. Guaranteed, there will be times when you'll need to fire off this name within a millisecond: "Max, off the table!" (Now try substituting *Mortimer, Christopher,* or *Isabella.*) So stick to simple pronunciations and one or two syllables.

While Max is one of the more neutral names, many perpetuate—or reinforce—the way we feel about our dog. Names like *Honey* and *Buddy* might engender warm sentiments. Other names summon

feelings of protecting (e.g., *Baby*) or being protected (e.g., *Brutu* *Duke*). Names like *Dodger* and *Rascal* might engender a gamely while those such as *Giggles* and *Pookie* may inspire giddiness.

Some names have negative connotations. So think twice b calling puppy *Dopey, Stinky,* or *Adolph.*

But remember, puppy's name, while possibly rich in meaning, ultimately be utilitarian. It will be a tool for identifying puppy, moning him, and getting his attention.

Dog monikers, as a whole, have always been a sign of the t When dogs were used mainly as workers long ago, they were outdoors and given simple, neutral appellations, like *Mutt* and *S*

That's changed over the years, as dogs have come inside become family members. We've given dogs gender-specific b (e.g., *Princess* and *Rex*), many of them human names (*Charlie, Molly,* and *Sandy* are among the top twenty). Some names stood the test of time (e.g., *Lady, Max,* and *Buddy*), while others signaled passing trends (e.g., *Lassie, Eddie,* and *Marley*).

Choose puppy's name carefully, because his name will outlas passing trends. While you can change puppy's leash, his sham his groomer or, if necessary, even his diet, his name is one thing should be his for life.

Top ten dog names*:

Male	Female
1. Max	1. Bella
2. Buddy	2. Molly
3. Rocky	3. Lucy
4. Bailey	4. Maggie
5. Jake	5. Daisy
6. Charlie	6. Sophie
7. Jack	7. Sadie
8. Toby	8. Chloe
9. Cody	9. Bailey
10. Buster	10. Lola

*VPI pet insurance registrations, 2008

Presidential dogs (partial list):

Drunkard, Sweet Lips, hounds (George Washington; 1789–1797)

Fido (Abraham Lincoln; 1861–1865)

Major, German shepherd (Franklin Delano Roosevelt; 1933–1945)

Checkers, cocker spaniel (Richard Nixon; 1969–1974)

Liberty, golden retriever (Gerald Ford; 1974–1977)

Grits, border collie (Jimmy Carter; 1977–1981)

Rex, cavalier King Charles spaniel; *Lucky,* Bouvier des Flandres (Ronald Reagan; 1981–1989)

Millie, English springer spaniel (George H. W. Bush (1989–1993)

Buddy, Labrador retriever (Bill Clinton; 1993–2001)

Barney, Scottish terrier; *Spot,* English springer spaniel (George W. Bush; 2001–2009)

Bo, Portuguese water dog (Barack Obama, 2009–)

Web sites for dog names:

www.babydognames.com

www.cat-dog-names.com

Tips for choosing dog names:

- Have household members make a short list of names.
- Select a name that everyone in the household agrees to use.
- Look for names that are easy to call out.
- Avoid names that are hard to pronounce.
- Avoid names with over two syllables.
- Avoid distasteful/controversial names.
- Avoid confusion: Steer clear of common dog names, and names that sound like commands or those of other household members.
- If unsure about a name, try it out for an afternoon.
- Once you select a name, don't switch it.
- It's okay to change the name of an adopted puppy.

Dogs can be named after:

- Animals (e.g., Bear, Bunny)
- Breed cultural/geographic origin (e.g., Brisbane, Australian cattle dog, Shannon, Kerry blue terrier)
- Colors (e.g., Blue, Copper)
- Dog's appearance (e.g., Freckles, Shorty)
- Dog's character traits (e.g., Champ, Pokey)
- Famous brands (e.g., Google, Nike)
- Famous movie dogs (e.g., Benji, Beethoven)
- Famous people (e.g., Hillary, Dutch)
- Foods (e.g., Hershey, Sushi)
- Hobbies (e.g., Kendo, Frisbee)
- Human movie characters (e.g., Gidget, Buzz)
- Musical artists (e.g., Arlo, Mozart)
- Nonsense words (e.g., Bobo, Muffy)
- People (e.g., Christy, Bob)
- Places (e.g., Denver, Sahara)
- Values/beliefs (e.g., Liberty, Justice)

GEOGRAPHICALLY SPEAKING...

Match puppy breed to weather and terrain in your neck of the woods

Mother Nature has given us many local gifts—and challenges. Depending on where you reside, it could be the winding waterways of the Chesapeake, the searing sun of the Sonoran Desert, the craggy hills of South Dakota, or the frosty Arctic tundra.

If you live in a place that has extreme conditions of weather or topography, you might want to find a breed especially suited to the idiosyncrasies of your region.

There are some 400 dog breeds, most created in harmony with their places of origin. Very few of these breeds—the American cocker spaniel, Boston terrier, Chesapeake Bay retriever, American Staffordshire terrier and its pit bull cousin, plus the coonhounds and spitz-type sled dogs of Alaska—actually originated in this country.

But their places of origin probably have American counterparts. The Mexican Chihuahua might feel at home in a warm state like Texas or Florida, for instance. The Portuguese water dog, developed along the Iberian coast, would probably enjoy the Jersey Shore.

Every breed comes in a unique package that includes specific hair coats, body structures, and sizes. Some are better suited to particular geographic regions. So too, there are breeds that don't do as well in certain places, without special accommodations.

A Siberian husky, for instance, will do fine in Miami. Just keep her clipped and give her an air conditioner. A miniature pinscher can survive Minnesota winters—as long as she is not outdoors for long periods, and is dressed warmly.

Some breeds fit in anywhere. Case in point: The current top five AKC–registered breeds in most major cities throughout the country are the Labrador and golden retrievers, German shepherd, Yorkshire terrier, and usually either the boxer or the bulldog.

But in Phoenix and other arid cities, the tiny Chihuahua—which loses body heat faster than a large dog—appears among the top five. In Honolulu, the Chihuahua shares top five ranking with two other small breeds, the Pomeranian and the dachshund.

Breed compatibility is also associated with different types of hu settlements, from rural farmland to congested cities. So is dog ership as a whole.

According to the APPA, slightly more dog owners than non-owners live in less populated rural areas. There is also a small graphic preponderance for dog ownership: while 16 percent c U.S. population lives in the South, 19 percent of dog owners are vened there.

Puppy-Place Match

Most dogs do fine just anywhere, as long as special accommoda are made when necessary. Because breeds were developed to their places of origin, as well as their "jobs," some dogs are particu compatible with certain areas and lifestyles.

Sled dogs, like Alaskan malamutes, are insulated from below temps by dense undercoats and hair between their pads.

Large, surefooted dogs, like Anatolian shepherds, Hungarian Kuv or Greater Swiss mountain dogs, would take to the Rocky Moun like an Irish water spaniel to a Louisiana bayou.

City Dog, Country Dog

Most dogs do fine in country or city, but some breeds are id suited to one versus the other. Where space is sparse and dwel congested, breeds that fit in best are generally smaller, have lc exercise needs, and bark less.

These include, respectively, miniatures, bulldogs, greyhounds, and the barkless basenji.

You can match outdoor country living with hardier, indepen dogs that have higher stamina. These include herding breeds, as collies, sheepdogs, the Australian cattle dog, and the Pemb Welsh corgi.

Some warm-weather breeds:
Chihuahua

Chinese crested

Miniature pinscher

Greyhound/Italian greyhound

Manchester terrier

Pharaoh hound

Canaan dog

Some cold-weather breeds:
Akita

Bernese mountain dog

Great Pyrenees

Norwegian elkhound

Samoyed

Alaskan malamute

Saint Bernard

Chow chow

Chesapeake Bay retriever

WEB SITES

Adopting

Adopt a Pet
www.adoptapet.com

The Humane Society
www.humanesociety.org/animals/pets

Petfinder
www.petfinder.com

The Senior Dog Project
www.srdogs.com

World Animal Net
www.worldanimal.net

AKC Canine

AKC Canine Good Citizen Program
www.akc.org/events/cgc/

Breed Information

Dog Breed Info Center
www.dogbreedinfo.com

Just Dog Breeds
www.justdogbreeds.com

Breed Organizations

American Kennel Club
www.akc.org

The Kennel Club
www.thekennelclub.org.uk

United Kennel Club
www.ukcdogs.com

The World Canine Organization
www.fci.be/default.aspx

Day Care

Central Bark Day Care
www.centralbarkusa.com
(866) 799-BARK

Dogtopia Day Care and Boarding
www.dogtopia.com

National Association of Professional Pet Sitters
www.petsitters.org
(856) 439-0324

Pet Sitters International
www.petsit.com
(336) 983-9222

Rover
www.rover.com

Disabled Dog Resources

Deaf Dog Education Action Fund
www.deafdogs.org

Pets with Disabilities
www.petswithdisabilities.org

Holistic Medicine

Academy of Veterinary Homeopathy
www.theavh.org

Alt Vet Med
www.altvetmed.com

American Academy of Veterinary Acupuncture
www.aava.org

American Holistic Veterinary Medical Association
www.ahvma.org

American Veterinary Chiropractic Association
www.animalchiropractic.org

Chi University
https://chiu.edu

International Association of Animal Massage and Bodywork
www.iaamb.org

International Veterinary Acupuncture Society
www.ivas.org

Mixed-breed Organizations
Mixed Breed Dog Clubs of America
https://mbdca.tripod.com

Negligence
Puppy mill abuse:
www.humanesociety.org/all-our-fights

Pet Insurance
ASPCA Pet Insurance
www.aspcapetinsurance.com

Pet Assure
www.petassure.com

Pets Best Insurance
www.petsbest.com

Veterinary Pet Insurance (VPI)
www.petinsurance.com
(800) USA-PETS

Pet Transportation
Dog-friendly cars ratings:
https://barkbuckleup.wordpress.com
www.dogcars.com
www.cars.com

Poison Control
ASPCA Animal Poison Control Center
(24-hour hotline)
(888) 426-4435

Spay/Neuter
Friends of Animals spay and neuter certificates:
(800) 321-PETS

Low-cost spay-neuter programs:
www.ASPCA.org

Spay Day USA:
www.humanesociety.org

Veterinary Information
American Veterinary Medical Association
www.avma.org

Dr. Patty Khuly
www.drpattykhuly.com

GEAR

Bedding and Housing Gear
Jeffer's
www.jefferspet.com

La Petite Maison
www.lapetitemaison.com

MidWest Homes for Pets
www.midwesthomes4pets.com

Collars and Leashes
Gentle Leader Headcollar
www.petsafe.com/product/gentle-leader-headcollar

Eco-friendly Gear
Earth Dog
www.earthdog.com

Earth Doggy
www.earthdoggy.com
Great Green Pet
www.greatgreenpet.com

Green Dog Pet Supply
www.greendogpetsupply.com

Pet Organics No-Dig Lawn and Yard Spray
https://nalabarry.com

Planet Dog
https://outwardhound.com/brands/planet-dog

General
Dogstuff
www.dogstuff.pet

8 in 1
www.8in1.eu/en

Jeffer's
www.jefferspet.com

Palmetto Pet Supplies
www.palmettopetsupplies.com

Robbins Pet Care
www.robbinspetcare.com

Grooming
SitStay
www.sitstay.com

Toys
Earth Dog
www.earthdog.com

Training
Invisible Fence
www.invisiblefence.com

Leerburg's Video & Kennel
www.leerburg.com

Travel Gear

High Country Plastics
www.highcountryplastics.com

Orvis
www.orvis.com

Pup Life
www.puplife.com

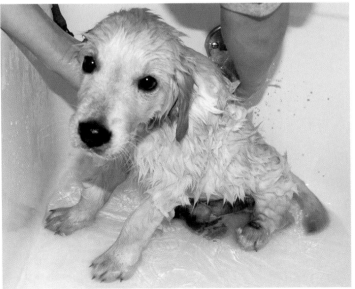

SPORTS, BEHAVIOR & TRAINING
Behavior and Training Organizations

Books

Aloff, Brenda, *Canine Body Language: A Photographic Guide Interpreting the Native Language of the Domestic Dog*, Dogwise Publishing, 2005

Ammen, Amy, and Kitty Foth-Regner, *Hip Ideas for Hyper Dogs*, Howell Book House, 2007

Donaldson, Jean, *The Culture Clash*, James & Kenneth Publishers, 1996

Millan, Cesar, *Cesar's Way: The Natural, Everyday Guide to Understanding and Correcting Common Dog Problems*, Three Rivers Press, 2007

Miller, Pat, *The Power of Positive Dog Training*, Howell Book House, 2008

Monks of New Skete, *Divine Canine: The Monks' Way to a Happy, Obedient Dog*, Hyperion, 2007

Rugaas, Turid, *On Talking Terms with Dogs: Calming Signals*, Dogwise Publishing, 2005

Web sites

Association of Professional Dog Trainers
www.apdt.com

Clicker Training Lessons
www.clickerlessons.com

K9 In Focus
https://k9infocus.com

National Association of Dog Obedience Instructors
www.nadoi.org

Whole Dog Journal
www.whole-dog-journal.com

RESOURCES

Dog Sports and Shows
www.workingdogweb.com/wdcompet.htm

www.dogplay.com

www.ukcdogs.com/about-all-breed-sports

www.akc.org/sports/

www.thekennelclub.org.uk/activities

Therapy Dog Organizations
Pet Partners
https://petpartners.org

Therapy Dogs International
www.tdi-dog.org
(973) 252-9800

RESOURCES

NUTRITION & HEALTH

Commercial Dog Food Manufacturers

Hill's Science Diet
www.hillspet.com/science-diet

Iams
www.iams.com

Pedigree
www.pedigree.com

Purina
www.purina.com

Food (Diets)

Natural or raw food diets:
www.aplaceforpaws.com
www.barfworld.com
www.olivegreendog.com

General Health

Virbac Animal Health C.E.T. Hextra
(800) 338-3659

General Information

Books

Billinghurst, Ian, *The BARF Diet,* SOS Printing, 2001

Dye, Dan, *Three Dog Bakery Cookbook,* Andrews McMeel Publishing, 1998

MacDonald, Carina, *Raw Dog Food: Make It Easy for You and Your Dog,* Dogwise, 2003

Pitcairn, Richard, *Dr. Pitcairn's New Complete Guide to Natural Health for Dogs and Cats,* Rodale Books, 2005

Web sites

Dog Food Analysis
www.dogfoodanalysis.com

The Dog Food Project
www.dogfoodproject.com

Nutrition

Hill's Pet Nutrition, Inc.
www.hillspet.com
(800) 445-0557

Treats

All kinds of treats:
www.dog.com

Training treats:
www.sitstay.com
www.zukes.com

DOG DEVELOPMENT & GROOMING

General Information

Books

Bonham, Margaret, *Dog Grooming for Dummies,* For Dummies, 2006

Eldredge, Debra, *Dog Owner's Home Veterinary Handbook,* Howell Book House, 2007

Fennell, Jan, *The Seven Ages of Man's Best Friend,* Collins Living, 2007

Gleeson, Eileen, *Ultimate Dog Grooming,* Firefly, 2007

Goldstein, Martin, *The Nature of Animal Healing,* Ballantine Books, 2000

Web sites

Groomer Locator
www.petgroomer.com

National Dog Groomers Association of America
www.nationaldoggroomers.com

Only Natural Pet
www.onlynaturalpet.com

World Veterinary Association
www.worldvet.org

More Grooming Needs

Grooming supply companies:
www.cherrybrook.com
www.petedge.com

MORE ON BREEDS

Dog Breed Web Sites

American Kennel Club guides to dog breeds, breeders, clubs and rescue groups:
www.akc.org

Breed info and links to breed clubs:
www.westminsterkennelclub.org

Directories of breed-specific rescue groups:

Directory of dog breeders:
www.breeders.net

General Breed Information

Dog Breed Info Center
www.dogbreedinfo.com

Just Dog Breeds
www.justdogbreeds.com

Mixed-breed Organizations

Mixed Breed Dog Clubs of America
mbdca.tripod.com

RESOURCES

ADDITIONAL READING

General Information Books

Dunbar, Ian, *Before and After Getting Your Puppy: The Positive Approach to Raising a Happy, Healthy, and Well-behaved Dog,* New World Library, 2004

Kern, Nancy, *The Whole Dog Journal Handbook of Dog and Puppy Care and Training,* The Lyons Press, 2007

Magazines

The Wildest
www.thewildest.com

Dogster
www.dogster.com

Dog's Life
www.dogslife.com.au

Fido Friendly
www.fidofriendly.com

Gun Dog
www.gundogmag.com

Modern Dog
www.moderndogmagazine.com

RESOURCES

Miscellaneous Books

Bloeme, Peter, *Frisbee Dogs, How to Raise, Train and Compete,* Sky Houndz, 1994

Donaldson, Jean, *The Culture Clash,* James & Kenneth Publishers, 1996

Kramer, Charles, *Rally-O—The Style of Rally Obedience,* 3rd Edition, Fancee Publications, 2005.

Pryor, Karen, *Don't Shoot the Dog,* Bantam Books, 1999

Simmons-Moake, Jane, *Agility Training: The Fun Sport for All Dogs,* Howell Book House, 1991

Theory and Breed Books

American Kennel Club, *The Complete Dog Book: 20th Edition,* Ballantine Books, 2006

Budiansky, Stephen, *The Truth about Dogs,* Viking Penguin, 2000

Coppinger, Raymond, and Lorna Coppinger, *Dogs: A Startling New Understanding of Canine Origin, Behavior and Evolution,* Scribner, 2001

Coren, Stanley, *Why We Love the Dogs We Do,* Simon & Schuster, 1998

235

PHOTO CREDITS

GLOSSARY

American Kennel Club: An American purebred dog registry that promotes and sanctions dog shows, sporting, and working events.

Agility: Dog sport in which handler and dog navigate an obstacle course, being judged on technique and speed.

Assistance dog: This is an umbrella term, like *service dog*, referring to dogs trained to work with disabled people.

BARF: Acronym for *bones and raw food* or *biologically appropriate raw food*. A term coined by Australian veterinarian Dr. Ian Billinghurst to describe a raw meat- and bones-based diet for dogs.

Bitch: The technical name for an adult female dog.

Brachycephalic breeds: Breeds with pushed-in faces, characterized by constricted nostrils and overlong soft palate. Examples are the pug, the bulldog, and the shih tzu.

Canadian Kennel Club: The Canadian purebred dog registry, promoting and sanctioning dog shows, sporting, and working events.

Chondrodysplasia: abnormal cartilage development causing disproportionate dwarfism (shortening of limbs) in affected breeds, such as dachshund and basset hound.

Clicker, clicker training: A clicker is a small handheld device that makes a distinctive "click" sound as a marker when a dog has performed the correct action. Clicking is paired with a treat reward to reinforce behaviors.

Conformation, dog show: Purebred dogs who are competing in the show ring for the distinction of which conforms most closely to the ideal breed standard.

Dam: The mother of a litter of puppies.

Deep chested: This term describes the depth of the dog's chest. A deep chest usually extends to or below the elbows. Examples include Dobermans, dachshunds, and Irish wolfhounds. The depth of the chest has nothing to do with the width, and many deep-chested dogs are rather narrow across the front.

Designer dog: A dog bred by breeding two dogs of different breeds (or breed mixes) for sale as a pet rather than for any working purpose.

Dewclaws: Extra toelike digits on the inside of a dog's ankles above the foot. A pup may be born with or without them, and they are sometimes removed from very young puppies. Some breeds, like briards, are born with double dew claws.

Dock diving: A relatively new sport in which dogs run and leap from the end of a dock into deep water after a thrown toy, competing for distance.

Double coat: Most dogs have a double coat. A softer, denser undercoat insulates the dog, and the coarser top coat provides some water resistance. All double-coated dogs shed to some degree.

Drive: A drive is a dog's urge to fulfill a working or instinctual need, such as herding, chasing, or defending territory. In very general terms, a high-drive dog is less suitable as an average family pet because of high exercise and training needs. Lower-drive dogs are more laid back and often easier to live with.

Dysplasia: Malformation of some sort, often applied to either the hip or elbow joints. Can be asymptomatic to crippling.

Earthdog: A terrier sport in which the dogs are dispatched down a narrow man-made hole to find a caged animal, usually a rat. The rat is typically unharmed.

Freestyle, canine freestyle: A sport in which the dog and handler perform a dance routine to music. It often includes some very complex moves and elements of formal obedience training, like precise heeling.

Handler: Any person who is training or showing a dog. A handler can be a paid professional at a dog show or the owner training or showing her dog.

Kennel Club: Usually referred to as "the Kennel Club," it is the United Kingdom purebred dog registry that promotes and sanctions dog shows, sporting, and working events.

Kibble: A dry food product for dogs, made by combining grains, meat products, and other ingredients and cooking them into dry pellets.

Lure coursing: A sport, primarily for sighthounds, that allows competitors to chase a lure via mechanized trolleys over a large field.

Neuter: This is technically the correct term for sterilizing a dog of either sex, although it is usually used to refer to male dogs. The testicles are removed, reducing testosterone production and making the dog unable to breed.

Obedience trial: A sanctioned event in which dogs compete for points toward obedience titles or championships.

Pack: The canine family structure that wild canids, such as wolves, form. Three or more dogs comprise a canine pack and may exhibit different behaviors as a group than singly.

Pedigree: The dog's family tree. Every dog has a pedigree. In registered purebred dogs, it is recorded with the registry.

Positive reinforcement: Any training technique that involves rewarding a dog for correct behavior with praise, treats, or play.

Puppy mill: There is no legal definition of the term. Usually considered to be a high-volume dog-breeding operation for profit. The dogs' value lies only in their worth as breeding stock or sales merchandise, and conditions are often unsanitary/inhumane.

Purebreed: Any dog with parents of a single recognized breed, registered or not.

Registry, registered dogs: Any dog or litter that is registered with an outside organization. The importance of the registration papers depends entirely on the validity of the registering body.

Schutzhund: A dog sport originating in Germany for working and police dogs. It gives equal importance to obedience, tracking, and protection.

Sighthounds: Dogs in the hound group who hunt primarily by sight, like greyhounds and whippets.

Single coat: Dogs like poodles, greyhounds, and some terriers that have a single coat, with no undercoat. They tend to shed minimally.

Sire: The father of a litter of puppies.

Spay: The medical procedure in which the ovaries and uterus are removed from a female dog, reducing estrogen and progesterone, eliminating heat cycles, and rendering her sterile. Sometimes only the uterus is removed, but complete removal of all reproductive organs is the most common procedure.

Therapy dog: A therapy dog provides comfort to others, usually in assisted living homes, hospitals, and schools.

Undercoat: The thick, dense insulating coat that many dogs have, covered by the top coat.

United Kennel Club: An American registry for both purebred and mixed-breed dogs. Although it sanctions and holds dog shows, its emphasis is on working and sporting events.

Weight pulling: A sport in which harnessed dogs compete to pull the most weight on a wagon or sled.

Whelp: Give birth to puppies.

Withers: The top of the dog's shoulders. Height of a dog is measured from the withers to the ground.

X-pen: A portable mesh pen for containing dogs.

INDEX